THE ARDEN SHAKESPEARE

GENERAL EDITORS: HAROLD F. BROOKS AND HAROLD JENKINS

THE MERRY WIVES OF WINDSOR

THE ARDEN EDITION OF THE
WORKS OF WILLIAM SHAKESPEARE

THE MERRY WIVES
OF WINDSOR

Edited by

H. J. OLIVER

LONDON
METHUEN & CO LTD

The general editors of the Arden Shakespeare have been W. J. Craig (1899–1906),
R. H. Case (1909–44) and Una Ellis-Fermor (1946–58).
Present general editors: Harold F. Brooks and Harold Jenkins.
The Merry Wives of Windsor was first published in the Arden Shakespeare in 1904
edited by H. C. Hart

This edition first published 1971

SBN 416 47690 2

Editorial matter © 1971 Methuen & Co Ltd

DISTRIBUTED IN THE U.S.A.
BY BARNES AND NOBLE INC.

PRINTED IN GREAT BRITAIN BY THE BROADWATER PRESS LTD
WELWYN GARDEN CITY, HERTFORDSHIRE

CONTENTS

INTRODUCTION

The question with which study of *The Merry Wives of Windsor* often begins, and the one with which it too often ends, is the relation of the play to Shakespeare's *Henry IV* and *Henry V*; criticism, understandably enough, centres on Falstaff, and the issue most likely to be debated is whether the Falstaff of *The Merry Wives* is the authentic Falstaff, as that life-like character is assumed to be in the two parts of *Henry IV*. The question, in so far as it is a real question, may be deferred, but the absurdity of pursuing it too far may be commented on even now. The links between the comedy and the Histories are certainly not made systematically, and it is difficult to say when exactly the action of *The Merry Wives* is supposed to take place. To be sure, when the audience needs to be reminded that Fenton is a romantic and desirable suitor, Master Page can reply to the Host's praise ('he capers, he dances, he has eyes of youth; he writes verses, he speaks holiday, he smells April and May') with an objection that the audience will probably interpret as a compliment—'he kept company with the wild Prince and Poins'; and such a statement, if taken literally, would place the action either in the reign of Henry IV, when Prince Hal was nearly breaking his father's heart by consorting with Falstaff and his Eastcheap companions in sin, or, at the latest, in the reign of Prince Hal himself as Henry V. Yet the Mistress Quickly of *The Merry Wives* does not seem to be the Eastcheap hostess of *Henry IV*, but does seem to be the speaker of lines about a Windsor Castle that has apparently just been identified as the home of 'our radiant Queen' who 'hates sluts and sluttery'. Indeed there is an important sense in which *The Merry Wives* is the one of Shakespeare's plays that most obviously deals with life in Elizabethan England, and it may even be not only the most topical of them but also the one most clearly designed for a specific (and royal) occasion. It would, then, be doubly unfortunate if the casual links with the other Falstaff plays, which would have added to the attraction of the comedy for its original audiences, happy to be reminded of old friends, were allowed to limit or spoil modern appreciation of the play.

I. THE TEXTUAL AND THEATRICAL HISTORY OF THE PLAY

Although, as will be shown, there is every reason to believe that the play was written in the last decade of the sixteenth century, the first mention of it is found in the Stationers' Register on 18 January 1602:

> Io. Busby. Entred for his copie vnder the hand of m^r Seton / A booke called. An excellent & pleasant conceited comedie of S^r Io ffaulstof and the merry wyves of windesor[.] vj^d

followed immediately by the transfer, in a different hand:

> Arthure Iohnson[.] Entred for his Copye by assignement from Iohn Busbye / A booke Called an excellent and pleasant con-ceyted Comedie of Sir Iohn ffaulstafe and the merye wyves of windsor[.] vj^d [1]

It is not known how Busby acquired his right in the text, but Johnson's claim could hardly have been disputed, since the transfer had been entered in the usual acceptable form; and in the same year he engaged Thomas Creede to print his text and duly pub-lished it, as a quarto, with the inviting title-page:

> A / Most pleasaunt and / excellent conceited Co- / medie, of Syr *Iohn Falstaffe*, and the / merrie Wiues of *Windsor*. / Entermixed with sundrie / variable and pleasing humors, of Syr *Hugh* / the Welch Knight, Iustice *Shallow*, and his / wise Cousin M. *Slender*. / With the swaggering vaine of Auncient / *Pistoll*, and Corporall *Nym*. / By *William Shakespeare*. / As it hath bene diuers times Acted by the right Honorable / my Lord Chamberlaines seruants. Both before her / Maiestie, and else-where. / [*ornament*] / LONDON / Printed by T.C. for Arthur Iohnson, and are to be sold at / his shop in Powles Church-yard, at the signe of the / Flower de Leuse and the Crowne. / 1602.

An attempt will be made later to show that this Quarto is a most corrupt version of the play not as it was presented before the Queen's Majesty but as it was no doubt divers times acted else-where. Nevertheless another printer, William Jaggard, reprinted this text with a few unimportant alterations in 1619 ('Q2'), ostensibly for Johnson but probably for Thomas Pavier, who published a series of genuine and spurious 'Shakespeare' texts in that year. Pavier's venture seems to have led to protests from the King's Men—on whose behalf the Lord Chamberlain wrote to the Stationers' Company forbidding further printing of King's Men plays without consent—and so, indirectly, it led to the publication by William Jaggard, his son Isaac, and others, in 1623, of the first

---

1. Register C, fo. 78, cited by W. W. Greg, *The Merry Wives of Windsor 1602*, Shakespeare Quarto Facsimiles, No. 3 (Oxford, 1957), p. i.

full collection of Shakespeare's plays, now known as the First
Folio.[1] The Quarto text of *The Merry Wives* was not reproduced
again until George Steevens in 1766 included a reprint of Q2 in
Volume 1 of his *Twenty of the Plays of Shakespeare, Being the whole
Number printed in Quarto During his Life-time, or before the Restoration*;
and although every editor of the play must refer to it, the Quarto
has not often been republished in the nineteenth and twentieth
centuries except in standard series of facsimiles (such as those of
Griggs, in 1881, corrected in 1888, and W. W. Greg, in 1939 and
1957) or because of its 'curiosity value' as an inferior or supposedly
earlier form of the fuller Folio text (e.g. by Halliwell in 1842 and by
Greg in 1910).

The version of the play published in the First Folio of 1623 is
almost twice the length of the Quarto text (which is the shortest of
all the Shakespearian 'Bad' Quartos) and is in nearly every way
markedly superior. Only odd lines or phrases in the Quarto have
no counterpart in the Folio, whereas the Folio has at least five
scenes that are not represented in the Quarto at all, the most important being the completely detachable 'Latin lesson' (Act IV,
Scene i). Not surprisingly, therefore, it was the Folio and not the
Quarto version that was republished as a further Quarto ('Q3') in
1630, although the new publisher Meighen did not take the step
until Johnson on 29 January of that year had assigned to him his
'estate' in the work. (It would seem that once an Elizabethan
stationer, by an entry on the Register, had established his right to
one text of a play, however corrupt, his fellows were normally
content to allow his right to other versions of that play, however
different.) The claim on the title-page that the text had been
'newly corrected' was no doubt intended to mean that this was the
first publication of the play *in quarto* to contain the 'corrected',
Folio, version and not that the Folio had been further corrected.
The First Folio text was reprinted with only the most minor of
variations in the later Folios; and the editorial history of the play
thereafter is related mainly to the use that each editor has been
prepared to make of the Quarto when he found the Folio 'wrong'
or, occasionally, inadequate.

The theatrical history of *The Merry Wives* in Shakespeare's own
day is harder to trace. There is no reason to doubt either the statement on the title-page of the 1602 Quarto that the play had been
acted 'divers times', both for the Queen 'and elsewhere', or its
implication that not only Falstaff but also Evans, Shallow, Slender,

1. See, e.g., E. K. Chambers, *William Shakespeare* (Oxford, 1930), I. 133–41;
W. W. Greg, *The Editorial Problem in Shakespeare* (Second edition, Oxford, 1951),
pp. 131–4.

Pistol, and Nym were popular characters with audiences. As will be seen later, there is also reason to think that the play may have been written for a special occasion as early as 1597. The first record of an actual performance, however, is in the Revels Accounts for 1604 (which seem now to have successfully survived allegations of forgery). Here it is recorded that the King's Men performed on 'Hallamas Day being the first of Nouembar A play in the Banketinge house att Whithall called The Moor of Venis' and 'The Sunday ffollowinge A Play of the Merry Wiues of Winsor'.[1]

There seems to be no substance in H. C. Hart's theory that a reference to the 'true heirs of Master Justice Shallow' in Dekker's *Satiromastix* (1601) means that the Children of Pauls, who are mentioned on the title-page of the 1602 edition of that comedy as having played it 'priuately', had also acted *The Merry Wives of Windsor*. The passage in question occurs in a speech by Horace (a caricature of Ben Jonson) when Horace is boasting to Crispinus that he has 'a set of' letters written to be sent to flatter 'any fresh suited gallant' who comes on the scene, the letters being intended to give impressive evidence of Horace's fluency and genius: 'We must haue false fiers to amaze these spangle babies, these true heires of Master Iustice Shallow'. Hart tries to link Horace's readymade letters with Falstaff's in *The Merry Wives*, of which Mistress Page says 'I warrant he hath a thousand of these letters, writ with blank spaces for different names...' (II. i. 71–2); but even if Dekker were thinking of Falstaff, the reference to the true heirs of Shallow seems to mean no more than 'fools like Shallow': Shallow is not connected in any way with Falstaff's letters in *The Merry Wives* and indeed (as Collier had already pointed out) Dekker may be thinking of the Shallow of *2 Henry IV*.[2]

It is just possible that the record of payment to the King's Men on 20 May 1613 for, among 'fowerteene severall playes', one called 'Sir John ffalstaffe' refers to *The Merry Wives*, since the very next entry includes another called 'the Hotspur';[3] but the next certain record is more than thirty years after the first: on 12 March 1638/9, the King's Men, through Lowin, Taylor, and Swanston, were paid for a performance at Court on 15 November 1638.[4]

1. E. K. Chambers, *The Elizabethan Stage* (Oxford, 1923), IV. 171 and 136–40.
2. H. C. Hart ed., *The Merry Wives of Windsor* (the original Arden edition, London, 1904, revised 1932), pp. 66–7; J. P. Collier, *The Works of William Shakespeare* (London, 1844), I. 175. The *Satiromastix* reference is to II. ii. 27–35 in the edition of Dekker by F. T. Bowers (Cambridge, 1953), I. 336.
3. Chambers, *Elizabethan Stage*, IV. 180. The point is made by William Bracy, *The Merry Wives of Windsor* (Columbia, Missouri, 1952), p. 10.
4. G. E. Bentley, *The Jacobean and Caroline Stage* (Oxford, 1941–68), I. 99; W. W. Greg ed., Malone Society *Collections*, II. 3 (Oxford, 1931), pp. 388–9.

After the Restoration in 1660, *The Merry Wives* was one of the first plays to be acted. It was among those allotted to Thomas Killigrew; and Pepys saw a performance in the Vere Street Theatre on 5 December 1660—and was not impressed. He thought 'the humours of the country gentleman [presumably Slender] and the French doctor very well done' but disapproved of Cartwright's Falstaff and 'the rest'. Performances on 25 September in the following year and on 15 August 1667 were no more to his taste. Downes also records a special performance 'at Court at St. *Jame's*', on 23 April 1704 or 1705, with what must have been one of the best casts ever seen in the play: Betterton was Falstaff; Dogget, Evans; Mrs Barry, Mistress Page; and Anne Bracegirdle, Mistress Ford. It may have been the acting rather than the play itself that disappointed Pepys, for Dennis recorded in 1702 that 'all those men of extraordinary parts, who were the Ornaments of that Court; as the late Duke of *Buckingham*, my Lord *Normandy*, my Lord *Dorset*, my late Lord *Rochester*, Sir *Charles Sidley*, Dr *Frazer*, Mr *Savil*, Mr *Buckley*, were in Love with the Beauties of this Comedy', and Downes recalled in 1708 that it was one of the 'Old Plays' which, being old, 'were Acted but now and then; yet being well Perform'd, were very Satisfactory to the Town'. Yet it is not difficult to believe that the Restoration audience would have thought unsophisticated a play in which country virtue triumphed so easily over courtly gallantry. (Indeed Dennis added that 'this Comedy had never upon Revivals had any great success, and that particularly when it was Revived in King *Charles* the Seconds time, the only character that pleased to a height was *Slender* acted by *Wintershal*'.)[1]

An attempt to 'improve' the play for early eighteenth-century audiences—inevitable in spite of its reasonable conformity to the unities of time, place, and action—was made by Dennis. *The Comical Gallant: Or The Amours of Sir John Falstaffe* was presented at Drury Lane in 1702, but not very successfully (Dennis blamed the actor who played Falstaff). As might have been expected, the plot was theoretically tightened up (Dennis complained that 'there are no less than three Actions in it that are independent one of another, which divide and distract the minds of an Audience'): Fenton becomes the principal character and is Mistress Ford's nephew; a second Host, the Host of the Bull Inn, is Mistress Ford's brother; Falstaff is persuaded by Fenton that Mistress Ford and Mistress Page are in love with him; instead of Falstaff's being thrashed as the supposed Witch of Brentford, Ford suffers the punishment at

1. John Downes, *Roscius Anglicanus*, ed. Montague Summers (London, [1928]), pp. 47, 9; John Dennis, Epistle Dedicatory to *The Comical Gallant* (London, 1702), A2, A2ᵛ.

the hands of Mistress Page—who is disguised as Captain Dingboy, the supposed lover of Mistress Ford; and, in the interests of symmetry, it is again Ford who is pinched and burnt and beaten by the 'fairies', when he, as well as Falstaff, is disguised as Herne the Hunter. Slender and Caius are tricked by the disguises into being 'married' to one another by the Host of the Garter disguised as a parson; and Fenton, too noble to marry Anne without her parents' consent, gains that consent because of the correctness of his sentiments. After all, as Dennis generously said, 'in so short a time as' Shakespeare was allowed to write his play, 'nothing could be done that is perfect'; but since Shakespeare 'performed more than anyone else could have done in so short a time', all that the reviser had to do was to 'Correct the foresaid Errours' (the plot, and the 'places' where the style was 'stiff and forced and affected').

In the 1720's Shakespeare's play, not Dennis's, became exceptionally popular, and it was produced by most of the famous companies and actor-managers of the eighteenth and nineteenth centuries, though often in an abridged form; Quin, for example, excelled as Falstaff, though Kemble (at first) and Kean preferred to play Ford. Kean's Mistress Ford was, of course, Ellen Tree; and Ellen Terry and Mrs Kendal later played the wives, with Beerbohm Tree as Falstaff. The play was also performed in America as early as 1770, in Philadelphia, and as early as 1773 in New York, and it was never quite lost to the United States theatre thereafter, although George Pope Morris informed the nation in *The New-York Mirror* of 13 November 1824 that 'there is no play in the English language of so exceptionable a character as this indelicate production of Shakespeare'.[1]

There have been many successful revivals in the twentieth century, not only in England and America but also, for example, in Europe (the play has been translated into most European languages); there is even record of a production in Japan. Experimental productions have included Oscar Asche's surprisingly unpopular 1911 'wintry' version, and his calamitous 1929 modern-dress variation (Anne 'rode pillion on Fenton's motor-bicycle'); Komisarjevsky's in 1935 with a Viennese background; a Yale Shakespeare Festival 1953 performance 'in the language of Shakespeare's day' (the actors being coached by Helge Kökeritz); a comic-ballet; and a 1957 production in Russia when 'in order to maintain the spirit of revelry and gaiety throughout the entire

1. Harrison T. Meserole, 'Shakespeare in New York, 1823–24: The *Mirror*, Morals, and The *Merry Wives of Windsor*', in G. R. Smith ed., *Essays on Shakespeare* (University Park, 1965), pp. 228–38. Augustin Daly's late nineteenth-century productions of the play were always carefully expurgated.

performance, a kind of merry fair was organized during the intervals, in which both the actors and the audience took part. This innovation was a great success, but the producer's rather free attitude to the text of the comedy has provoked some disagreement.'[1] Suffice it to add that although some theatre-goers naturally prefer Shakespeare in a more serious mood, such a production of *The Merry Wives* as that by Glen Byam Shaw in the 1955 season at Stratford-upon-Avon showed that even a sophisticated audience can be delighted when the play is presented as the light-hearted comedy it really is. *The Merry Wives* also has the distinction of having been used for the librettos of at least nine operas, including those by Reynolds (1824), Balfe (1838), Nicolai (1849), Vaughan Williams (*Sir John in Love*, 1929), and, above all, Verdi (*Falstaff*, 1893).[2]

2. THE RELATIONSHIP OF QUARTO AND FOLIO

It was inevitable that the Quarto of 1602, which, in approximate figures, has only 1,600 lines, as against the Folio's 2,700, and is in all judgements inferior to it, should once have been taken to be an earlier version of the play or even a first draft.[3] This was commonly thought to be the status of several Shakespeare texts, such as the First Quartos of *Hamlet* and *Romeo and Juliet*, and even *The Taming of a Shrew*; and although Collier, Grant White, P. A. Daniel, and others had reservations and alternative theories, most critics did not abandon the 'first sketch' explanation altogether until A. W. Pollard made his famous distinction between 'good' and 'bad' Quartos and pointed the way to the full demonstration that many published plays once thought to be sources or first versions were in fact later, debased, 'reported' or 'pirated' forms of the authentic Shakespeare texts. As early as 1910, however, W. W. Greg argued

1. Y. Shvedov, in 'International Notes', *Shakespeare Survey 12* (Cambridge, 1959), p. 118. Fuller details of various twentieth-century productions are given in other volumes of *Shakespeare Survey* and *Shakespeare Quarterly* and in J. C. Trewin, *Shakespeare on the English Stage, 1900–1964: A Survey of Productions* (London, 1964). For the earlier stage history, see e.g. E. L. Avery, *The London Stage 1660–1800* (Carbondale, Ill., 1960–); C. B. Hogan, *Shakespeare in the Theatre. 1701–1800* (Oxford, 1952, 1957); G. C. D. Odell, *Shakespeare from Betterton to Irving* (New York, 1920); W. Winter, *Shakespeare on the Stage* (Third series, London, 1916), pp. 383–430; O. J. Campbell and E. G. Quinn ed., *The Reader's Encyclopedia of Shakespeare* (New York, 1966), pp. 536–8; and Harold Child, 'The Stage-History of *The Merry Wives of Windsor*', in Quiller-Couch and J. Dover Wilson ed., *The Merry Wives of Windsor* (Cambridge, 1921, 1954), pp. 135–8.

2. See, e.g., Winston Dean, 'Shakespeare and Opera', in Phyllis Hartnoll ed., *Shakespeare in Music* (London, 1964).

3. This was the opinion of, e.g., Pope (who knew the 1619 Quarto), Theobald (who also knew of the earlier one), Johnson, Capell, and even Malone.

convincingly that the Quarto of *The Merry Wives* was just such a corrupt 'report'.[1] There have, it is true, been dissentients—notably William Bracy, but his '*The Merry Wives of Windsor.' The History and Transmission of Shakespeare's Text* (1952), while entering a few caveats, failed to destroy the theory of memorial reconstruction. The facts must be set out in some detail.

P. A. Daniel first pointed out[2] that the Quarto version of the part of the action covered in Folio's Act iv Scene v hardly makes sense and could best be explained as a failure to reproduce correctly a larger version of the scene such as Folio's.[3] In the Quarto, Slender's servant Simple, in quest of 'the wise woman of Brainford', has the following conversation with Falstaff:

> *Sim.* Marry sir my maister *Slender* sent me to her,
> To know whether one *Nim* that hath his chaine,
> Cousoned him of it, or no.
> *Fal.* I talked with the woman about it.
> *Sim.* And I pray sir what ses she?
> *Fal.* Marry she ses the very same man that
> Beguiled maister *Slender* of his chaine,
> Cousoned him of it.
> *Sim.* May I be bolde to tell my maister so sir?
> *Fal.* I tike, who more bolde.
> *Sim.* I thanke you sir, I shall make my maister a glad
> man at these tydings, God be with you sir

(and although no exit is marked, Simple apparently leaves). In Daniel's words, 'Simple, therefore, is made to say that he will make his master a glad man with the news that he has been cozened of his chain'—and, even allowing that Simple is stupid enough for most things, that is rather surprising. The Folio text presents no problems here. When Simple receives Falstaff's answer that 'the very same man that beguil'd Master *Slender* of his Chaine, cozon'd him of it', he is not satisfied but replies 'I would I could haue spoken with the Woman her selfe, I had other things to haue

---

1. A. W. Pollard, *Shakespeare Folios and Quartos* (London, 1909) and *Shakespeare's Fight with the Pirates* (Cambridge, 1920); Peter Alexander, *Shakespeare's 'Henry VI' and 'Richard III'* (Cambridge, 1929); *Shakespeare's 'Merry Wives of Windsor' 1602*, ed. W. W. Greg (Oxford, 1910). Also valuable, though out of date in some respects, is Alfred Hart, *Stolne and Surreptitious Copies* (Melbourne, 1942). See, too, Leo Kirschbaum, 'An Hypothesis concerning the Origin of the Bad Quartos', *PMLA*, lx (1945), 697–715, and for proof that the Quarto of *Henry V* is a reported text, G. I. Duthie, in *Papers Mainly Shakespearian*, coll. G. I. Duthie (Edinburgh, 1964), pp. 104–30.

2. Preface to William Griggs's facsimile of the First Quarto (London, 1881, revised edition 1888), p. x.

3. The Quarto has no act and scene divisions; the references given are always those of the Folio, with the line-numbering of the present edition.

spoken with her too, from him', and we soon learn what they are, namely, 'they were nothing but about Mistris *Anne Page*, to know if it were my Masters fortune to haue her, or no':

> *Fal.* 'Tis, 'tis his fortune.
> *Sim.* What Sir?
> *Fal.* To haue her, or no: goe; say the woman told me so.
> *Sim.* May I be bold to say so Sir?
> *Fal.* I Sir: like who more bold.
> *Sim.* I thanke your worship: I shall make my Master glad with these tydings.

Obviously this makes better sense; and it is hard to believe either that somebody composed the Quarto version first or that somebody deliberately shortening the Folio version would have omitted the question about Anne Page and retained the one about the chain. It will also be noticed that Simple's 'May I be bold to say so Sir' has been retained in the Quarto version, albeit as a comment on the first, not the second question—as if somebody's memory jumped a few lines—and that the Quarto's 'I tike, who more bolde' could most easily be explained as some kind of corruption of Folio's 'I Sir: like who more bold' (meaning 'be as bold as you please' or 'as bold as the boldest')—possibly a simple misprint ('t' for 'l' in 'like'), perhaps an attempt to 'improve', conceivably even a confusion of the line being recalled with such another as 'Base Tyke, cal'st thou mee Hoste' from *Henry V* (II. i. 31).

There is another tell-tale omission, in the Quarto scene corresponding to Folio's I. iv.[1] When Caius finds Simple hiding in the 'Counting-house' (itself an odd substitution for the Folio 'Closset'), Simple denies being a thief, with the words

> O Lord sir no: I am no theefe,
> I am a Seruingman:
> My name is *Iohn Simple*, I brought a Letter sir
> From my M. *Slender*, about misteris *Anne Page*
> Sir: Indeed that is my comming

whereupon Caius writes out a challenge not to Slender but to Sir Hugh Evans. Now it is true that the *audience* has already seen Evans send Simple to Quickly with the letter, on Slender's behalf, but there has been nothing whatever to cause Caius to associate Evans with the matter (and Bracy's insistence on 'the skill with which the essential plot is advanced' throughout the Quarto is seen to be quite wrong). Again the Folio makes all clear: the Quarto has omitted Mistress Quickly's volunteering to Caius of the information 'I beseech you be not so flegmaticke: heare the truth of it. He

---

1. According to Harness's edition of 1825, it was first noticed by James Boaden.

B

came of an errand to mee, from Parson *Hugh*' and has reproduced only the general sense of Simple's 'Tale' of why he came: 'To desire this honest Gentlewoman (your Maid) to speake a good word to Mistris *Anne Page*, for my Master in the way of Marriage'. No dramatist could have *composed* the Quarto scene as it stands, to tell the story; and no sane reviser of the play trying to save space or time would have left out the only statement that makes sense of the action.

One further instance of Quarto lines that are meaningless in themselves, and can be understood only if the Folio text is taken into account, occurs in ii. iii. Caius waits for Evans to appear and fight the duel for which he sent the challenge in i. iv; and Shallow, Page, the Host, and Slender come instead. (At least, the Quarto stage direction says that all four of them come, but Slender does not speak, and Caius asks 'Vat be all you, Van to tree com for, a?'; in the Folio, Slender does speak, and Caius, consistently, asks 'Vat be all you one, two, tree, fowre, come for?') To the Host's question whether Evans has already been killed, Caius replies (in both texts) that Evans has not dared to show his face. In the Quarto, Shallow thereupon comments: 'He hath showne himselfe the wiser man M. Doctor: / Sir *Hugh* is a Parson, and you a Phisition'. Why should a parson not meet a physician, one wonders? The Folio alone gives the answer: in that text, Shallow's reply to Caius is 'He is the wiser man (M. Doctor) he is a curer of soules, and you a curer of bodies: if you should fight, you goe against the haire of your professions', and it is a few lines later in the scene that he says: 'M. Doctor *Caius*, I am come to fetch you home: I am sworn of the peace: you haue show'd your selfe a wise Physician, and Sir *Hugh* hath showne himselfe a wise and patient Churchman'. Whoever was responsible for the Quarto remembered, apparently, that something was said about the professions of Caius and Evans but forgot what was said; and because he forgot exactly what was said, he set down a phrase that misses the whole point of Shallow's first comment.

The only theory that will explain all the corruptions already listed is that somebody (singular or plural) was trying to reconstruct either the Folio text or one similar to it. Although the Quarto text was published first, it cannot possibly represent either an early draft of a text like the Folio's or *only* a version of it shortened for performance. There is no feature of the Quarto that is inconsistent with the theory that it is a 'reported' text; and there are many features that cannot be otherwise explained.

The Quarto stage directions, for example, sometimes bring on characters who have nothing to say and no part in the action: presumably their presence on stage was remembered (and, of course, a reviser preparing a deliberately abridged version of the play would have removed them from the stage directions too). One instance has already been noted—Slender's presence in the Quarto stage direction in II. iii, although his Folio line "Giue you good-morrow, sir' has been dropped (but Caius does refer to him—in a speech where lines, perhaps by a compositor's error, have been run into those that should be spoken by the Host—'M. *Page* and M. *Shallow,* / And eke cauellira *Slender,* go you all ouer the fields to Frogmore?'). Then in the next scene, corresponding to III. i of the Folio, the Quarto has a stage direction '*Enter Page, shallow, and Slender*' but Slender neither speaks nor is spoken to, whereas in the Folio version he wanders round sighing 'O sweet *Anne Page*'. Even more significant, in the opening scene the Quarto has the stage direction: '*Enter Syr* Iohn Falstaffe, Pistoll, Bardolfe, *and* Nim', but Bardolph does not speak, and Slender does not include him in his accusations of those who robbed him. Where the Folio has 'I haue matter in my head against you [Falstaff], and against your cony-catching Rascalls, *Bardolf, Nym,* and *Pistoll*', the Quarto has 'I haue matter in my head against you and your cogging companions, *Pistoll* and *Nym*' and the Folio's later charge that 'he in the red face had it' is missing, as are Bardolph's replies (and Evans's comment on the first of them). Again it is the stage direction that gives the game away.[1]

There are also, as Alfred Hart noted,[2] many of the superfluous and 'descriptive' stage directions that either repeat or replace dialogue and are rarely if ever found in good texts. They include, in the order in which they occur in the Quarto (the Folio act and scene references for comparison being given in parentheses):

(i) *Quic.* . . . For Gods sake step into the Counting-house . . .
        He steps into the Counting-house.
    . . . Are you come home sir alreadie?
        And she opens the doore. (I. iv)

(ii) *Doc.* . . . *Iohn Rugby* giue a ma pen
    An Inck: tarche vn pettit tarche a little.
        The Doctor writes. (I. iv)

(iii)   *Enter Mistresse* Page, *reading of a Letter*
    (cf. Folio, II. i: *Mist Page.* What, haue scap'd Loue-letters in the holly-day-time of my beauty, and am I now a subiect for them? let me see? . . .)

1. Curiously, in III. i, although Bardolph is not on the stage, according to either the Folio or the Quarto stage directions, the Quarto has the Host say '*Bardolfe* laie their swords to pawne' where the Folio has only 'Come, lay their swords to pawne'. Presumably any name was good enough for the reporter here.
2. *op. cit.,* pp. 429–31.

  (iv) *Ford.* A word with you sir.
                     Ford *and the Host talkes.*
      (Folio, II. i: *Ford.* Good mine Host o'th' Garter: a word
      with you. / *Host.* What saist thou, my Bully-Rooke?)

  (v) *Mis. For.* O Lord step aside good sir *Iohn.*
                Falstaffe stands behind the aras.
      (cf. Folio, III. iii: *Fal.* She shall not see me, I will ensconce
      mee behinde the Arras. / *M. Ford.* Pray you do so, she's a
      very tatling woman.)

  (vi) *Sir Iohn goes into the basket, they put cloathes ouer him, the two*
      men carries it away: Foord meetes it, and all the rest, Page,
      Doctor, Priest, Slender, Shallow
      (all based on the Folio dialogue, III. iii).

 (vii)   *Enter mistresse Page.*
      [*Mis. For.*] Gods body here is misteris *Page,*
          Step behind the arras good sir *Iohn.*
                He steps behind the arras.
      (cf. Folio, IV. ii, 'Step into th' chamber, Sir *Iohn*'. The
      Quarto confuses, and weakly repeats, the similar but
      different action in III. iii.)

 (viii) *Enter M. Ford, Page, Priest, Shallow, the two men carries the*
      basket, and Ford meets it.
      (cf. the Folio dialogue, IV. ii, as in this edition; but cf. also
      vi, above.)

  (ix) *Enter Falstaffe disguised like an old woman, and misteris Page*
      with him, Ford beates him, and hee runnes away.   (IV. ii)

  (x) The stage directions recorded in the collations to this
      edition at v. v. 30, 37, and 103.

The Quarto also often confuses and conflates incidents or
speeches that are similar but distinct in the Folio—and often gets
into the earlier of the two episodes words that belong properly in
the later (a phenomenon, incidentally, that practically rules out
any theory that the Quarto text is an inaccurate shorthand report
of the Folio). For example, in II. i in the Folio, when the proposed
'duel' between Evans and Caius is being discussed, Page says to
Shallow, 'I haue heard the French-man [Caius] hath good skill in
his Rapier' and Shallow in his reply speaks of the modern technique
of fencing ('your Passes, Stoccado's, and I know not what') contrasted with the practice of his own youth: ''tis the heart (Master
Page) 'tis heere, 'tis heere: I haue seene the time, with my long-
sword, I would haue made you fowre tall fellowes skippe like
Rattes'. In II. iii, after Shallow has told Caius that Evans 'is the
wiser man' for not appearing, Page, to make conversation, comments, 'Master *Shallow*; you haue your selfe beene a great fighter,

though now a man of peace' and Shallow, flattered, agrees: 'if I see
a sword out, my finger itches to make one . . . we are the sons of
women (M. *Page*.)' The Quarto, which has nothing similar in
II. iii, gets Page's comment into II. i and conflates the two thus:

> *Pa.* Maister *Shallow* you your selfe
> Haue bene a great fighter,
> Tho now a man of peace:
> *Shal:* M. *Page* I haue seene the day that yong
> Tall fellowes with their stroke & their passado,
> I haue made them trudge Maister *Page*,
> A tis the hart, the hart doth all: I
> Haue seene the day, with my two hand sword
> I would a made you foure tall Fencers
> Scipped like Rattes.

(The weak repetitions of 'tall' and 'I haue seene the day' should be
noticed too.)

Again, in Folio III. iv, Slender's unforgettable 'wooing' of Anne
Page (which the Quarto manages to botch so badly that it is hardly
funny at all) ends with Anne's desperate question 'I meane (M.
Slender) what wold you with me?' and Slender's equally desperate
reply 'Truely, for mine owne part, I would little or nothing with
you: your father and my vncle hath made motions: if it be my
lucke, so; if not, happy man bee his dole, they can tell you how
things go, better then I can: you may aske your father, heere he
comes'. The Quarto confuses this with the other time when Anne
and Slender are left alone on the stage, in I. i, and 'reproduces' it
there thus:

> *Anne.* Now forsooth why do you stay me?
> What would you with me?
> *Slen.* Nay for my owne part, I would litle or nothing with you. I
> loue you well, and my vncle can tell you how my liuing
> stands. And if you can loue me why so. If not, why then
> happie man be his dole.

(Even worse, if worse can be imagined, is the reply that the Quarto
gives to Anne—a reply that proves that whoever was responsible
for the Quarto had not the least understanding of her character:

> *An.* You say well M. *Slender*.
> But first you must giue me leaue to
> Be acquainted with your humor,
> And afterward to loue you if I can.

Anne love Slender, indeed!)

In Folio IV. ii, after Falstaff, at his second assignation with
Mistress Ford, has had to step hurriedly 'into th' chamber' when

Mistress Page appears, Mistress Ford whispers to her fellow-conspirator 'Speake louder' (that Falstaff may not fail to be terrified by what she is saying). The Quarto contrives to get Mistress Ford's 'Speake louder' into the scene of the first assignation with Falstaff when—on the Quarto's own showing—Mistress Page is in no danger of not being heard, since Falstaff is only behind the arras. Equally absurd is the transference of Ford–Brook's flattery of Falstaff in II. ii, 'Sir, I heare you are a Scholler . . .' to Page in III. i: when Page should be saying to Evans, 'We are come to you, to doe a good office, M^r. Parson' and frightening him by telling him how angry his opponent Caius is, he is made to say, astoundingly, not only, 'Well Sir *Hugh*, we are come to craue / Your helpe and furtherance in a matter' but also 'Now Sir *Hugh*, you are a scholler well red, and verie perswasiue, we would intreate you to see if you could intreat him to patience'.

Not to labour the point, there are at least four other instances of Quarto's confusing situations thus. It gets the part of Ford's soliloquy involving devils' names, at the end of II. ii, into his other soliloquy at the end of III. v. It transfers from III. iii both Evans's acceptance of Page's invitation to breakfast, 'If there is one, I shall make two in the Companie' and Caius' unfortunate addition, 'If there be one, or two, I shall make-a-the turd' and puts them both in III. ii, as answers to *Ford's* invitation to *dinner*. It omits from Falstaff's speech in IV. v about being cozened the lines 'if it should come to the eare of the Court, how I haue beene transformed . . . they would melt mee out of my fat drop by drop, and liquor Fishermens-boots with me: I warrant they would whip me with their fine wits, till I were as crest-falne as a dride-peare' (ll. 89–95), and puts a version of them into his reflections in v. v on his being deceived by the supposed fairies 'Well, and the fine wits of the Court heare this, / Thayle so whip me with their keene Iests, / That thayle melt me out like tallow, / Drop by drop out of my grease'. Again, in II. ii, in Falstaff's blustering description of Ford to 'Brooke', for the Folio's 'They say the iealous wittolly-knaue hath masses of money', the Quarto substitutes 'For they / Say the cuckally knaue hath legions of angels', confusing it with Falstaff's earlier account of the Fords to Pistol and company in I. iii, 'Now, the report goes, she has all the rule of her husbands Purse: he hath a legend of Angels' (which the Quarto renders in the right place as 'She hath legians of angels'). It is even likely that the Quarto has Falstaff say to Shallow in I. i 'youle complaine of me to the Councell, I heare?' where the Folio has 'Now, Master *Shallow*, you'll complaine of me to the King?' not because the Folio text was

altered after the Quarto was derived from it or because the Quarto
was trying to remove any inconsistency between a King's reign and
the Queen's, but simply because the Council had been mentioned
earlier in the scene and was mentioned again a few lines later. With
the possible exception of this last example, none of the transferences
is of the kind that can be attributed to a compositor carrying words
in his mind from what he has just set up or from reading his copy
ahead.

In reported texts it is common to find also the mistaken introduction of, or confusion with, similar lines in other plays—perhaps
plays in which the reporter had acted. Such conflation is found in
the Quarto of *The Merry Wives* but fewer conclusions than usual
can be drawn from it. For example, the line 'What is the reason
that you vse me thus?' (spoken by Mistress Ford to her husband, in
place of lines to the same general effect but quite different in word-
ing in Folio IV. ii), occurs in *Hamlet* (V. i. 312). It is not an exceptional line, however; conceivably the reporter (half-remembering
Mistress Ford's 'You vse me well, M. *Ford*? Do you?', from III. iii[1])
could have invented it, or it could be a standard phrase used
frequently in conversation. Some of the other 'inter-play borrowings' listed by Alfred Hart and H. R. Hoppe[2] are unconvincing for
much the same reason ('caught you a the hip', for example, 'Haue
you importuned her by any means', 'Ifaith I know not what to say',
'led in a fooles paradice', and 'tis not vnknown to you'). It is also
far from certain that Mistress Page's 'Why what a bladder of
iniquitie is this?' (II. i) is a recollection of Falstaff's 'a plague of
sighing and griefe, it blowes a man vp like a Bladder' (*1 Henry IV*,
II. iv. 366) as conjectured by E. K. Chambers.[3] More convincing is
the hypothesis that Pistol's 'When *Pistoll* lies do this' in the same
scene is a transference from *2 Henry IV*, V. iii, of the identical words,
spoken by the same character.

More important are lines in Nym's speeches that suggest that the
reporter knew *Henry V* and was confused about Nym's speeches in
the two plays (and perhaps that the actor who had played Nym in
both plays was one of the 'reporters' of the Quarto *Merry Wives*).
Editors have spoilt some of the evidence here by introducing lines
from the Quarto unnecessarily into their texts (see particularly
II. i. 133 and note). In the Folio, Nym constantly uses and misuses

1. In III. iii, what should be Mistress Ford's line is given quite nonsensically
to Evans in the form 'You serue me well, do you not?'

2. Hart, *Stolne and Surreptitious Copies*, pp. 393–4; Hoppe, 'Borrowings from
Romeo and Juliet in the 'Bad' Quarto of *The Merry Wives of Windsor*', *Review of
English Studies*, xx (1944), 156–8.

3. *William Shakespeare*, I. 429.

the word 'humour', but he does not once say 'that's the humour of it'. This idiom is his 'signature tune' in *Henry V*, where he uses it at least five times (II. i. 63, 74, 101, and 121; and II. iii. 63). In the Quarto *Merry Wives*, in the form 'there's the humor of it', the phrase is introduced into four of Nym's nine speeches—and of the other five, two are 'Let vs about it then' and 'By *Welkin* and her Fairies' and neither into these nor into the other three could the full phrase easily be fitted even by a reporter. The four speeches in the Quarto in which Nym does say 'There's the humor of it' all have Folio counterparts: the Quarto has simply added the phrase to two of the four, and in the others has substituted it for 'is not the humor conceited?' (I. iii. 21–2) and, perhaps most significant of all, for 'that is the very note of it' (I. i. 152).[1]

The borrowing from *Henry V* seems certain (and incidentally proves that the Quarto *Merry Wives* cannot have been put together until after *Henry V* had been played). With this clue, it then becomes interesting to note other verbal links with *Henry V*, which in themselves could not prove the dependence of one play on the other but perhaps provide a kind of corroborative evidence. Where, for example, in the Folio *Merry Wives*, Pistol says 'word of deniall in thy *labras* here' (I. i. 147), the Quarto has 'I do retort the lie / Euen in thy gorge'—and '*Couple a gorge*, that is the word. I defie thee againe' is found, spoken by Pistol, in *Henry V* (II. i. 75–6 in the 'Globe' division but Act 1 in the Folio's). In *The Merry Wives* II. ii. 264, where the Folio has 'ther's my haruest-home', the Quarto reads 'there's my randeuowes'—and 'rendezvous' is used twice in *Henry V* (once by Nym, II. i. 18—'that is the rendeuous of it', once by Pistol, v. i. 88—'and there my rendeuous is quite cut off'). Less significant, perhaps, but interesting, is Quarto's 'egregious' in Falstaff's 'I suffered three egregious deaths', where the Folio has 'I suffered the pangs of three seuerall deaths' (III. v. 98–9): 'egregious' occurs twice in *Henry V*, at II. i. 49 and IV. iv. 11— both times spoken by Pistol. One expects Shakespearian characters to have each an idiom of his own, and it is natural that some phrases will tend to be common to plays written about the same time (and there are verbal links of this kind between the Folio *Merry Wives* and *Henry IV* and *Henry V*); but the noted substitution in the Quarto, for different phrases in the Folio, of words spoken in *Henry V*—particularly when so many of them concern Nym and Pistol—seems explicable only as memorial contamination.

1. William Green (*Shakespeare's 'Merry Wives of Windsor'*, Princeton, 1962, pp. 90–4) points out that the 'Bad', 1600, Quarto of *Henry V* similarly substitutes 'there's the humor of it' for comparable phrases of the good, Folio, text. But it does *not* follow that the *Merry Wives* reporter must have known the *Henry V* Quarto.

That so much of the Quarto is printed as if it were verse, when it must be prose, may be the compositor's fault, but there are instances where the Quarto verse corresponds to the Folio verse—and the difference between them is instructive. For example, for the Folio's

> Albeit I will confesse, thy Fathers wealth
> Was the first motiue that I woo'd thee (*Anne:*)
> Yet wooing thee, I found thee of more valew
> Then stampes in Gold, or summes in sealed bagges:
> And 'tis the very riches of thy selfe,
> That now I ayme at (III. iv. 13–18)

the best that the Quarto can do is:

> Thy father thinks I loue thee for his wealth,
> Tho I must needs confesse at first that drew me,
> But since thy vertues wiped that trash away,
> I loue thee *Nan*, and so deare is it set,
> That whilst I liue, I nere shall thee forget.

The tortured syntax and word-order of the Quarto are more easily explained as the price paid in a desperate attempt to recall ideas that were half-remembered (and remembered to be in verse) than as a probable part of a 'first shot' at the speech.

The examples of Quarto's retaining the sense of the Folio, but not the words; of its spoiling the very point of what it is trying to say; and of its omitting the only words and phrases that can make sense of what it retains, are far too numerous to list. The following, however, are typical:

(1) F. I. i. 112. *Eu. Pauca verba*; (Sir *Iohn*) good worts.
    Q.   *Sir. Hu.* Good vrdes sir *Iohn*, good vrdes.

(2) F. I. i. 40–59, and 187–238. Evans proposes the match between Slender and Anne Page ('there is also another deuice in my praine. . . There is *Anne Page*, which is daughter to Master *Thomas Page*, which is pretty virginity'), and mentions her 'goot gifts'; and Shallow and Evans try to prompt Slender and to 'description the matter' to him, but he is not 'capacity of it'.
    Q. *Shal.* . . . M. *Page* . . . For you
              Syr, I loue you, and for my cousen
              He comes to looke vpon your daughter.
       Pa. And heres my hand, and if my daughter
              Like him so well as I, wee'l quickly haue it a match

—and this before Slender's idiocy has been demonstrated. (Quarto's words probably represent a confusion with III. ii. 52–6.)

(3) F. I. i. 270–5. *Sl.* I haue seene *Sackerson* loose, twenty
     times, and haue taken him by the Chaine; but (I
     warrant you) the women haue so cride and shrekt
     at it, that it past: But women indeede, cannot abide
     'em, they are very ill-fauour'd rough things.

   Q. *Slen.* . . . Ile run yon to a Beare, and take her by the
     mussell,
     You neuer saw the like.
     But indeed I cannot blame you,
     For they are maruellous rough things.

(4) F. I. ii. 2–5. *Eu.* . . . one Mistris *Quickly*; which is in the
     manner of his Nurse; or his dry-Nurse; or his Cooke;
     or his Laundry; his Washer, and his Ringer.

   Q. *Sir Hu.* . . . one mistris *Quickly*, his woman, or his try
     nurse.

(5) F. I. iv. 88–99. *Qui.* [to Simple, of Caius] . . . ye French
     Doctor my Master, (I may call him my Master,
     looke you, for I keepe his house; and I wash, ring,
     brew, bake, scowre, dresse meat and drinke, make
     the beds, and doe all my selfe:)

   Simp. 'Tis a great charge to come vnder one bodies
     hand.

   Qui. Are you a-uis'd o' that? you shall finde it a great
     charge: and to be vp early, and down late: but
     notwithstanding, (to tell you in your eare, I wold
     haue no words of it) my Master himselfe is in loue
     with Mistris *Anne Page.*

   Q. *Quic.* . . . my M. hath a great affectioned mind to mis-
     tresse *Anne* himselfe. And if he should know that I
     should as they say, giue my verdit for any one but
     himselfe, I should heare of it throughly: For I tell
     you friend, he puts all his priuities in me.

   Sim. I by my faith you are a good staie to him.

   Quic. Am I? I and you knew all yowd say so:
     Washing, brewing, baking, all goes through my
     hands,
     Or else it would be but a woe house.

   Sim. I beshrow me, one woman to do all this,
     Is very painfull.

   Quic. Are you auised of that? I, I warrant you,
     Take all, and paie all, all goe through my hands.

(Here it will be noticed that although, exceptionally, the Quarto
is not shorter, it is still thinner; the subtler indecencies of the
Folio have been reduced to one obvious malapropism; Simple's
two comments between them do not provide as good a 'lead' as
'one bodies hand'; and Quickly's twice-used 'all goes through
my hands' misses the joke.)

(6) F. II. i. 4–19. Falstaff's letter to Mistress Ford (substantially as in this text).

Q. *Mis. Pa.* Mistresse *Page* I loue you. Aske me no reason,
Because theyr impossible to alledge. Your faire,
And I am fat. You loue sack, so do I:
As I am sure I haue no mind but to loue,
So I know you haue no hart but to grant[.]
A souldier doth not vse many words, where a knowes
A letter may serue for a sentence. I loue you,
And so I leaue you.
Yours Syr Iohn Falstaffe.

(and the Quarto manages only a twenty-line summary of the ensuing discussion of the letter by Mistress Page and Mistress Ford—about seventy lines in the Folio).

(7) F. II. ii. 52–76. Quickly's long-winded attempt to give Falstaff the message from Mistress Ford is followed by Falstaff's plea 'But what saies shee to mee? be briefe my good shee-*Mercurie*'.

Q reduces Quickly's lines to five; and in those five she does give Falstaff some information (that Mistress Ford has received his letter); yet Quarto retains 'Nay prethy be briefe my good she *Mercury*'.

(8) F. II. ii. 259. *Fal.* [to 'Broome', of Ford] Hang him (poore Cuckoldly knaue) I know him not...
267–8. *Fal.* Hang him, mechanicall-salt-butter rogue; I wil stare him out of his wits.

Q. *Fal.* Hang him poore cuckally knaue, I know him not...
Fal. Hang him cuckally knaue, Ile stare him Out of his wits.

(9) F. III. ii. The Folio begins with the cross-chat of Ford, Mistress Page, and Robin (not in the Quarto at all), then has a soliloquy by Ford (eighteen lines—reduced to five feeble lines in the Quarto); then has Slender and Shallow decline an invitation to dinner at Ford's home, giving as their excuse their earlier invitation to dine with Anne.

Q. (apparently remembering that Anne was not present but was relevant somehow)
For. Welcome good M. *Page*,
I would your daughter were here.
Pa. I thank you sir, she is very well at home.

(10) F. IV. ii. 113–16. *Page.* Why, this passes M. *Ford*: you are not to goe loose any longer, you must be pinnion'd.
Euans. Why this is Lunaticks: this is madde, as a mad dogge.
Shall. Indeed M. *Ford*, thi[s] is not well indeed.

> Q. *Pa.* Fie M. *Ford* you are not to go abroad if you be in
> these fits.
> *Sir Hu.* By so kad vdge me, tis verie necessarie
> He were put in pethlem.

The 'reporting' process that seems to be illustrated by this analysis of the relation of the Quarto to the Folio text may have taken place in different ways and for at least two possible purposes (the preparation of a text specifically for sale to a publisher or the attempt to reconstruct one for acting). The theory that the play was taken down, inadequately, in shorthand would not account for the misplacings or for the kinds of misunderstanding and substitution noted above, whereas a theory of 'memorial reconstruction' does cover them all; and that the reporters were members of a company that had acted the play is made probable by the variation in the quality of the reporting from scene to scene and from character to character.

Of the important parts, those of Page, Ford, Mistress Ford, Mistress Page, Mistress Quickly, and Fenton, in particular, are badly reported; speeches by these characters are nearly always inaccurate and are sometimes cut almost to nothing. (Three of these roles, significantly, may have been played by boys—who are less likely to play the same part over a period of years, if only because the boy's voice 'breaks' in time.) By contrast the lines spoken by the Host are reproduced with remarkable accuracy. A theory that the reporter was the actor who played the Host was modified by its original proponent, Sir Walter Greg, to the form 'Perhaps it would be safer to assume an independent reporter relying generally on mine Host's assistance';[1] in fact, however, the reasons given for withdrawing the original theory are questionable. Greg admitted that the horse-stealing scenes were not evidence either way, for they may also have been known on the stage in a form different from that in which they appear in the Folio; and if 'there are errors in his speeches that perhaps suggest mishearing rather than the blunders of a compositor (IV. v. 85, "I am cozened Hugh and coy Bardolf" for "hue and cry"!)',[2] that need mean no more than that the Host was himself dictating to an amanuensis (and in fact 'coy' may be a printing error for 'cry' or even a misreading of it by the compositor). Greg's other concession that 'the superiority of the scenes in which he appears is not quite uniform (for instance the beginning of II. ii, when he is off, is better than the end of II. i, when he is on)' is even more misleading: the Host's own few words in II. i, as distinct from Shallow's, are repeated with

---

1. *The Editorial Problem in Shakespeare*, p. 71.   2. *ibid.*

more than reasonable accuracy: 'God blesse you' instead of 'How now', for example, may be an accurate memory of what was in the unexpurgated text—and the omission of 'will you go An-heires?' may signify only that the actor had no more knowledge than have later editors of what the words were supposed to *mean*. More disturbing, perhaps, is another fact, that where the Folio has in the duel scene (III. i. 71–2), '*Host.* Disarme them, and let them question: let them keepe their limbs whole, and hack our English', the Quarto divides the speech thus: '*Host.* Disarme, let them question. / *Shal.* Let them keep their limbs hole, and hack our English'; yet the mistake, if it is one, is not impossible for an actor, or the alteration may have been an attempt by compositor or 'editor' to 'improve', or the Folio may even be in error.

The good reporting of II. ii, of course, is not evidence against the Host as reporter: it is evidence—and only part of overwhelming evidence—that the actor who played Falstaff was *another* of the reporters. Many of his set speeches are reproduced accurately (I. iii and III. v give good examples);[1] and in a scene such as II. ii it is noticeable how much better Falstaff's part is than either Quickly's or Ford's—and that when Falstaff's fails, it is often because the right cue is missing from the other actor's part. (Actors do not always listen carefully to, let alone remember, what is said *to* them on stage.) IV. ii is not as good—but again the main failing is in the words of other characters, and Falstaff himself has relatively little to say anyway.

Allowing, then, for the possibility of assistance from a 'bookholder' or prompter, and for the other possibility (see pp. xxi–xxii above) that the actors who played Pistol and Nym may have had some share in the reporting (since there are conflations of their parts in *The Merry Wives* with their parts in *2 Henry IV* and *Henry V*), the best hypothesis would seem to be that the Quarto text was put together, at some time after *Henry V* had been produced and perhaps not until 1602, by a small group of adult actors, including at least the two who had played (or, conceivably, understudied?) the parts of Falstaff and the Host of the Garter Inn.[2]

The theory that the state of such a text as the Quarto *Merry Wives* can best be explained as memorial reconstruction is not

1. 'A mountaine of money' (for 'mummy') at III. v. 17 is odd, but may be a compositor's misreading.

2. Speculation whether a leading actor such as William Kemp would have stooped to 'reporting' a play, even after he had left a company, is hardly worth while. There is nothing to say that the Chamberlain's Men did not use understudies; and circumstances must have made it necessary sometimes for a minor actor to step into a leading role. Indeed, the actor who normally played the Host may have been the understudy for Falstaff.

weakened at all by a demonstration that the text also contains occasional errors of other kinds, such as foul case, misreading of secretary or italic script, setting out of prose as verse, or even mishearing. What the reporters have reconstructed must still be written down somehow (for example, by one of the actors, or by a separate amanuensis, to whom the speeches are dictated); and what is written down must still be set in type by a compositor. *If*, then, Quarto's '*Hugh*, and coy *Bardolfe*' is a mishearing of 'Hue and cry', that may mean no more than that what the *reporter* said was misheard (and, in addition to the chance of a simple printing error—perhaps foul case—there are the possibilities that the actor learnt some of his part in the first place from dictation, or that the compositor worked for a while from dictation); and the same explanations would cover, if indeed they are mishearings or 'aural' misunderstandings, Quarto's 'gongarian' for 'hungarian' (I. iii. 19); 'by my sword were steele' for 'by my side weare Steele' (I. iii. 72); 'de Hearing be not so dead . . .' for 'de herring is no dead, so . . .' (II. iii. 11); 'is a dead bullies taile' for 'is he dead bully-Stale' (II. iii. 27–8); and 'thou shalt wear her' for 'thou shalt wooe her' (II. iii. 82–3). 'Betmes' for 'buttons' (III. ii. 63) is probably the compositor's misreading rather than the reporter's misremembering; and the constant setting out of prose as verse may be misunderstanding (or attempted inflation) by either compositor or reporters.

A more difficult problem is presented by the omission from the Quarto of passages or whole scenes of the full text. Here there are at least three possibilities: that the reporters simply forgot parts of the original; that they (or their 'editor', if they assigned to one of their number, or to another, the authority to patch up, or put together, the text) deliberately cut the original; or that the version they were trying to recall was itself a cut version of the full text as preserved, for example, in the Folio.

The first explanation covers the omission of many single lines and whole speeches and the general abbreviating where the Quarto dialogue retains the gist of what had been spoken but leaves out much of the detail and most of the colour. It is thus valid for the kinds of inadequacy already noted (pp. xxiii ff.); for the omission of the talk about Page's 'fallow Greyhound' by Slender, Shallow, and Page in I. i and of Quickly's words with and about Rugby before she questions Simple in I. iv; for the truncating of some of Ford–Brook's speeches to Falstaff in II. ii; and possibly for the omission of Mistress Page's discussion with Robin, and discussion of Robin with Ford, at the beginning of III. ii.

One cannot argue that Robin has been deliberately cut from the

Quarto version: his entry and exit in I. iii forbid this. (It is true that he does not speak, but he does not speak here in the Folio either; in both texts he is addressed by Falstaff and given the task of carrying the letters to Mistress Page and Mistress Ford.) Accordingly his omission from II. ii (where his only line in the Folio is to introduce Mistress Quickly—'Sir, here's a woman would speake with you'—and his only other function is to accompany her out) and from III. iii (where in the Folio he announces Falstaff's arrival and later Mistress Page's approach) may both be accidental: in neither scene is he essential to the plot and he certainly has nothing memorable to say. Nevertheless, the possibility that the part had been cut to a minimum before the Quarto was 'reported', in some intermediate version, so that it could be played by—for example—the boy who also played Anne Page, cannot be dismissed (although no company could easily have played *The Merry Wives* if it were short of boys: they are needed as fairies in the final act).

The reduction of Fenton's part in the Quarto raises a similar question. The Quarto omits altogether Fenton's interview with Quickly at the end of I. iv. The first mention of him in the Quarto is thus the Host's question to Page, in III. ii: 'But what say you to yong Maister *Fenton*? . . .' and he first appears, in an abbreviated version of III. iv, with Quickly and Anne. IV. vi is reported well enough, just, to make clear his final plot to marry Anne; and he duly enters with her at the end of the play, but has only two poor lines instead of a formal speech of eleven. Forgetfulness by the reporters may explain this; the alternative explanation is that the reduction has been made to avoid any unnecessary re-telling or fore-telling of what is seen happening on the stage.

This may well be the explanation of the omission from Falstaff's speech in III. v, describing to Ford his sad fate in the buck-basket, of lines 86–98, which recapitulate the stage-action of III. iii—and it will be remembered that Falstaff's part is generally well reported. There can be little doubt that v. i, v. ii, v. iii, and v. iv are omitted because they add nothing to the story. Yet that v. i was not omitted *before* the reporting is proved by the fact that one phrase from it ('this is the third time: I hope good lucke lies in odde numbers') gets into the Quarto version of v. v.

The Latin lesson, IV. i, must have been left out—whether by the reporters or in an intermediate version they were reporting—because it would lose all its fun for an audience that did not know Latin, and most of it for an audience that had not been brought up on William Lilly's Latin grammar text. (The omission of IV. i in turn made necessary the reordering of III. iv and III. v to avoid two consecutive Falstaff scenes.) Presumably Caius' longer French phrases were dropped from I. iv for auditors who could not be assumed to know French; and the jokes in I. i on 'Coram' and '*Cust-alorum*' and on coats of arms with 'Luces' in them would naturally go out for performance before an audience that could not be expected to understand them. Probably, too, such lines as 'What Duke should that be comes so secretly' (IV. iii) and '*Germanes* are honest men' (IV. v) were private or 'in' jokes, not appropriate for all occasions.[1]

Behind the Quarto text, then, there would seem to be a version of *The Merry Wives* that was designed for an audience not aristocratic and not primarily intellectual, whereas the full Folio text has much that would appeal only to the more sophisticated. Here perhaps lies also the explanation of the main differences between the two forms of the final scene (V. v).

In the Quarto, the action may not be convincing but it is relatively straightforward (though rendered hopelessly confusing because of its own confusion over the colours). Falstaff enters and is joined by Mistress Ford and Mistress Page (arriving together); Sir Hugh '*like a Satyre*' and Mistress Quickly '*like the Queene of Fayries*' come on with boys dressed as fairies, and Quickly instructs them to pinch black and blue any mortal they find; Evans gives pointless orders to 'Peane' and 'Pead'; and Falstaff is found, and 'tested' for virtue by tapers put to his fingers' ends. While the fairies '*sing about*' Falstaff, Caius '*steales away a boy in red*' (which is what Fenton had said was Mistress Page's plan); Slender takes another boy '*in greene*' (though Page has previously said that Anne would be in white for Slender, and Fenton had confirmed this); '*And Fenton steales misteris Anne, being in white*'. The entry of Ford, Page, and company immediately disconcerts Falstaff—whose question 'What hunting at this time at night? / Ile lay my life the mad Prince of *Wales* / Is stealing his fathers Deare' does not seem to refer specifically to any action the audience knows of except the appearance of these others. Ford demands the return of £20 borrowed by Falstaff from 'Brooke', but at his wife's request agrees to forgo it. Caius enters complaining that his expected bride turned out to be a boy; Slender likewise has discovered that his wife is a boy, though 'I came to her in red as you bad me'; and Fenton and Anne return, and are forgiven largely because the accomplished fact cannot be undone. But Mistress Page is glad that her husband's plan failed, he is glad that hers miscarried, and Falstaff gets satisfaction from knowing that both their arrows

1. See below, pp. xlvi–xlix.

'glanced'. They are happy to go home to laugh at Slender and Caius. Although this would be far more effective if the reconciliation had not taken place *before* Slender, Caius, Fenton, and Anne returned, the spirit is sustained for the 'happy ending', the interest is entirely in that ending, and there is nothing to connect the scene with any particular occasion or ceremony.

In the Folio, however, not only are the opening speeches fuller and more amusing (Falstaff thinks Mistress Ford is alone and has to be told 'Mistris *Page* is come with me (sweet hart)'), but also there are two specific references to Windsor Castle: one is Pistol's instruction to 'Cricket' to leap to 'Windsor-chimnies' and pinch any lazy maids because 'Our radiant Queene, hates Sluts, and Sluttery', the other is Quickly's long and, in a sense, irrelevant set speech (ll. 56–77) packed with references to the Order of the Garter and apparently directing the elves to prepare the Castle and St George's Chapel for a ceremony connected with that Order. Falstaff is 'discovered' and tested in much the same way as in the Quarto; but he is not let off as easily and is ridiculed and teased by all who are in a position to gloat over him. There is not even the suggestion that he will be let off the repayment of the £20 he had from 'Broome':[1] indeed 'his horses are arrested for it' and 'to repay that money will be a biting affliction'. It is at this point that Page first invites Falstaff 'to be cheerefull', by laughing at Mistress Page who does not know that Slender 'hath married her daughter'. Slender enters and disabuses him: he took a fairy in green, who proved to be a boy. (In iv. vi. 34–7 and v. ii. 5–10, however, it has been made quite clear that Slender should have taken the fairy in *white*.) Mistress Page announces that Caius has taken Anne in white—and Caius enters to complain that the white fairy too was a boy. (And, of course, although Mistress Page originally said in iv. iv. 70–1 that Anne was to be in white—and meant to deceive the others by changing the colour later—the real plan, of iv. vi. 37–41, was for Caius to find Anne in green.) The entry of Fenton and Anne clears up the main mystery and makes it possible for Falstaff for the first time to feel that others cannot afford to laugh at him: 'I am glad, though you haue tane a special stand to strike at me, that your Arrow hath glanc'd'. Mistress Page's 'Good husband, let vs euery one go home, / And laugh this sport ore by a Countrie fire, / Sir *Iohn* and all' saves—so to speak—*everybody's* face.

It would seem, then, that once again the Quarto has all the

1. For discussion of the Brook–Broome problem throughout the play, see below, pp. xxxiv–xxxv and lvi–lviii.

C

marks of the 'reported' text: the reordering of speeches and events robs them of meaning, and perhaps the Quarto confusion over the colours is a relic of confusion in the original text, helped (in one sense, and made worse in another) by the remembrance that the third colour in the denouement was red.[1] But it is far from certain that what the Quarto is reporting here is the Folio text. The complete omission of the Windsor Castle and Garter speeches (though the action is still left in 'Windsor forrest') may indicate this time that those speeches were not in the text being reported: that, in short, there was an alternative ending to the play for use—probably on the public stage—when, perhaps, the special occasion for which the original text was prepared was simply not relevant.

The general superiority of the Folio does not mean that the Quarto is invariably inferior. No matter how corrupt a reported text may be, there is always the chance that a reporter will have remembered correctly what the scribe who copied the good text, or the compositor who set it up in print, accidentally omitted, misread, or otherwise got wrong; and if the better text had been revised or in any way altered *after* the production or productions that the reporter knew, then the more corrupt text may in some respects be nearer to the original than is the generally superior one. Both these possibilities seem to have been realized with *The Merry Wives*.

The clearest example of the first is towards the end of III. i, where the Host is (he thinks) scoring over Caius and Evans and reconciling them to each other. In the words of the Folio,

> Shall I loose my Doctor? No, hee giues me the Potions and the Motions. Shall I loose my Parson? my Priest? my Sir *Hugh*? No, he giues me the Prouerbes, and the No-verbes. Giue me thy hand (Celestiall) so: Boyes of Art, I haue deceiu'd you both.

---

1. Interestingly, the Quarto report of IV. iv is particularly poor in *all* respects. In dressing Anne in white when Fenton elopes with her, the Quarto may be influenced by the idea that this is the appropriate colour for a bride; but since there are three specific statements in the Folio that *Slender* must expect her in white (IV. iv. 70–4, IV. vi. 34–7, V. ii. 5–10), and since the boy whom Caius takes must be in green, Anne probably wears a third colour for Fenton—which will be red, if the Quarto reporter, confused as he was, remembered correctly the colours involved. The suggestion, made, for example, by Schücking (*M.L.R.*, XIX, 1924, 338–40), that Fenton distinguished Anne by the 'Ribonds-pendant, flaring 'bout her head'—words that the Quarto puts in the speech in which Fenton describes (to the Host) how he will recognize her—does not explain the Quarto's other confusions about the colours, and does not begin to explain how the words appear in the Folio in Fenton's description of how *Caius* will recognize Anne.

The Quarto, though not right, comes to the rescue here:

> Shall I lose my doctor? No, he giues me the motiōs
> And the potions. Shall I lose my parson, my sir *Hu*?
> No, he giues me the prouerbes, and the nouerbes:
> Giue me thy hand terestiall,
> So giue me thy hand celestiall:
> So boyes of art I haue deceiued you both.

The reporter, although he has apparently forgotten two words ('my Priest'), has remembered the crucial words 'Give me thy hand terrestrial, so' (though either he or the compositor erred over 'terrestrial'), which the Folio omitted, presumably because the compositor's (or scribe's) eye skipped to the parallel word 'celestial'.[1]

Many editors have thought that there are other examples, but these are open to another explanation. For instance, where the Folio has Falstaff say (IV. v. 97–8) 'well, if my winde were but long enough; I would repent', the Quarto has 'and my winde / Were but long inough to say my prayers, / Ide repent', and there is no doubt that the additional words make the joke obvious—but perhaps so obvious that a reporter is more likely to have put them into Falstaff's mouth than is Shakespeare. Similarly, there is no good reason for believing that the Quarto's opening to II. ii

> *Fal.* Ile not lend thee a peny.
> *Pis.* I will retort the sum in equipage.
> *Fal.* Not a pennie

is other than a weaker version of the Folio's

> *Fal.* I will not lend thee a penny.
> *Pist.* Why then the world's mine Oyster, which I, with sword will
>   open.
> *Fal.* Not a penny.

So far from preserving a line dropped from the Folio, the Quarto reporter may be only substituting one semi-proverbial phrase for another.[2] Again, in I. i, Slender's specific charge against Pistol and Nym in the Quarto that 'They carried mee to the Tauerne and made mee drunke, and afterward picked my pocket' has been retained by most editors as a lead to Falstaff's later question in the Folio (and in the Quarto), '*Pistoll*, did you picke M. *Slenders* purse?' Is it not probable, however, that Falstaff's question, since nobody

---

1. For an illustration of the similar dropping of a necessary line from a good text (*2 Henry VI*) and its preservation in a reported text (*The Contention*) see Alfred Hart's *Stolne and Surreptitious Copies*, pp. 301–2.
2. See note on II. ii. 2–3.

in the Folio text has mentioned the charge, shows a prior knowledge of the crime—because he has been involved in it? (As Pistol
afterwards says to him on a similar matter, 'Didst not thou share?
hadst thou not fifteene pence?') The Quarto, confusing Falstaff's
later question with Slender's accusation, misses the subtlety completely. Finally, if the Quarto's version of Nym's briefing of Page
in II. i:

> *Nym.* . . . . Farwell, I loue not the humor of bread and cheese:
>   And theres the humor of it.   *Exit Nym.*
> *Pa.* The humor of it, quoth you:
>   Heres a fellow frites humor out of his wits.

is compared with the Folio's far fuller one, ending

> *Nim.* . . . adieu, I loue not the humour of bread and cheese:
>   adieu.
> *Page.* The humour of it (quoth 'a?) heere's a fellow frights
>   English out of his wits

it may be concluded, not that the Quarto preserves a phrase ('And
theres the humor of it') wrongly dropped from the Folio, but that
the Quarto is monotonously repeating one phrase (possibly imported from *Henry V*)—and that in the Folio Page catches up
Nym's single word 'humour', not a whole phrase.[1]

There are two, or perhaps three, examples in the play of Quarto's
preserving the original text where the Folio preserves a revised and
possibly un-Shakespearian reading. One of these concerns the
pseudonym that Ford adopts when in disguise he bribes Falstaff,
as he thinks, to demonstrate Mistress Ford's unfaithfulness. In the
Folio the pseudonym is, always, 'Broome'; in the Quarto it is
'Brooke'. 'Brooke' or 'Brook' is obviously a more natural second
name for a Ford than is 'Broome'; and indeed there are lines in the
Folio that make sense only on the supposition that 'Broome' must
be replaced by 'Brook'. The best instance is Falstaff's comment
(II. ii. 145–6) when he is told that the visitor has sent him 'a
mornings draught of Sacke': 'such *Broomes* are welcome to mee,
that ore'flowes such liquor'. The Quarto reads 'Such *Brookes* are
alwaies welcome to me', which is far better sense, but, most
significantly, omits the following words, 'that ore'flowes such
liquor', which are necessary to give point to the jest—an almost

1. See above, p. xxi; and see note on II. i. 133. It may be added that in the
lines corresponding to I. iii. 90 and 91, the Quarto has Nym and Pistol say that
they will report Falstaff's ambitions to Page and Ford, as they later do, whereas
the Folio has it the wrong way round. The Quarto may be either rationalizing
here or recalling a performance in which the confusion had been 'tidied up'.
See, however, the note on I. iii. 90, 95.

certain proof that the Quarto did not invent the name 'Brooke' but
was once again recalling a joke without being able to recall the
exact words that made it a joke. Other Folio phrases that perhaps
lose their point with the substitution of 'Broome' for 'Brooke' are
(III. v. 126–8): 'you shall haue her (Master *Broome*) Master
Broome, you shall cuckold *Ford*' and the final couplet of the play 'To
Master *Broome*, you yet shall hold your word, / For he, to night,
shall lye with Mistris *Ford*'. The only logical explanation seems to
be that Shakespeare wrote 'Brook(e)' and that 'Brooke' was spoken
on the stage, since the Quarto remembers it, and that at some *later*
time 'Broome' was substituted for it.[1]

The second way in which the Folio text seems to have been
altered for the worse after the original performances concerns the
oaths and other asseverations. In II. ii. 49–50, for instance, the Folio
has Quickly say 'heauen-blesse them, and make them his Seruants',
while the Quarto has 'Now God blesse them, and make them his
seruants'. In II. iii. 18 in the Folio, Shallow's greeting is ''Saue you
M^r· Doctor *Caius*'; in the Quarto the line (given to Page) is 'God
saue you M. Doctor *Cayus*'. For Evans's ''Plesse my soule: how full
of Chollors I am, and trempling of minde' (III. i. 11–12), the Quarto
has 'Ieshu ples mee, how my hart trobes, and trobes'; and for the
Folio's ''Mercie on mee, I haue a great dispositions to cry', the
Quarto reads 'Now so kad vdge me, my hart / Swelles more and
more. Mee thinkes I can cry / Verie well'. The last two examples
are perhaps good enough reason for suspecting that the Quarto
cannot be trusted to have the oaths exact, since it has only a vague
paraphrase of the words that the oaths introduce (and a study of
other bad texts such as the First Quarto of *Romeo and Juliet* confirms
that reporters improvise asseverations more readily than most
other phrasing). Nevertheless the Folio text has obviously been
censored. The expurgation of dramatic texts became more common, though not invariable, after the *Acte to Restraine Abuses of
Players* (3 Jac. I, c.21–27 May 1606), which provided a penalty of
£10 for 'jestingly or prophanely' speaking or using 'the holy Name
of God or of Christ Jesus, or of the Holy Ghoste or of the Trinitie' in
any 'Stageplayes, Interludes, Maygames, Shewes' or pageants;
and there was some 'censorship' of printed plays also, at least after
Sir Henry Herbert took office as (virtually) Master of the Revels, in
1623—what Greg calls 'a purely literary tradition of expurgation'.
It seems that plays were sometimes expurgated by scribes or
'editors' as a precaution before being presented for licensing; and
it is generally said that the expurgating of the plays in the Folio of

1. See below, pp. lvi–lviii.

1623 is more severe in those that were printed, or prepared for printing, after Herbert's succession—i.e. in the Histories and Tragedies.[1] Here, however, in *The Merry Wives*, is a comedy that has been expurgated—which may be some kind of reason for thinking that the offending phrases were removed for stage purposes, after 1606 but before the transcript or other copy was prepared for the printing of the Folio.

The New Cambridge editors have argued (p. 125) that the Quarto's references to '*Horne* the hunter' also preserve an original name that has been corrupted in the Folio to 'Herne'. It is not certain that there was a legend of a former keeper in Windsor Forest who haunted an oak in the neighbourhood (although *after* Shakespeare's day there was an oak that apparently became famous as Herne's or Falstaff's oak, until it was cut down towards the end of the eighteenth century); but whether there was such a tradition or not, it seems far more likely that the Quarto, always ready to make more obvious or otherwise vulgarize, would have substituted 'Horne' for 'Herne' and then invented the line saying that Falstaff was to be persuaded to come 'Disguised like *Horne*, with huge horns on his head', than that Folio would have replaced 'Horne' by 'Herne', for no good reason at all. (Various claims to have discovered the name 'Herne' or 'Horne' 'in the old Windsor Registers of Shakespeare's period' or on a list of yeomen guilty of poaching in Henry VIII's reign seem, like W. S. Gilbert's flowers that bloom in the spring, to have nothing to do with the case.[2]) What is curious is that Mistress Ford's and Mistress Page's explanations to their husbands (IV. iv) of their third and final plan to disgrace Falstaff do not, in the Folio, specify that Falstaff is to be disguised like Herne with horns on his head; many editors, not content with Mistress Page's later 'We'll . . . dis-horne the spirit', therefore incorporate the Quarto line, even if they change 'Horne' to 'Herne' in the process.[3]

One other slight difference between the Quarto and the Folio should be mentioned. In I. iv in the good text, Mistress Quickly hides Simple in the 'Closset' where Caius keeps his green box and his other 'simples'; and it is in the 'Closset' that Caius discovers the hidden visitor. The Quarto refers consistently not to a closet but to a 'Counting-house' (three times in the dialogue and once in a stage direction). Many commentators have found it difficult to believe that a counting-house and a closet were so similar that the

1. See, e.g., Chambers, *Elizabethan Stage*, IV. 338–9; Greg, *The Shakespeare First Folio* (Oxford, 1955), pp. 149–52 and 169–72.

2. H. C. Hart, *The Merry Wives of Windsor*, pp. li–lii.

3. See note on IV. iv. 28–45.

reporter of the Quarto could himself have substituted one for the other and they have suspected that the Quarto is, so to speak, a London version of the play. It has thus also been thought significant that the Quarto replaces some of the references to Windsor Castle in the final scene with the lines 'Where is *Pead*? go you & see where Brokers sleep, / And Foxe-eyed Seriants with their mase, / Goe laie the Proctors in the street, / And pinch the lowsie Seriants face'. Yet it replaces others with lines about 'these shady groues', and 'Peane' is told to go 'to the countrie houses'; John Munro has shown that 'counting houses' were known in country homes (the house-keeping accounts were kept there); and, as he says, 'Brokers, Serjeants, and Proctors were not peculiar to London'.[1] The Quarto's variations again look like poor improvisation rather than logical substitution. It is just possible, however, that the version of the play used on the public stage presented Caius as the kind of dealer in herbs and other medicines with which a typical London audience would have been familiar. Another theory, that the Quarto—for some reason—is closer to a supposed source play about London citizens, is contradicted by all the evidence showing that the Folio text was in fact the earlier.[2]

3. THE PRINTING OF THE QUARTO AND THE FOLIO

The printer of the 1602 Quarto of *The Merry Wives*, T[homas] C[reede], printed two other bad Quartos, *The First Part of the Contention betwixt the Two Famous Houses of Yorke and Lancaster* (1594)—for T. Millington—and *The Cronicle History of Henry the fift* (1600)—for Millington and Busby (and Busby, it will be remembered, assigned *The Merry Wives* to Arthur Johnson, just before the publication of the Quarto in 1602). It might be unwise to infer that either Busby or Creede habitually dealt in pirated texts: apparently publishers and printers did not always inquire into the good faith of those who sold dramatic texts or wanted them printed—although failure to inquire, even in the days before copyright, may itself suggest an incriminating lack of concern.

The printing of the Quarto is careless and also rather odd. There is some reason for thinking that at least two compositors were involved: one preferred the spellings 'Ford' and 'here' and was addicted to the colon as a mark of punctuation (there are some twenty-one colons on E2, for example—counting both dialogue and speech-prefixes); the other normally spelt 'Foord' and 'heere' and

1. 'Some Matters Shakespearian', *Times Literary Supplement*, 13 September 1947.
2. See not only pp. xiii–xxvi above but also pp. lx–lxi.

could set a whole page with but a single colon (E3, for instance). The second seems to have been more willing than the first to set prose as prose—but throughout the Quarto the intention was presumably to set everything possible as verse, largely, perhaps, to spread it all out more, over as great a number of pages as possible, though there are many abbreviations and turned-over lines. (E2ᵛ, which is nearly all prose, is quite exceptional.) Probably the existence of the two compositors, working simultaneously but from two different cases of type, is connected also with the curious use of the italic capital '*I*' for the roman on many pages. The italic '*I*' is first found on B3ᵛ, but not in the first seven lines, in which there are four roman capital 'I's; Quickly's speech in line 8 begins '*Is* he quoth you' and the italic capital is used in the remainder of that page and throughout B4 (but not at all in B4ᵛ—where suddenly there is prose, in the speech by Mistress Page following the reading of Falstaff's letter, although the rest of the page, after Mistress Ford's entrance, is set as 'verse'). This looks like two compositors setting at this stage by formes—with the compositor who set the inner forme running out of the roman capital 'I', and resorting to the italic, before the end of his stint.[1] No such clear-cut pattern emerges in the remainder of the play, although the two compositors may have continued to divide the work, unsystematically, throughout: perhaps once the type was distributed after the printing of the 'B' gathering, and after the setting of some of 'C', the roman and italic capital 'I's were mixed up, in one case: there are pages in which none of the italic capitals occur—namely C1, C1ᵛ, and C2, and then C3, C4ᵛ, D1, D1ᵛ, F1, F1ᵛ, G2ᵛ, G3, and G3ᵛ; at least one which has them only at the top of the page (C4); others which have them only after a certain point (C2ᵛ, C3ᵛ, D4); and many which have a mixture (D2, D4ᵛ, etc.).

Unfortunately there is nothing in the facts or hypotheses concerning the printing of the Quarto to help determine the nature of the copy from which it was set. No one character's speeches, for example, are more consistently in prose than another's, and none has a characteristic spelling. The only useful guess might be that most of the copy was in prose; that the persistent setting out as verse was a matter of 'editorial' or 'compositorial' policy and, occasionally, of *ad hoc* decisions based on the spacing of the page; and that since Fenton, on his few appearances, *always* speaks verse, albeit sometimes very poor verse, the reporter (who was certainly not the actor who played Fenton) may have remembered that the

---

1. It may be significant of a general scarcity of type that on these same two pages—B3ᵛ and B4—the compositor resorts to roman 'VV' for 'W'.

part, exceptionally, was mostly blank verse in the original text.

There are five surviving copies of the Quarto—in the British Museum; the Bodleian Library; the Wren Library of Trinity College, Cambridge; the Folger; and the Huntington.[1] They have all been collated, and no variants have been found, other than a 'variant' apparently caused by the dislodging of a piece of type.

The Folio, although a longer and better text than the Quarto, is certainly not perfect. As has already been shown (pp. xxxii ff.), in at least one speech the Folio dropped, by accident, a line that must have been in the play as written and that, by good luck, is preserved in the Quarto; the text has been expurgated, at some indefinable time between the composition of the play and the publication of the Folio (but probably after 1606); and at the beginning of I. iii either the scribe or the compositor has perpetrated an obvious and understandable error with the stage direction '*Enter Falstaffe, Host, Bardolfe, Nym, Pistoll, Page*': Page does not appear in this scene at all and could not conceivably do so, for he is discussed in his absence, but 'the Page', Robin, is needed and must be meant.

The stage directions in the Folio are all of the kind just cited: that is to say, at the beginning of every scene (and the Folio has a full, systematic, division into acts and scenes) there is a list of all the characters who appear at any time during the scene—i.e. a so-called 'massed entry'; but no other entries or exits are marked during a scene, no matter how many characters may come and go. There is only one exception: '*Enter Fairies*' at v. v. 37—an entry which is still cryptic, for it covers the disguised Evans, Pistol, and Quickly as well as the children.

The massed entries, made 'under the influence of the neo-classical drama of the Continent',[2] are part of the evidence for the generally accepted theory that the 'copy' given to the printer for the Folio *Merry Wives* was a transcript made by the professional scribe, Ralph Crane. Crane—whose transcripts of Middleton's *Game at Chess* and *The Witch* and Fletcher's *Demetrius and Enanthe*, and other works, have survived and been carefully studied for evidence of his scribal habits—is thought to have been employed, as a matter of policy, to transcribe for the printer what were to be the first four plays in the Folio, namely *The Tempest, The Two*

1. The original *Short-Title Catalogue*, compiled by A. W. Pollard and G. R. Redgrave in 1926, mistakenly lists four other copies, which are in fact of the 1619 Quarto.

2. Greg, *Editorial Problem*, p. 137. Greg convincingly refutes the earlier theory that massed entries were an indication of a text made up from players' parts and a 'plot' (a summary of exits and entrances, action and properties).

Gentlemen of Verona, *The Merry Wives of Windsor*, and *Measure for Measure*. *The Two Gentlemen of Verona* also has the massed entries (though *The Tempest* and *Measure for Measure* have not). Other characteristics of Crane found in *The Merry Wives* are his addiction to parentheses—'that same knaue (*Ford* hir husband) hath the finest mad diuell of iealousie in him (Master *Broome*) . . .'; his extravagant use of colons; his fondness for hyphens—'an old-fat-woman', 'rag'd-hornes', 'ranting-Host', 'mary-her'; a strange use of the apostrophe—'go't's' (='Got's'), 'do's' (='does'), 'if he ha's'; and some favoured spellings ('troa' for 'trow' may be one: compare 'doa' for 'doe' in both *The Witch* and *Demetrius and Enanthe*).[1] Perhaps too the occasional setting-up as 'verse' of what can only be prose—as in Mistress Page's comments on Falstaff's letter in II. i[2]—occurs because the compositor follows Crane, who, although he does not necessarily begin every line with a capital, has a most confusing trick sometimes of setting out in separate lines like verse what must have been prose in his copy. On the other hand, Crane elsewhere has careful stage directions marking exits and entrances during scenes (notably in *The Witch*). It must be added that *any* inference about what was in the printer's 'copy' for an Elizabethan play is in a sense guesswork, since Elizabethan compositors felt free to space and punctuate as seemed to them fitting at the moment.

That true verse does occur at times in the Folio text of *The Merry Wives* need not mean that there was anything odd about the copy. If, as will be argued later (p. lxxvi), the verse is used appropriately for some of the more romantic or serious parts, there is no necessity for a theory that the verse sections represent copy by a different playwright or copy from an earlier stage of composition (although it is certainly not impossible that *The Merry Wives* involves revision of an earlier play). Nor can much be inferred from the presence in v. v of the only stage direction within a scene. The entry of so many characters at once is itself exceptional in the action of the play; and in other respects Act v Scene v seems to be no different from the rest: it has the massed entry at the beginning of the scene, and other 'Crane' mannerisms. It is true that Evans's Welsh accent is not indicated in the speeches he utters while in

1. On Crane, see, e.g., F. P. Wilson, 'Ralph Crane, Scrivener to the King's Players', *The Library*, 4th Ser. VII (1927), 194–215; W. W. Greg, 'Some Notes on Crane's Manuscript of *The Witch*', *The Library*, XXII (1942), 208–22; Middleton's *A Game at Chesse*, ed. R. C. Bald (Cambridge, 1929); the Malone Society editions of *Demetrius and Enanthe* (1951) and *The Witch* (1950); and T. H. Howard-Hill, 'Ralph Crane's Parentheses', *Notes and Queries*, N.S. XII (1965), 334–40.
2. Even the Quarto, exceptionally, reports this, albeit very badly, as prose—a probable indication that it was prose in the original.

disguise as a fairy or satyr or whatever it is; but since Falstaff does notice some accent ('Heauens defend me from that Welsh Fairy'), the explanation may be that the actor playing Evans is being encouraged to give the impression that he 'tries' to alter his accent while speaking his prepared or given lines, and fails.

The printing of the Folio text has been fully analysed by Charlton Hinman in *The Printing and Proof-Reading of the First Folio of Shakespeare* (Oxford, 1963). That *The Merry Wives* was printed immediately after *The Two Gentlemen* is proved by, for example, the error in using the running title '*The Merry Wives of Windsor*' for the last two pages of the preceding play (D1 and D1^v); but there may have been interruptions because of the need to work concurrently on, and sometimes give priority to, another book (Wilson's *Christian Dictionary*). Probably for this reason, several compositors (three or even four) seem to have set parts of the text, and Hinman has more than the usual difficulty in identifying them from spelling habits or from typographical evidence. In such conditions, printing errors are to be expected, but there is nothing to suggest any special care in reading proofs. Only five trivial variants in different copies of the Folio have been found: on D2 the final letter was dropped in the catchword and wrongly replaced (so that some copies have, correctly, '*Shal.*' but others have the point before the 'l' and the 'l' upside down); on E2 uncorrected copies have a wrong character (for which 'y^e' had to be substituted) and a blotch (probably an inked quad) that had to be removed; and the uncorrected E5^v has 'id' for 'in', and another inked quad. There was obviously some 'casting-off' of copy (i.e. calculating in advance how much copy was required to fill a particular page and forme); and on D2^v, for example, the compositor can be seen resorting to abbreviations, as he approaches the foot of the second column, so that he can fit all the necessary words and speeches in.

There is an oddity, at the head of the first column of E1, that makes one wonder whether for the minute the compositor had his eye on the Quarto. The relevant lines, as set out in the Folio, are:

Cai. I, dat is very good, excellant.
Host. Peace, I say: heare mine Host of the Garter,
  Am I politicke? Am I subtle? Am I a Machiuell?
  Shall I loose my Doctor? No, hee giues me the Potions
  and the Motions. Shall I loose my Parson? my Priest?
  my Sir *Hugh*? No, . . .

The setting-up of the Host's first two lines as verse is odd (there is room to spare for 'Am' at the end of the first line, and for 'Shall' at the end of the second); and the Quarto is thus:

[D3]   *Doc.* This is verie braue, excellent.
      Host. Peace I say, heare mine host of the garter,
[D3ᵛ]   Am I wise? am I polliticke? am I Matchauil?
           Shall I lose my doctor? No, he giues me the motiōs
           And the potions. Shall I lose my parson, my sir *Hu*?
           No, . . .

It will be apparent, however, that the differences far outweigh the resemblances (indeed it is later in this speech that the Folio omits the words that the Quarto has in the form 'Giue me thy hand terestiall, / So'); and the probable explanation of the passing similarity is that the Host's lines were set out thus (as in the Folio) in Shakespeare's original script, and in the actor's part transcribed from it, and that the actor who played the Host (and was almost certainly one of the reporters of the Quarto, and a good one) has remembered and reproduced, as actors sometimes do, the *look* of his lines as they were written out for him. The same explanation covers a vague typographical similarity in the Folio (D5) and the Quarto (C2ᵛ) of a speech by Falstaff (II. ii. 4–12), noted by the New Cambridge editors.[1] There is, then, no good reason for thinking that the Folio was at any time set up from the Quarto.

4. THIS EDITION

In accordance with the practice of the Arden series, the text of this edition is in modern spelling, with modern punctuation. All possible weight has been given to the seventeenth-century punctuation, but any attempt to retain in a modernized text a system so different from our own leads to hopeless inconsistency and invites misunderstanding of Shakespeare's meaning.

Necessarily, in view of what has been said in the preceding sections of this Introduction, this edition is based on the Folio. Readings from the Quarto are adopted very rarely and only when one can be reasonably certain that the Quarto preserves a reading that is right where the Folio, exceptionally, omits it by accident (e.g. III. i. 97) or gets it wrong through misreading or misprinting (as, probably, in I. iii. 14) or, possibly, through rationalization (as in the speech prefix of II. i. 203). The Quarto has also been followed for Ford's pseudonym 'Brooke' as against the Folio's 'Broome', the justification being that the dialogue shows that Shakespeare must have written 'Brook(e)' and that even if he had to put up with 'Broome' for particular performances, he cannot have preferred it.[2] The oaths present a problem. Undoubtedly the Folio text has

---

1. pp. 95–6.   2. See above, pp. xxxiv–xxxv, and below, pp. lvi–lviii.

been expurgated and yet only by following it can one achieve any consistency at all; the Quarto may sometimes have the oath that Shakespeare wrote down, but all one's experience with reported texts suggests that the reporter had at best an even-money chance of being right on such a question. For once, then, Bertrand Russell's famous dictum may be reversed: it may be better to be consistently 'wrong' (with the Folio) than to be occasionally right (with the Quarto) at the certain cost of importing actors' improvisations that neither Shakespeare nor Heminge and Condell would necessarily have approved. Nor is it impossible that Shakespeare himself, however reluctantly, made the alterations for the expurgated text.

Whereas the Folio entries are massed at the head of each scene, the Quarto often gives a stage direction in the correct place; it therefore has authority of a kind here, although no Quarto stage direction has been adopted unless it can also be inferred from the full text. Stage directions which are in neither the Folio nor the Quarto are, in accordance with Arden practice, invariably placed in square brackets. Once or twice it happens that an early editor (say, Rowe) has a stage direction similar to a Quarto stage direction, in a scene so badly reported in the Quarto that there is no precise parallel between the Quarto and the full text; the stage direction is then put in square brackets and the collation reads, exceptionally, 'Rowe (as Q)'. Imaginary settings of the scene are not given in the stage directions but the collations include a sampling of those invented by earlier editors, generally in complete misunderstanding of the principles of the bare Elizabethan stage.

The collations are essentially selective. Every Folio reading of any importance not adopted in this edition is collated, but it has not been thought necessary to record aberrant Folio line-division where it is obviously typographical in origin—i.e. where verse lines have been cramped into prose length to save space or where prose lines have been spaced out as if verse, to spread insufficient text over a page. Wrong fount is not retained in citations of either the Folio or the Quarto. It is impossible in collations to give all the different readings of the Quarto; but none have been omitted that are conceivably right or have any special interest as evidence of the reporting process.

Emendations made in the later Folios and by subsequent editors are listed only where they are accepted in this edition, or are plausible, or have been so widely accepted as to be familiar to many readers of the play, or have had their place in the historical process of emendation, pointing the way to a better emendation made by a later editor. The collations do not record, for instance, all Pope's scene divisions (a few examples are given) or the attempts of editors to 'normalize' Shakespeare's syntax or their attempts to 'regularize' Evans's bad English (e.g. by altering 'good' to 'goot' or 'cheese' to 'seese').

The Folio reading is given in the exact spelling (except for the long 's') if it is not adopted, as in

27. Galen] *Rowe; Galien F*

but is not necessarily given exactly when it is adopted, as in

50. will hack] *F*

where the Folio actually reads 'will hacke', or even

ACT II SCENE I] *F*

where the Folio has '*Actus Secundus. Scæna Prima*'. If, however, the Folio spelling could conceivably be otherwise interpreted or could be relevant to a textual (as distinct from a purely bibliographical) theory, it is shown thus:

152. we] *F* (wee).

5. THE PROBABLE OCCASION OF THE PLAY AND THE THEORIES OF PERSONAL SATIRE

The tradition, now often repeated as if it were fact, that *The Merry Wives of Windsor* was written by Shakespeare to please Queen Elizabeth is first recorded in print in John Dennis's dedication to George Granville of *The Comical Gallant* in 1702. Dennis's adaptation had not succeeded on the stage: some of his ill-wishers, he says, believed the original play 'to be so admirable, that nothing ought to be added to it; the others fancied it to be so despicable, that anyones time would be lost upon it'; and it is in this context that he makes his now famous statement:

> That this Comedy was not despicable, I guess'd for several Reasons: First, I knew very well, that it had pleas'd one of the greatest Queens that ever was in the World, great not only for her Wisdom in the Arts of Government, but for her knowledge of Polite Learning, and her nice taste of the Drama, for such a taste we may be sure she had, by the relish which she had of the Ancients. This Comedy was written at her Command, and by her direction, and she was so eager to see it Acted, that she commanded it to be finished in fourteen days; and was afterwards, as Tradition tells us, very well pleas'd at the Representation. (A2)

(He repeats in his Prologue the assertion about the fourteen days.) A few years later, in the biography published with his 1709 editions of Shakespeare, Rowe added to the details:

She was so well pleas'd with that admirable Character of *Falstaff*, in the two Parts of *Henry* the Fourth, that she commanded him to continue it for one Play more, and to shew him in Love. This is said to be the Occasion of his Writing *The Merry Wives of Windsor*. How well she was obey'd, the Play it self is an admirable Proof.

(pp. viii–ix)

Then in 1710 Gildon, probably relying only on Dennis and on Rowe (whose edition he and his publisher Curll were supplementing unasked) but also at least drawing attention to the relevance of parts of Act v, wrote:

The *Fairys* in the fifth Act makes a Handsome Complement to the Queen, in her Palace of *Windsor*, who had oblig'd him to write a Play of Sir *John Falstaff* in Love, and which I am very well assured he perform'd in a Fortnight; a prodigious Thing, when all is so well contriv'd, and carry'd on without the least Confusion.[1]

There is no reason to believe that Dennis, Rowe, or Gildon knew of the 1602 Quarto. They were therefore presumably not indebted to its title-page for their information that the play had been presented before the Queen. (It is nevertheless not impossible that the tradition of the Queen's command had begun, years earlier, from that same title-page.) Pope (who knew only the 1619 Quarto) and Theobald (who rediscovered that of 1602) made the connection, but unfortunately concluded that the play written in a fortnight for the Queen must have been the Quarto version, which they thought of as a 'first imperfect sketch'.[2] They thereby started criticism on a wrong track, along which it ran happily for over a hundred years.

Gildon was more probably correct when he associated the royal command with the lines in Act v of the play (v. v. 56–74)—found only in the *Folio* text—that instruct the fairies to prepare Windsor Castle for, apparently, some special ceremony and allude to the Order of the Garter. It does not follow, however, that the play was performed *at* Windsor; and easily the most persuasive explanation of the occasion and date of the play is that advanced by Leslie Hotson in his *Shakespeare versus Shallow* (London, 1931), although unfortunately it falls short of final proof.[3]

Hotson argues that the play was performed at the Garter Feast celebrated not in Windsor but in the royal Whitehall Palace, in

1. 'Remarks on the Plays of Shakespear', in *The Works of Mr. William Shakespear* [ed. Rowe]. *Volume the Seventh*. (London, 1710), p. 291.
2. Pope, *The Works of Shakspear*, 1. 233; Theobald, *The Works of Shakespeare*, 1. 223.
3. William Green's *Shakespeare's 'Merry Wives of Windsor'* tries to build on Hotson's argument but adds little to it.

Westminster, on St George's Day, 23 April 1597. (A decree made early in Elizabeth's reign permitted the celebration 'Where the *Soveraign* should then happen to be'.) This feast, which marked the first election of knights to the Order of the Garter for four years, preceded by one month the formal installation of the knights in St George's Chapel at Windsor, an installation which the Queen did not attend. The Fairy Queen's speech in Act v of the Folio is thus explained adequately as a direction to the fairies that they must now start getting Windsor Castle, and in particular the Chapel, ready for the installation, by scouring the 'Chaires of Order', cleaning the coats of arms and other insignia, and 'writing' in flowers the motto of the Order of the Garter, '*Hony Soit Qui Mal-y-Pence*'. Nor should one overlook the simple fact that a play about Windsor would have been appropriate for the purpose.

Hotson further pointed out that there was a very special reason for the involvement of Shakespeare's company, the Chamberlain's Men, in the London celebrations in April 1597, for one of the five knights being honoured by election to the Order was George Carey, Lord Hunsdon, who became patron of the company after the death of his father Henry in July 1596, and who on 17 April 1597 had just become Lord Chamberlain following the death in March of his father's successor, William Brooke Lord Cobham. Hunsdon seems to have been a great favourite with the Queen (Hotson quotes, on p. 116, a few of her letters to him, one including, in modernized form, the sentence 'And in what place soever you be, you shall find us a mother and a wife to minister unto you all the best effects of that tender and kind affection which we may possibly extend to one whom for many respects we hold so near and dear unto us'); he had decided to make a grand occasion of his election and is known to have borrowed extensively to do so; and he would thus presumably have been most eager to have his company, through its greatest playwright, obey any command the Queen may have given.[1]

The theory that *The Merry Wives of Windsor* was written for the Garter Feast in 1597 has the added attraction that it alone makes sense of allusions in the play that were first discussed by Charles Knight in his 1839 'Pictorial Edition' of Shakespeare. These are the allusions supposed to be to Frederick, Duke of Württemberg and formerly Count of Mömpelgard, allusions which were once

1. F. P. Wilson (*Shakespearian and Other Studies*, Oxford, 1969, p. 88n.), arguing that there is 'no record of payment to the Chamberlain's men' on this day, and that the Queen would not have been likely to pay for the performance herself, overlooks the probability that, if Hotson's theory is correct, Hunsdon would have borne the expenses.

thought to gain their point from their supposed connection with the stealing of the Host's horses but which are now seen to be humorous rather because of their relevance to the Garter ceremonies in 1597. As Count Mömpelgard, Frederick had visited England in 1592, had travelled to Maidenhead, Reading, and Windsor, among other places, and had afterwards developed a 'burning desire' to be elected to the Order of the Garter; after his return home and his becoming Duke of Württemberg, he kept pestering Elizabeth about an alleged promise she had made him that he would be elected. (She denied this to his envoy in 1595.)[1] Probably for political reasons, he was finally elected, in 1597, but *in absentia*; Elizabeth, thanks to a clause introduced by Henry VIII, was not obliged to tell him immediately of his success and conveniently forgot to do so (and James I had to pay for the insignia in 1603 after her death). To a court audience in April 1597, then, there would be special fun in the Host's reply to Bardolph's statement in IV. iii (of the Folio text only) that 'the Duke himselfe will be to morrow at Court, and they are going to meet him': 'What Duke should that be comes so secretly? I heare not of him in the Court'. Mömpelgard was coming very 'secretly' indeed; since he had not been invited, he was not coming at all. The same jest is to be found in Caius' 'it is tell-a-me, dat you make grand preparation for a Duke *de Iamanie*: by my trot: der is no Duke that the Court is know, to come' (IV. v. 81–4—also only in the Folio). At a time when relations between England and the German states were deteriorating, the Host's earlier comment 'doe not say they be fled: *Germanes* are honest men' (ll. 66–7, Folio only) may also have been as gleefully received as would have been a statement on the English stage in the 1930's that Germans were modest and retiring.

Whether there was further point in associating Mömpelgard in particular, or Germans in general, with horse-stealing or post-horses is far from clear. It will be remembered that in the earlier part of the comedy (III. i. 106–15 and III. iii. 221–5) Caius and Evans vow vengeance on the Host for the practical joke he has played on them by arranging the 'duel' and then making them look silly when it is not fought. Only a very naïve reader, surely, could fail to link this with the gloating way in which, one after the other, they come in (IV. v. 68–84) to add to the Host's misery by giving him corroborative detail about the theft of his post-horses—

1. See Elias Ashmole, *The Institution, Laws & Ceremonies Of the most noble Order of the Garter* (London, 1672); W. B. Rye ed., *England as seen by Foreigners in the Days of Elizabeth and James the First* (London, 1865), pp. iv-ciii and 3–53; Victor von Klarwill ed., *Queen Elizabeth and Some Foreigners*, trans. T. H. Nash (London, 1928), pp. 347–423; Green, *op. cit.*, pp. 121–50.

D

a theft of which Bardolph (no doubt bribed for the purpose) has just told him. The relevant lines of Caius' contribution have already been quoted; Evans's lines, in the Folio version (70–7), are 'Haue a care of your entertainments: there is a friend of mine come to Towne, tels mee there is three Cozen-Iermans, that has cozend all the *Hosts* of *Readins*, of *Maidenhead*; of *Cole-brooke*, of horses and money: I tell you for good will (looke you) you are wise, and full of gibes, and vlouting-stocks: and 'tis not conuenient you should be cozoned. Fare you well.' The puns on cousins-germane, Germans who could be addressed as 'cousin' (a frequent polite term of aristocratic address), Germans who 'cozen' or cheat, and those who 'cozen' by pretending to be Germans may all be disentangled fairly easily, but that Shakespeare is associating the particular German, Mömpelgard, with any incident involving post-horses is improbable. The corresponding Quarto passage, 'Now my Host, I would desire you looke you now, / To haue a care of your enter-tainments, / For there is three sorts of cosen garmombles, / Is cosen all the Host of Maidenhead & Readings . . .', has been thought to provide evidence for such a connection, 'garmombles' being taken to be a word invented as a quibble on Mömpelgard's name (and one theory is that the Quarto here retains an original jest removed in a post-1602 revision and not preserved in the Folio). On the other hand, 'garmombles' may be only another bad attempt by the Quarto to recall the general sense of what was spoken on the stage (and perhaps the actors themselves became confused between the jokes on Mömpelgard—which would quickly lose their point—and the others, really distinct, about German horse-thieves). The word 'garmomble' probably did exist—see note on IV. v. 72—and even W. B. Rye (p. xcviii) was prepared to grant that 'if the word be archaic, and a meaning found for it, we are willing to yield the point', i.e. willing to concede that 'garmombles' did not neces-sarily refer to 'Mömpelgard'.

J. E. V. Crofts[1] has shown that there is no reason for associating Mömpelgard with misappropriation of post-horses; indeed the Duke was given an official warrant enabling him to use them without charge. Crofts's alternative theories, however—that Shakespeare transferred from Frenchmen to Germans a scandal in-volving de Chastes, the visiting Governor of Dieppe, in 1596 and in revising alluded rather to another, involving only Englishmen, in November 1597—have little to recommend them.[2] There is

1. *Shakespeare and the Post Horses* (Bristol, 1937).
2. Crofts's attempts at textual analysis of the Quarto and the Folio, and Green's further explanation (pp. 169ff.) of how 'the fertile brain of the playwright toyed with the incident' (of de Chastes), have even less.

really no need to suppose that the stealing (or unofficial borrowing) of horses had any topical reference at all; the 'source' for the incident may have been, as the text itself suggests, Marlowe's *Doctor Faustus*, undoubtedly a play about Germans, and whether this sub-plot was ever any clearer in a version of which even the Folio is not a true representation is highly problematical.

The connection of Lord Hunsdon and Count Mömpelgard with the Garter Feast of April 1597 was, paradoxically, less important in the mind of Leslie Hotson, who first showed the connection, than another supposed reference that he thought pointed to the same date—a reference that has not seemed nearly so certain to later writers on the subject. Hotson discovered that in 1596 one William Wayte took out a writ of surety against William Shakespeare, Francis Langley (the owner of the Swan theatre), and two women, and that a writ of attachment was duly issued, returnable on 29 November. He also discovered that, a little earlier, Langley had taken out a writ of surety against Wayte and Wayte's step-father William Gardiner, a Surrey justice of the peace. Finding that Wayte was elsewhere described as 'a certain loose person of no reckoning or value, being wholly under the rule and commandment of the said Gardiner'; building up a not fully convincing case against Gardiner as a rogue;[1] and arguing, also not very convincingly, that Gardiner was one of the chief opponents and prosecutors of the theatre,[2] Hotson went on to suggest that Gardiner and Wayte were satirized in *The Merry Wives* as Shallow and Slender, particularly in the first scene.

It is true that if one could be sure that, exceptionally, Shakespeare was here making fun of living people—and relying on his audience's knowing the facts in so much detail that all the jokes could be appreciated (which is rather harder to believe[3])—this first scene would be more amusing, and what seem to be loose ends in the play, having no connection at all with the later actions of Shallow and Falstaff, would at least be explicable. It is true, for example, that Gardiner, like Shallow (ll. 1–4 and 32), was given to threats of legal action (as were many other Elizabethans!); that

1. J. E. Hannigan, 'Shakespeare vs. Shallow', *Shakespeare Association Bulletin* VII (1932), 174–82, enters some important caveats and shows how, e.g., Hotson takes conventional legal phraseology too literally.

2. Hotson's evidence on this question perhaps proves no more than that as a justice of the peace Gardiner naturally received instructions to put into effect decisions made by his superiors.

3. Cf. Peter Alexander's comment that to see satire here 'is to attribute to Shakespeare a sad deficiency of gall, and to the audience an appreciation of Shakespeare's allusions rivalling that of later investigators' (*Shakespeare*, London, 1964, p. 41).

he was a member of the quorum but could hardly hope to be custos rotulorum, and that William Wayte would probably not have known the difference (ll. 5–8); that he had luces in his coat of arms, and only by quartering, since his first wife was the widow Frances Wayte, née Luce or Lucy; that he had married Wayte off to an heiress, possibly to swindle him of her money; and that he had a deer park, perhaps acquired by shady methods. April 1597 would also be exactly the right time for a caricature of Gardiner, after the writs of November 1596 and well before Gardiner's death on 26 November 1597. It is also true, however, that there are no signs of any satire on Gardiner in the portrait of Shallow in *2 Henry IV*; that Shallow is supposed to be over eighty; that he comes from Gloucestershire; that the setting of the play is Windsor; and that the audience for which the play was first written was probably an aristocratic one. Perhaps Shakespeare was allowing himself a sideglance or two at a pompous opponent; it is difficult to be certain.

If Shakespeare is here indulging, even for a passing moment, in personal satire, Gardiner may be a better candidate for the distinction than is the traditional one, Sir Thomas Lucy. The Lucy story is familiar to most students of Shakespeare in the version of Rowe:

> He [Shakespeare] had, by a Misfortune common enough to young Fellows, fallen into ill Company; and amongst them, some that made a frequent practice of Deer-stealing, engag'd him with them more than once in robbing a Park that belong'd to Sir *Thomas Lucy* of *Cherlecot*, near *Stratford*. For this he was prosecuted by that Gentleman, as he thought, somewhat too severely; and in order to revenge that ill Usage, he made a Ballad upon him. And . . . it is said to have been so very bitter, that it redoubled the Prosecution against him to that degree, that he was oblig'd to leave his Business and Family in *Warwickshire*, for some time, and shelter himself in *London*.   (p. v)

Rowe later adds:

> Amongst other Extravagances, in *The Merry Wives of* Windsor, he has made him [Falstaff] a Dear-stealer, that he might at the same time remember his *Warwickshire* Prosecutor, under the Name of Justice *Shallow*; he has given him very near the same Coat of Arms which *Dugdale*, in his Antiquities of that County, describes for a Family there, and makes the *Welsh* Parson descant very pleasantly upon 'em.   (p. xviii)

(Rowe is referring here to a coat repeated in four quarterings, so that the three luces of the Lucy coat of arms become twelve, as in the play.)

Rowe can hardly have known that the same tradition had already
been recorded in some manuscript notes by Richard Davies, who
died in 1708. Davies had written that Shakespeare was

> much given to all unluckinesse in stealing venison & Rabbits
> particularly from Sʳ   Lucy who had him oft whipt &
> sometimes Imprisoned & at last made Him fly his Native
> Country to his great Advancem! but His reveng was so great that
> he is his Justice Clodpate and calls him a great man & yᵗ in
> allusion to his name bore three lowses rampant for his Arms.¹

Obviously Davies knew of, but did not fully understand, the allegation that Mr Justice Shallow was a caricature of Lucy; yet his
mention of rabbits, as well as 'venison', and of whipping, and his
inability to give Lucy's christian name, suggest that his source of
information may not have been exactly the same as Rowe's.

Malone, finding no evidence that Lucy had a deer-park, rejected
the story outright and has been followed by others who maintain
that the play does not support the tradition and that in fact the
tradition arose from the play. Perhaps there was confusion in
somebody's mind because Lucy's grandson, the third Sir Thomas
Lucy, did bring a charge in Star Chamber in 1610 against 'a gentleman who had stolen deer from his park at Sutton'; and it is true
that it was not until 1618 that this Sir Thomas was licensed to
impale his park at Charlecote.² Yet even as cautious a scholar as
Chambers hesitates to reject the deer-stealing tradition. The first
Sir Thomas Lucy, he points out, did at least have a free-warren,
in which he may have been entitled to run roe-deer, if not fallow
deer;³ and indeed there may have been advantages in not licensing
one's park until one had to.

The best reasons for not accepting the opinion that Shakespeare
caricatured, or cast side glances at, Lucy in the person of Shallow
in *The Merry Wives* are, again, that there are no traces of such
allusions in the Shallow of *2 Henry IV*; that Lucy was not the kind
of man one could safely satirize in a play written for performance
at Court (and there would have been no special reason for thinking
of him in 1597); and that not even the Court audience could have
been expected to see the point (if indeed there is one: 'satire' is
almost a misnomer for cryptic references of the kind suspected in
the opening scene). It may perhaps be confessed, nevertheless, that
if ever there were a place in Shakespeare's art for laughing comment on individuals (comment that most readers would feel to be

1. The MS is reproduced by Chambers, *William Shakespeare*, II. 257.
2. Recorded in Mark Eccles, *Shakespeare in Warwickshire* (Madison, 1961), p. 75.
3. *William Shakespeare*, I. 18–20.

foreign to his ways of thought), then, provided that he could have
relied on his audience to identify the persons concerned, that place
would have been in such a topical play as *The Merry Wives* seems to
have been.

6. THE RELATIONSHIP OF THE PLAY TO SHAKESPEARE'S HISTORIES; AND THE 'BROOKE'–'BROOME' PROBLEM

Inevitably, since many of the characters of *The Merry Wives*
appear also in the better-known First and Second Parts of *Henry IV*
or in *Henry V*, there has been considerable discussion of the connection of the comedy with the 'Histories'. The discussion has taken
two main forms: an attempt to determine when the action of *The
Merry Wives* is supposed to have occurred, in relation to the events
dramatized in *Henry IV* and *Henry V*; and an attempt to establish
the exact order of composition of the four plays.

The first question is answerable only if it is assumed, in an old-
fashioned way, that Shakespeare thought of the characters as real
people whose biographies could, as it were, be written from the
plays—and may not be answerable even then. That *The Merry
Wives* presupposes an audience familiar with *1 Henry IV* is made
certain by Page's comment on Fenton that 'he kept company with
the wild Prince and Poins' (III. ii. 66–7)—which if taken seriously
would date the action in the reign of Henry IV or V; yet elsewhere,
as has been shown, the action seems rather to be in Elizabethan
England, and not only does Fenton not know Falstaff (perhaps
not as inconsistent a fact as Wheatley supposed) but also Falstaff
does not know Mistress Quickly. Moreover while Quickly has both
the same name as the character in *Henry IV* and *Henry V* and the
same manner of digressive speech larded with malapropisms, she
is in many other ways a different person. The most that can be said
is that Falstaff's 'If it should come to the ear of the court how I have
been transformed, and how my transformation hath been washed
and cudgelled, they would melt me out of my fat drop by drop, and
liquor fishermen's boots with me; I warrant they would whip me
with their fine wits till I were as crest-fallen as a dried pear' clearly
presupposes a time when he is on jesting terms with Prince Hal, a
time *before* his disgrace at the end of *2 Henry IV*.

Whether the words may have been more easily *written* before the
end of *2 Henry IV* is another question; but some evidence does
suggest that *The Merry Wives* may have been composed at the same
time as the second part of the trilogy, and none of the available
facts contradicts such an hypothesis.

The First Part of *Henry IV* is now normally dated in the winter of

1596–7. The play, which must be later than *Richard II*, was entered on the Stationers' Register on 25 February 1597/8 (and published in 1598); and Meres, in his *Palladis Tamia* (S.R. 7 September 1598) mentions it, though he lists it as proving Shakespeare's ability in tragedy (he has no separate category of 'history').[1] It is known that Falstaff in Part 1 was originally called 'Oldcastle' ('my old lad of the Castle' survives in the dialogue as a form of address to him); and in the epilogue to the Second Part, there occurs the famous promise and retraction: 'If you be not too much cloyed with fat meat, our humble author will continue the story, with Sir John in it, and make you merry with fair Katharine of France: where, for any thing I know, Falstaff shall die of a sweat, unless already a' be killed with your hard opinions; for Oldcastle died a martyr, and this is not the man.'[2] (In fact Falstaff does not appear in *Henry V*— except for the announcement of his death—although it has been conjectured that he was originally in the play and was taken out on second thoughts.[3]) The generally accepted theory is that the name 'Oldcastle' was changed because of protests from the influential Cobham family, who objected to the denigration of a distinguished ancestor (and of course *if* the protest came from William Brooke, Lord Cobham, when as Lord Chamberlain he was in a strong position to see that his objection was not overruled, it must have been before his death in March 1597; but there is nothing to prove that his son, Sir Henry, was not the one to speak up: it was he who was satirically called 'S^r Io. Falstaff' in a private letter by Essex in February 1598).[4]

1. For discussion of the dating of *1 Henry IV*, and further evidence suggesting the 1596–7 date, see *King Henry IV Part I*, the (New) Arden edition, ed. A. R. Humphreys (London, 1960), pp. xii–xiv. It has been conjectured that because Meres lists the play as tragedy, he must have been thinking of 'the dark tone of Part II'. May he not rather have been thinking of the death of Hotspur? Incidentally, Meres does not mention *The Merry Wives*, but it has long been clear that his list is made up more from a desire for neat parallels than from any desire for completeness; and if *The Merry Wives* had been originally produced at Court and not quickly transferred to the public stage, he may not have seen it or known of it by, say, early 1598.

2. There may or may not have been an earlier version of the epilogue without these lines. Even if there were one, it does not follow that the name 'Oldcastle' was not altered until the later version; an apology is never *too* late.

3. See *King Henry V*, the (New) Arden edition, ed. J. H. Walter (London, 1954), pp. xli–xliii.

4. Humphreys, *op. cit.*, p. xii. The hypothesis, advanced by H. N. Paul, Humphreys, and others, that Shakespeare chose 'Falstaff' as the substitute name because in *1 Henry VI* he had (wrongly) associated the historical Sir John Falstaff (1378–1459) with conduct unworthy of a knight of the Garter is incapable of proof. Incidentally 'Falstaff' was just as unfair, if one thought of the man of the same name in history, as was 'Oldcastle'.

The alteration of 'Oldcastle' to 'Falstaff' must have been made before the entry of *1 Henry IV* on the Stationers' Register on 25 February 1597/8, for the entry mentions 'the conceipted mirthe of Sir Iohn Falstoff'; and there is really nothing to suggest that the character in *The Merry Wives* or *2 Henry IV* was ever called anything but 'Falstaff', although the name 'Oldcastle' may well have remained, as it were, in Shakespeare's subconscious after it was officially abandoned. It would be natural for him to *think* of the character as 'Oldcastle'; and this is sufficient explanation of the occurrence of the speech prefix '*Old.*' at I. ii. 137 in the Quarto of Part II and is also sufficient explanation, if explanation is needed, of the pun, if any, in *Merry Wives*, IV. v. 5, 'There's his chamber, his house, his castle' (but would anybody ever have seen a pun on 'Oldcastle' here, or in the Quarto version of the lines, if not going out of the way to look for it?).

Queen Elizabeth could have seen *1 Henry IV* at Court on 26 or 27 December 1596, 1 or 6 January, or 6 or 8 February 1597: on all those dates the Lord Chamberlain's Men played before her.[1] She could then have expressed a wish to see Falstaff in love, and a performance of *The Merry Wives* would have followed most opportunely in April.[2] The unlucky 'Oldcastle' name had probably already been changed (why would the Brookes wait until the offence had been repeated before protesting?); and by this time Shakespeare may well have been working on *2 Henry IV* (a second part having been in his mind from the beginning or—as Harold Jenkins has argued[3]—having become necessary as he found he had too much material while writing Part I). There is no good reason for putting the completed *2 Henry IV* before late 1598 (and some slight reasons—e.g. a possible use of Gerard's *Herball*—for not putting it earlier); and it is difficult to agree that '*The Merry Wives* . . . assumes that the spectators already know Justice Shallow, and they could do so only through *2 Henry IV*. Similarly, Pistol is elaborately introduced into *2 Henry IV* whereas in *The Merry Wives* Slender mentions him, with Nym and Bardolph, as a matter of course'.[4] The introduction of Shallow in *The Merry Wives* is even more 'elaborate' than that of Pistol in *2 Henry IV*, which could be interpreted as the fanfare to introduce an old friend; and no earlier knowledge of Pistol, Nym, and Bardolph is neces-

1. Chambers, *Elizabethan Stage*, IV. 165.
2. To this extent, I agree with a suggestion made by H. N. Paul in a letter to the editor of the New Variorum edition of *1 Henry IV* (Philadelphia and London, 1936), p. 355; I cannot accept other parts of his theory.
3. *The Structural Problem in Shakespeare's 'Henry the Fourth'* (London, 1956).
4. Humphreys, *op. cit.*, p. xiii.

sary for an understanding or appreciation of their roles in the
comedy.

The theory that *2 Henry IV* and *The Merry Wives* were being
written at the same time—the composition of the former having
been interrupted for the hasty writing of the latter—has two minor
advantages. It 'explains' the occurrence in the two plays of words
and phrases not found elsewhere in Shakespeare ('by cock and pie';
'pippin'; 'tester'; 'red-lattice'; 'cavalier(o)'; 'Ephesian'; 'said I
well?', plus perhaps the Jove–bull joke and the pun on 'cheater'
and 'escheator'[1]); and it perhaps solves the problem of Falstaff's
curious out-of-the-way journey to Gloucestershire on his way north
from London that has so puzzled editors of *2 Henry IV*. A. R.
Humphreys has written: 'The conscientious insertion of locations
by editors has concealed the fact . . . that Shakespeare makes no
mention of Gloucestershire as Justice Shallow's habitat until
2 Henry IV, IV. iii. 80, 126–7. Shallow is "a poor esquire of this
county" in III. ii, but no county is named [though Lincolnshire is
implied]. . . When . . . [Falstaff] is due to return, it transpires that
his second visit to Shallow is to take place in Gloucestershire, and
thereafter the place-names relate to that county. . . Why [Shake-
speare] apparently shifted the location thus can hardly be ascer-
tained'.[2] The answer may be that, having meanwhile made
Shallow a justice of the peace in Gloucestershire (which is not so
far from Windsor) in *The Merry Wives*, Shakespeare decided that he
might as well live with it.[3] For the little it is worth, one other
observation may be made: any request from the Queen for
Falstaff to be shown 'in love' may have been more easily made if
she had not yet seen the Doll Tearsheet scenes of *2 Henry IV*.

It would seem, then, that the weight of probability, including
not only Hotson's interpretation of topical allusions most relevant
on a particular occasion but also the relationship of *The Merry
Wives* to the Henry IV plays, favours as the date of the comedy not
1599 or 1600 or even 1602, as once thought, but 1597, after the
production of the first part of *Henry IV* and probably before the

---

1. *Wiv.*, I. i. 279 (Page); I. ii. 12 (Evans); I. iii. 83 (Pistol); II. ii. 25 (Falstaff);
II. i. 186 etc. (Host); IV. v. 16 (Host); I. iii. 11 (Host); V. v. 3 (Falstaff); I. iii. 66
(Falstaff); *2H4*, V. i. 1 (Shallow); V. iii. 2 (Shallow); III. ii. 297 (Falstaff); II. ii.
86 (a page); V. iii. 62 (Shallow); II. ii. 164 (a page); III. ii. 227 (Shallow); II. iii.
192 (Hal); II. iv. 111 (Quickly).

2. *The Second Part of King Henry IV*, the (New) Arden edition (London, 1965),
pp. 235–6.

3. Although he does not say so, H. N. Paul perhaps had this in mind when he
suggested, with unnecessary precision, that Shakespeare interrupted *2 Henry IV*
at IV. iii. See above p. liv, n. 2. Humphreys also mentions the possibility
(*2 Henry IV*, p. xvii, n. 3).

lvi THE MERRY WIVES OF WINDSOR

completion of the second. *Henry V* certainly followed *2 Henry IV*
and thus almost certainly, for the reasons already given, *The
Merry Wives*.[1] It is not possible to say whether the final omission of
Falstaff from the action of *Henry V* had anything to do with his
having been used for another full play, *The Merry Wives*, that was
not part of the historical sequence as originally contemplated. On
the whole it is unlikely, particularly if *2 Henry IV* was not completed
until after *The Merry Wives*; and the Falstaff comedy of the latter
is too far removed from the Histories to make acceptable the otherwise tempting theory that Falstaff scenes first planned or written
for *Henry V* were hurriedly transferred from it and adapted for the
play that had to be written in 'a fortnight'. Yet another conjecture,
that the omission was forced on Shakespeare when Kemp left the
acting company, carries weight only if one believes firmly both
that Kemp played Falstaff and that nobody else could have done so.

To add to the confusion, there is the problem of Ford's pseudo-
nyms, 'Brooke' in the Quarto, 'Broome' in the Folio. It has been
shown (p. xxxiv) that Shakespeare must originally have written
'Brook(e)'; and in the days when the Quarto was thought of as a
first sketch of the play, it was natural to argue that 'Brooke' was
used in the first performances and altered to 'Broome' for later
performances—in particular at Court—because of protests, or
feared protests, from the Cobham family who, having objected to
the name of their ancestor 'Oldcastle' in *1 Henry IV*, were similarly
put out by the occurrence of their family name in *The Merry Wives*
(although exactly why its use should have offended them, or been
thought likely to do so, has never been made clear). Now that the
1602 Quarto is seen to be a later, debased version of the play, and
the 1623 Folio probably very close to the text of a first Court
performance, the problem is more difficult. The Quarto could
hardly read 'Brooke' unless that was the name spoken on the public
stage;[2] and so one must infer *either* that 'Brooke' was altered to
'Broome' for the original Court performance and altered back to

1. There may also be something in the argument that Nym is taken for granted
when first seen in *Henry V* (II. i), as if he were already known from *The Merry
Wives* (he does not appear in *2 Henry IV*). The contrary reasoning, that he would
not have been called 'Corporal' in *The Merry Wives* if he had not earlier been
seen on the battlefield in *Henry V*, is not conclusive, for he is associated with
Bardolph, who is seen serving under 'Captain' Falstaff in *1 Henry IV*. The title-
page of the Quarto, which has been dragged into the discussion, is irrelevant. All
that it proves is that *by 1602*, Pistol, Nym and the others were well known, from
performances on the stage of any of the plays—not excluding *The Merry Wives*.

2. Green's theory (p. 119) that the Host-reporter restored in the Quarto the
name that he had first learnt but had later had to abandon *during rehearsal* is
surely desperate.

'Brooke' for the public theatre—and that the Folio was printed from the still unchanged Court text—*or* that 'Brooke' was spoken on all stages until at least the time of the compilation of the Quarto but was subsequently altered in the text that finally became, directly or indirectly, 'copy' for the Folio (if only in the sense that a transcript was made from it, by Crane or somebody else, for the printer). The second explanation seems the better. If 'Brooke' once gave offence, it could hardly have been put back, before 1602, while Sir Henry was still able to take offence (certainly 'Oldcastle' was never restored and in 1600, when *2 Henry IV* was printed, in a good text, the apology for it stood); and if 'Brooke' ever had been restored on the stage, it is also difficult to believe that it would not have been put back in the acting company's texts of the play. It is not as if the manuscript behind the Folio had been left unchanged in all other respects since, shall we say, April 1597; for one thing, as has been shown, it had been expurgated. Even accepting, then, that the Folio text is a 'Court' text, and that the Quarto is based on a 'public' one, an hypothesis of alteration to the former *after* the latter had been published is the more acceptable. Two such explanations have been proposed. One, proffered by Crofts, that 'Broome' was substituted during the printing of the Folio, to placate the York Herald, Ralph Brooke, who had fallen out with the publisher Jaggard over the printing of his book in 1619, has been convincingly rejected by Green, for the very good reason, among others, that Jaggard was more concerned to score off Brooke than to placate him.[1] The other, first proffered by Alfred Hart,[2] that the substitution was made in 1604, at least has nothing against it. *The Merry Wives* was performed before James I on 4 November 1604; in December 1603 George Brooke (brother of Henry, Lord Cobham) had been executed for his part in the Bye Plot, and Sir Henry Brooke had been arrested and sentenced to death for his in the Main Plot, to depose James and put Arabella Stuart on the throne, and in February 1604 Sir Henry, although reprieved from death and imprisoned instead, had been expelled from the Order of the Garter. Hart's reasoning that 'Brooke' would be removed in November 1604 from the text of a play presented before the King, lest the name 'revive unpleasant memories', is certainly not answered by Green's demonstration that the King had shown some clemency to Brooke; and Hart's theory does

---

1. *Shakespeare and the Post Horses*, p. 103; Green, p. 109.
2. *Stolne and Surreptitious Copies*, pp. 89–90. David M. White was apparently developing the same idea at the same time in an unpublished thesis, and later published a note on it, 'An Explanation of the *Brook–Broome* Question in Shakespeare's *Merry Wives*', *Philological Quarterly*, xxv (1946), 280–3.

explain both why the Quarto reads 'Brooke' and why the Folio, if based on a manuscript that had been used for the 1604 revival of the full original Court play, should have the inferior reading.

7. LITERARY SOURCES OR ANALOGUES

The search for the work or works on which Shakespeare may be presumed to have based *The Merry Wives* has been so unsuccessful, in one sense, that Kenneth Muir, in a standard book on Shakespeare's sources, notes the suggestions made by others and is content to add 'In the present state of our knowledge it is useless to pursue the matter further.'[1] In another sense, no further investigation is necessary, inasmuch as for nearly every incident and situation in the plot of the play an analogue or a vaguely possible source has been found in earlier European fiction and farce or in English stories and translations.[2]

The Falstaff–Ford–Brook story belongs to a group of tales in which a lover unwittingly tells a husband of the progress of an affair with the latter's wife. The closest analogue is probably the second 'novella' of the second day of Ser Giovanni Fiorentino's *Il Pecorone* (a collection that also seems to have given Shakespeare the idea for the 'pound of flesh' in *The Merchant of Venice*).[3] A young man Buccivolo, a student in Bologna, consults a professor about the science of love, follows the advice, and reports his progress, until the assignation is made with the lady who is, of course, the professor's wife. The husband suspects the truth and follows the lover, who has to be concealed under a heap of damp washing ('un monte di panni di bucato, i quali non erano ancora rasciutti'); but after the search for him is unproductive, the gallant is successful with the wife and duly tells the professor so. Interrupting the second assignation, the husband stabs the pile of washed clothes— as Ford searches the buck basket—and is similarly considered mad (and treated accordingly). The lover, however, now identifying the professor as the husband, visits the house a third time, to console him, and then leaves the city to return to his native Rome. No English translation of this story is known to have been available to Shakespeare, but it is at least closer to *The Merry Wives* than is the

1. *Shakespeare's Sources. I. Comedies and Tragedies* (London, 1957), p. 260.

2. Most of these are discussed, and some are given, in Geoffrey Bullough, *Narrative and Dramatic Sources of Shakespeare*, Vol. 2 (London, 1958), pp. 3–58. Earlier studies not listed elsewhere in these notes include K. M. Lea, *Italian Popular Comedy* (Oxford, 1934), II. 431–3.

3. The relevance for *The Merry Wives* was first pointed out by Carlo Segré in 1911. See S. G. Thomas, 'Source of *The Merry Wives of Windsor*', *Times Literary Supplement*, 11 October 1947, p. 528.

'source' favoured by H. C. Hart and others, 'The Tale of the two Lovers of Pisa' in *Tarltons Newes out of Purgatorie* (1590), another version of the lover's confiding in the husband, but with the difference that the lover is unsuccessful (until after the husband's death). That this husband, like Caius, is an elderly foolish doctor, who is chosen by the wife's parent (her father, in fact), hardly strengthens the case for 'borrowing'.

Not fully convincing either is the claim that the tale 'Of Two Brethren and their Wives' in Barnaby Riche's *Riche his Farewell to the Militarie Profession* (1581) is a direct source.[1] Here a wife plays off against each other three unwanted (but previously acceptable) lovers; and one, a lawyer, is nearly suffocated when he is persuaded to allow himself to be wrapped in a bag or knapsack, and is beaten, while the second lover is a doctor, who is employed to carry the bag from the house, believing it to contain the wife, and is startled to find that 'she' has a beard. The third lover, a soldier, is used to disconcert and beat the other two, but is later sent to foreign wars— and the lady and the husband live happily ever after. The differences between this and *The Merry Wives* far outweigh any resemblances, although a few verbal 'parallels' have been suspected; and in any case Riche is known to have based others of his stories on Italian originals, which may have come independently to Shakespeare's notice.

The evidence may be summarized by saying that Shakespeare did not need to *invent* a husband who receives 'progress reports' on the attempted seduction of his wife; a lover who is the victim of a clever wife's schemes, involving near-suffocation in her washing; a jealous husband who, having learnt how he has been tricked once, assumes that he is being tricked a second time in the same way; women who tell each other of the approaches made to them by the one man; or a lover who escapes by pretending to be a woman. All these, however, may have leapt to his mind when required, from reading done over a period of years; a source, in the stricter sense, was unnecessary.

Similarly, it seems superfluous to propose as the source of the Anne Page story a play by Plautus, *Casina* (of which there was no available English translation):[2] again the differences far outweigh

1. Dorothy Hart Bruce, '*The Merry Wives* and *Two Brethren*', *Studies in Philology*, 39 (1942), 265–78. Of course this tale is generally accepted as a source for part of the Malvolio story in *Twelfth Night*.
2. R. S. Forsythe, 'A Plautine Source of *The Merry Wives of Windsor*', *Modern Philology*, 18 (1920), 401–21. Bullough, *op. cit.*, p. 9, understates the difficulties, but still has to admit that 'The *Casina* could not be followed closely because Falstaff, unlike Lysidamus, was not meant to lust after Anne Page'.

the resemblances, and there must have been many such plots
where the suitor favoured by the young lady wins the day against
suitors favoured by her parents. It remains barely possible that
Shakespeare, had he been able to examine his subconscious, might
have been prepared to admit that schoolboy memories of Plautus
gave him the 'idea' for the disguises and confusion of Slender and
Caius and their 'wives' in the final scene.

Not content with 'sources' for parts of the plot, some commentators have argued that the whole play is only a rewriting of an un-
discovered, non-extant, original. The favourite candidate, proposed by F. G. Fleay and adopted by the New Cambridge editors,
is *The Jealous Comedy*, a lost play that Shakespeare's company had
acted in 1593;[1] and the 'evidence' includes the loose ends, such as
the deer-stealing allegations of the first scene; Ford's telling
Falstaff (II. ii. 174) 'Sir, I hear you are a scholar' (apparently
flattery never extends to improbabilities); and speeches that are
said to be uncharacteristic of the 'real' Falstaff (i.e. Falstaff as some
readers think him to be in *1 Henry IV*), such as (v. v. 127–9) 'See
now how wit may be made a Jack-a-Lent, when 'tis upon ill employment!' (apparently Falstaff is considered incapable of a wry
and rueful glance at his own folly—in spite of 'No more of that,
Hal, an thou lovest me!' after the Gadshill exposure in *1 Henry IV*,
III. iv. 312–13). The Quarto also is dragged in, the references to
sergeants and proctors in Act v being taken as relics of a 'London'
original;[2] and even the preponderance of prose, with only sparing
and uneven use of verse, is said to indicate a source in verse that
Shakespeare had not time or energy to rewrite fully in blank
verse—as if his predecessors, such as Greene, had not pointed the
way to the use of prose for comedy in certain tones, including the
farcical, and as if Shakespeare was never to write *As You Like It*[3] or
Dekker *The Shoemaker's Holiday* and *The Honest Whore*.

J. M. Nosworthy would go further and would identify the source
of *The Merry Wives* as *The Two Merry Women of Abingdon*, an unfinished play that Henslowe in 1599 commissioned from Henry
Porter, presumably because of the rather inexplicable success of
his *Two Angry Women of Abingdon*.[4] Obviously, since the proposed

1. F. G. Fleay, *A Chronicle History of the Life and Work of William Shakespeare*
(London, 1886), pp. 210–13.

2. See above, pp. xxxvi–xxxvii.

3. See below, p. lxxvi. At the time of the earlier volumes in the New Cambridge series, of course, the editors did argue—consistent in this—that *As You
Like It* was a revision of a verse play. The theory was later withdrawn. Fleay
(*op. cit.*, p. 211) maintained that the predominance of prose in *The Merry Wives*
was proof of haste, as in *Much Ado* (and forgot *As You Like It* altogether).

4. *Shakespeare's Occasional Plays* (London, 1965), pp. 86–127.

source does not survive, the 'evidence' must consist mainly of alleged parallels in incident, setting, and phrasing between *The Merry Wives* and the surviving Porter play; and, again, the argument depends partly on the Quarto, which is said to be in some respects, and particularly in the last scene, closer to the lost source. Beyond recording the opinion that another plot as thin as that of *The Two Angry Women of Abingdon* would have given Shakespeare next to nothing to work on, there is little that one can say in reply to so tenuous an argument; presumably it is no use protesting that Porter's deliberate and often humourless style is at the opposite extreme from the gaiety of *The Merry Wives*, for the answer will be that vivacity was precisely what Shakespeare may have added to his hypothetical original.

Nothing is more likely, if the story of the royal command to write a play in a short time is correct, than that the dramatist should have made use of any materials that were at hand; but until stronger evidence is produced, the theory that he rewrote an earlier play falls far short of proof. If the 1597 date for *The Merry Wives* is right, Nosworthy's nomination of the supposed lost source is automatically wrong; and perhaps the signs of inadequate 'revision' that others have found in Shakespeare's play also indicate no more than hasty composition.

Literary sources may have played minor parts in the writing of some sections of Shakespeare's comedy. For example, Tyrwhitt thought that the merry Host of the Garter was indebted to the immortal Harry Bailly, Chaucer's host of the Tabard Inn in Southwark and 'governour' of his Canterbury pilgrims.[1] No doubt Harry Bailly's jovial and exclamatory manner of speech and his general character, intolerant of fuss and hypocrisy, are like Shakespeare's Host; but we may have to allow for a tradition of merry Hosts before *The Merry Wives*, as there was certainly such a tradition after it, including the Host in *The Merry Devil of Edmonton*,[2] and extending at least to Farquhar's Boniface in *The Beaux' Stratagem* (1707).

The fairy scene in Lyly's *Endimion* may or may not have contributed something to the punishment of Falstaff by the 'fairies' in the last act of *The Merry Wives* (see note on v. v. 103). Perhaps, too,

---

1. Malone was sceptical of the verbal echo ('said I well?') that Tyrwhitt thought he had found, but granted the possible general indebtedness. (The point is made by Sailendra Kumar Sen, ' "The noblest Roman of them all": Malone and Shakespearian Scholarship', *Shakespeare Commemoration Volume*, Presidency College, Calcutta, 1966, pp. 67–8.)

2. Noted by Chambers, *Elizabethan Stage*, IV. 30. The date is probably between 1599 and 1604.

there was some lost account of a 'wise woman' of Brentford that
suggested Falstaff's method of escape when he is trapped for the
second time in Ford's house. Again, however, the Quarto may be
responsible for a red herring. In the Folio, Mistress Ford begins
the relevant section with the line 'My Maids Aunt the fat woman
of *Brainford*, has a gowne aboue'; we are told that Ford, who
'cannot abide' her, 'sweares she's a witch' (IV. ii. 67–8, 77–8); and
Ford addresses 'her' in appropriate language, and outlines her
methods of witchcraft (158–65). Simple and Slender also know of
the repute of 'the Wise-woman of *Brainford*' (IV. v. 24–5), but the
only name that she is ever given is when Mistress Page addresses
her as 'mother *Prat*' (IV. ii. 168)—and the name may have suggested
itself to Shakespeare for the sake of Ford's reply.[1] It is the Quarto
that has Mistress Page twice identify the old woman as 'my maids
Aunt *Gillian* of *Brainford*' (though the second time it is 'my maidens
Ant')—and so it may have been the reporter and not Shakespeare
who made the connection between the 'character' in the play and
the perhaps proverbial Gillian of Brentford whose comic 'Testament' had been written by Robert Copland, in 1560 or there-
abouts, and who is referred to thrice by Nashe (though he once
calls her 'Joane'), and once by Harington (both probably recalling
Copland) and was apparently to have been a character in a play
'called fryer fox & gyllen of branforde' written by—or possibly only
commissioned by Henslowe from—Samuel Rowley and Thomas
Dowton in February 1598/9.[2] (It must be pointed out, however,
that Copland's Gillyen is in no sense a witch—she is a 'mery widow'
and is notable only for the curse-like series of legacies she dictated
to her Curate.) Alternatively, the Quarto reporter may merely
have made explicit what Shakespeare assumed could safely be left
to the audience—the identification of the old woman named in the
play with a notorious practiser of fortune-telling 'and such dawbry
as this is', of whose doings they had read or heard in ballad and
story.

For the Latin lesson (IV. i), Shakespeare could have found a
model—had he needed one—not in earlier English drama but in
the French. M. L. Radoff has shown that 'by the beginning of the
sixteenth century this comic device had become very popular in the
[French] farces' and has argued that since John Heywood drew on

1. See note on IV. ii. 170.
2. Robert Copland, *Gyl of braintfords Testament. Newly Compiled* (n.d.); Thomas
Nashe, *The Works*, ed. R. B. McKerrow, supp. F. P. Wilson (Oxford, 1958),
III. 235, 314; IV. 421; V. 195; [Sir John Harington] *Vlysses vpon Aiax* (London,
1596), B4; *Henslowe's Diary*, ed. R. A. Foakes and R. T. Rickert (Cambridge,
1961), p. 104.

these French plays, Shakespeare could have known them too.[1] At least it can be said that the parallels are closer than one normally finds in alleged sources: they include not only the schoolboy, his master, his mother, and a female who asks unfortunate questions but also some of the indecencies.

In one other way *The Merry Wives* may have been indebted to earlier literature, and particularly drama, for comic material. During the last quarter of the sixteenth century, writers began to see the literary possibilities arising from the theory of 'humours'—the four fluids that existed in different proportions in the composition of different men and thus determined a man's character or disposition. The word 'humour' achieved a 'vogue' comparable with the popularity of 'complex' in the psychology or pseudo-psychology of, say, the second quarter of the twentieth century; fools boasted of their 'humours', and took comfort from them, as their successors did from their 'inferiority complexes' and even 'Oedipus complexes'.

'Humour' appears frequently in the work of writers such as Thomas Nashe (in e.g. *Christ's Tears over Jerusalem,* in 1593); and Nashe may have coined 'humorously' (in the same work) and, in the corresponding sense, the noun 'humourist'.[2] In drama, Lyly, for one, had found the word convenient for naming phases of character; and Shakespeare himself had adopted it in some of his early comedies, including *Love's Labour's Lost* (III. i. 23–4) and, notably, *The Taming of the Shrew,* where it is used often, and at least three times of Kate's shrewishness or of Petruchio's imitation of it: Peter says 'He kills her in her own humour' (IV. i. 183); Petruchio, 'And thus I'll curb her mad and headstrong humour' (IV. i. 212); and Baptista, 'Such an injury would vex a very saint, / Much more a shrew of thy impatient humour' (III. ii. 28–9). Chapman was thus perhaps not so very original when he made great play with the word in *The Blind Beggar of Alexandria,* one of the most popular dramas of 1596, and had Irus use it of his assuming the role of one 'Count Hermes', noted for his 'mad-brain' conduct, mood, or 'humour'. Chapman may have been the first, however, to see the possibilities of fun in the abuse and over-use of the cliché; and presumably (the text is truncated and corrupt) the Spaniard Bragadino is comic partly because of this verbal mannerism: 'you know my intent, my humour is insophisticated and plain'; 'put up thy pistol; 'tis a most dangerous humour in thee'; 'I do not like this

1. 'Influence of the French Farce in *Henry V* and *The Merry Wives*', *Modern Language Notes,* 48 (1933), 427–35.
2. See, e.g., Jürgen Schäfer, '"Humour" in the *O.E.D.*', *Notes and Queries,* N.S. 13 (1966), 290–2; and Bracy, *op. cit.,* pp. 115–17, citing, particularly, C. R. Baskervill, *English Elements in Jonson's Early Comedy* (Austin, Texas, 1911).

E

humour in thee in pistoling men in this sort; it is a most dangerous and stigmatical humour'.[1] Here, if precedent is needed, is precedent for Nym's murdering of the word in *The Merry Wives*.

Chapman's influence is thought by some to go beyond the mere word and to extend to the dramatic method of basing characterization on 'humours', the method that Jonson was to make his own in *Every Man in his Humour* (1598) and *Every Man Out of his Humour* (1599). In the final Jonsonian formula, the comic characters each had one mannerism or eccentricity; and only when that eccentricity became, or was caused to be, extreme could the possessor be made aware of it or otherwise be brought 'out' of it, and so cured. In earlier versions of the formula, any character with a predominating mannerism, mood, passion, or affectation—or even a character in disguise pretending eccentricity—could be presented for laughter, in what came to be known as a 'humours comedy'; and perhaps the first of these was Chapman's *An Humourous Day's Mirth* (first acted in May 1597) in which Lemot virtually describes the play when he says 'thus will I sit, as it were, and point out all my humourous companions' (ii. 20–1). In this sense, however, it is debatable whether *The Merry Wives of Windsor* should be called a humours comedy at all; and it may be suspected that Nym's abuse of the word, combined with uncertainty in dating the play, has given a false lead. Pistol, with his speech made up of quotation from, and imitations of, earlier popular drama, may possibly be thought of as a 'humours' character, but he has other qualities, such as bluster and an affected sense of honour, that make such simple classification difficult; and although jealousy is a favourite 'humour' with Chapman and Jonson, Shakespeare's drawing of Ford is really too subtle to be reduced to one-dimensional presentation of character.

If *The Merry Wives* is correctly dated April 1597, then the connections between it and Jonson's *Every Man in his Humour* can only be Jonson's emulation of Shakespeare, or friendly rivalry, or (if one must think in terms of opposition) Jonson's attempt, with his portraits of the jealous husband Thorello (Kitely in the 1616 version) and the country fool Stephano (Stephen) to show Shakespeare how such humours ought to have been displayed in Ford and Slender. The further suggestion made by the New Cambridge editors[2] that Shakespeare caricatured Jonson, as Nym, 'prating of

---

1. *The Comedies of George Chapman*, ed. T. M. Parrott (London, 1914), Scene i, ll. 326–43; Scene ii, ll. 74, 82–3, 114–16.

2. *op. cit.*, pp. xxxi–xxxii. The New Cambridge editors apparently overlooked Sarrazin's 1904 article, 'Nym und Ben Jonson' (*Shakespeare Jahrbuch*, 40, pp. 213–22). Sarrazin argued that Nym may have been taken by Jonson as a caricature but was not necessarily meant as one.

his "humours", reiterating the word until its boredom became comic, under a make-up which ridiculed Jonson in person and even in face' would similarly be ruled out by date, even if it had not already been ruled out by improbability. (Why, one may ask, should Shakespeare have wished at this time to ridicule Jonson? Another tradition says that it was Shakespeare who persuaded his company to act Jonson's play. And how could Shakespeare have afforded to be critical of Jonson for over-frequent use of a word that, as has been shown, he had not failed to exploit himself?)

Similarly, the resemblances between *The Merry Wives* and Chapman's probably contemporaneous *An Humourous Day's Mirth* seem to come to no more than comedy deriving from misuse of the word 'humour', together with another jealous husband, Labervele (but his suspicions of his wife's frailty are in fact justified, if he only knew it, and his manner of speech and his final resolve never to 'be suspicious more' owe so much less to observation than to the 'humours' theory that they clearly had nothing to teach Shakespeare). Chapman's still later *All Fools* (1599?) hardly comes into the story at all: it too has a jealous husband, Cornelio—or, if we believe his final pronouncement, as probably we should not, a husband who merely pretends to be jealous—but while it is conceivable that Chapman took some hints from Shakespeare in showing how the jealous man can 'justify' his jealousy as the alternative to foolishness ('No, let me still be pointed at, and thought / A jealous ass and not a wittolly knave', II. i. 286–7), Chapman had sufficient precedent in his own earlier portraits of the type.

The alleged 'humours' content of *The Merry Wives*, then, is so slight that even if the order of the relevant plays were shown somehow to be quite different, there would be no reason to suspect Shakespeare of indebtedness to either Chapman or Jonson and no reason to alter one's opinion of his originality or of his superiority when he chose to use fashionable literary material.

8. THE PLAY

Whether the tradition of the royal command is true or not, *The Merry Wives of Windsor*, in the Folio text, may be seen as a superb medley of all that would be likely to amuse an aristocratic audience towards the close of the sixteenth century. First and foremost there was a revival, in whatever sense, of Falstaff, the finest comic character the English stage had yet known or was perhaps ever to know; and with him from the merry gang of *1 Henry IV* came not only his red-nosed crony Bardolph but also, albeit in a different role, Mistress Quickly, whose unlucky uses of the English tongue, both decent ('I am nothing to thank God on, I would thou shouldst know it') and indecent, must have made her immediately popular with audiences, though her part was small. For good measure there was a first taste (or—if the dating be disputed—further taste) of loud-mouthed Pistol, Falstaff's colleague in a memorable scene (II. iv) in *2 Henry IV*, and of Mr Justice Shallow, and also of Corporal Nym, who was to ring further changes on his favourite word and add to his qualifications as a humorist in *Henry V*. Then to assist Quickly, Pistol, and Nym in what we must nowadays refer to as 'the cold-blooded murder of the English tongue', there were introduced a jovial Host, a Welsh parson-schoolmaster, and a French doctor—all conceivably variations on types of character already popular on the stage.

For the educated audience that could be flattered by the assumption that it was educated, there were included for good measure the Latin scene (showing Quickly at her best, or worst) and occasional wit of a literary kind, such as Parson Evans's confusion of a Marlowe lyric with a psalm, and the essentially unromantic Falstaff's incongruous accosting of Mistress Ford with a line from Sir Philip Sidney's sonnet sequence *Astrophel and Stella*.

Perhaps Shakespeare added the spice of personal satire, with passing suggestions of living people, in Shallow and even Slender; certainly he put in the all-but-compulsory dash of romance, with the story of 'sweet Anne Page' and her wooer Fenton, who, by carrying her off in spite of the rivalry of less worthy suitors favoured by otherwise likeable parents, shows once again that though the course of true love never did run smooth, love will prevail. Yet *The Merry Wives* is not primarily satiric comedy, nor is it—whatever John Dennis might think about the desirability of making Fenton the central character—either comedy of intrigue or romantic comedy as Shakespeare had already developed that genre in *The Two Gentlemen of Verona* or *A Midsummer Night's Dream* and was to develop it further in *As You Like It* and *Twelfth Night*. *The Merry Wives* is in essence citizen comedy, of the kind also made famous by Dekker in *The Shoemaker's Holiday*, by Chapman, Jonson, and Marston in their fine collaborative work *Eastward Ho* (and by Webster and Dekker in the rival comedies *Westward Ho* and *Northward Ho*) and later by Middleton, and by Massinger in, for example, *The City Madam*. Instead of being set in London, however, it has the added charm of being a portrait of life in an English country town; the characters cross fields and climb over stiles, match their greyhounds or go a-birding, and can always go home to laugh the sport o'er by a country fire, even at the close of a 'raw rheumatic day'.

Gravely to discuss the theme of a play put together in this way is to risk breaking the butterfly upon the wheel. In so far as *The Merry Wives* may be said to have one theme, however, it is the old one of the natural superiority of plain 'honesty' or virtue to the sophisticated or sophistical arts of the gallant or courtier; or if true comedy always involves incongruity, the humour may be said to be based on the incongruity between Falstaff as he sees himself and Falstaff as he is seen by Mistress Page and Mistress Ford, with whom he never stands a chance.

That Falstaff should come off second best in any encounter is, in the eyes of some critics, the height of Shakespeare's offending. Allan Gilbert has answered this in part: it is, he points out, 'the nature of comedy' that 'demands his discomfiture, or a repentance that to his idealizers is still more distasteful. The objection to Falstaff's defeat in the *Merry Wives* is, then, an objection to the very nature of comic drama.'[1] It is also necessary to insist, however, that the Falstaff of *Henry IV* is likewise often discomfited: in spite of 'the incomprehensible lies' that the fat rogue tells when he meets the Prince and others at supper, he loses the battle of wits over the Gadshill robbery and is not allowed to forget it (as when Hal tells him 'I lack some of thy instinct'); even Hal loses patience with him when he has a bottle of sack instead of a pistol in his holster on the battlefield ('What, is it a time to jest and dally now?'); and if the Prince's contemptuous 'Why, thou owest God a death' does not discomfort him, since he is hardly capable of shame, it does lower him for ever in the eyes of any perceptive audience; and though he gets away with his monstrous lie that he killed Hotspur, that is only because Hal is above contradicting it. There is not such a gap as has often been alleged between that Falstaff and the one who can so easily be made to look foolish by the kind of honest woman of whom he has little experience, or between the Falstaff who is frightened of being found by a jealous husband and the one who ran away at Gadshill. Nor is the Falstaff who admits to beating the servants of a justice of the peace, killing his deer, and breaking open his lodge, and at another time (II. ii) to having used influence to keep guilty cronies out of gaol and to sharing the profits of their crimes, a different man from the one who on hearing the news that Hal had become king announces 'Let us take any man's horses; the laws of England are at my commandment. Blessed are they that have been my friends; and woe to my lord chief-justice!'

1. *The Principles and Practice of Criticism* (Detroit, 1959), p. 88.

Shakespeare has also been gravely censured for obeying the
Queen's command and showing Falstaff in love.[1] Of course, he
did no such thing; the Queen might give what commands she
pleased but if she did give this one, Shakespeare sidestepped it, and
showed Falstaff pretending to be in love *because* he was hard-up:
'I will be cheaters to them both, and they shall be exchequers to
me: they shall be my East and West Indies, and I will trade to
them both'. Dr Johnson saw this quite clearly and in a 'general
observation' contributed to the 1773 Steevens edition wrote:
'Shakespeare knew what the queen, if the story be true, seems not
to have known, that by any real passion of tenderness, the selfish
craft, the careless jollity, and the lazy luxury of Falstaff, must have
suffered so much abatement, that little of his former cast would
have remained. Falstaff could not love, but by ceasing to be
Falstaff. He could only counterfeit love, and his professions could
be prompted, not by the hope of pleasure, but of money.' The
Quarto reporters, incidentally, also had no illusions on this point:
having proclaimed that he must 'cheat' and 'cony-catch', Falstaff
first mentions the wives with the announcement of his policy: 'I do
intend to *make loue* to Foords wife' (my italics).

Falstaff, then, is not 'infatuated' at all but is the victim of
another disease, that incurable 'consumption of the purse' that
he suffers from again in *2 Henry IV*; and he is prepared to play a
different role in the hope of 'earning' money. The audience awaits
the result. The fun will be in the ways in which he is victimized, and
the laughs will come partly from the conflicts of character and
from the farce-like incidents. They come also, however, not from
the lies that the fat rogue tells of his adventures (indeed, in *The
Merry Wives* he often tells the truth) but from the incomparable
idiom in which he tells of them. And if the Falstaff of *The Merry
Wives* shares one quality above all others with the Falstaff of
Henry IV, that quality is, surely, the idiom.

It is heard immediately on his entrance: 'I will answer it straight:
I have done all this. That is now answered'; it is clear in his description of Mistress Ford's and Mistress Page's alleged interest
in him, with its characteristic trick of seeming to deprecate, or
depreciate, himself without really doing so ('sometimes the beam
of her view gilded my foot, sometimes my portly belly'—compare,
for example, from *2 Henry IV*, 'I do here walk before thee like a sow
that hath overwhelmed all her litter but one', and the following

---

1. M. R. Ridley has complained, for example, that we are 'apparently being
solemnly, or at least seriously, invited to suppose' that the old Falstaff 'could . . .
be no better than an infatuated gull' (*William Shakespeare: A Commentary*, London,
1936, p. 74).

interview with the Chief Justice); and it is unmistakable when, equally characteristically, he parodies his own style, among others, and, tongue in cheek, writes a letter: 'I love thee. I will not say pity me—'tis not a soldier-like phrase—but I say, love me. By me, / Thine own true knight, / By day or night / . . . *John Falstaff*'. This could not be more like his letter to Hal in *2 Henry IV*, II. ii. 136ff., 'I commend me to thee, I commend thee, and I leave thee. . . Thine, by yea and no, which is as much as to say, as thou usest him, *Jack Falstaff* . . .'.

He is made to speak with exactly the same gift for the unexpected nouns in the most vivid of similes and the repetition of a word to form a startling pun: 'I have *grated* upon my good friends for three reprieves for you and your *coach-fellow* Nym—or else you had looked through the *grate*, like a *geminy* of *baboons*'. In the wry self-communion that is as close as he comes to self-pity, the phrases 'you may know by my size that I have a kind of alacrity in sinking... The water swells a man; and what a thing should I have been when I had been swelled! I should have been a mountain of mummy' are comparable with 'I were better to be eaten to death with a rust than to be scoured to nothing with perpetual motion' (*2 Henry IV*, I. ii. 246–8). Of his subsequent retelling to Ford of his ducking in the Thames (III. v. 75–113), one need say perhaps only that there is no finer comic prose in the whole of English drama. It is ungracious to ask for more, and Hazlitt was surely wrong when he said that Falstaff's 'wit and eloquence have left him'.[1]

One other aspect of Shakespeare's 'revival' of Falstaff in *The Merry Wives* should be noticed—its masterly avoiding of what could have become major problems. For example, Mistress Quickly's second interview with Falstaff (III. v), to invite him to visit Mistress Ford the second time, is kept very short; and the main part of the third, when obviously it would be more difficult for her to evade questions about his earlier discomfiture, takes place off-stage (it is merely introduced in IV. v). Finally, Falstaff's face is saved after the Herne the Hunter farce, when the disclosure is made that those who have played tricks on him have themselves been deceived: Anne has married neither her father's nor her mother's choice, so that her parents, trying to trick each other, have both been tricked, and Caius and Slender have failed to marry their promised brides. Page's invitation to Falstaff to laugh at Mistress Page falls flat, and indeed nobody can afford to laugh at anybody else. Not only has the previously realistic play been turned in Act V into a kind of courtly masque, in which characters

---

1. *Characters of Shakespeare's Plays* (1818, rep. London, 1890), p. 230.

can step out of their main roles to play other parts, particularly for the purpose of compliment, in true masque style; but also now the masque has, as it were, been allowed to fade out, that the characters of the main play may step forward again and *all* be seen in their true colours. As J. W. Mackail once put it, 'it is a wonderful feat of sleight-of-hand. . . . Managed light-handedly as it is, and taken light-heartedly as it should be, it is as good reading as it is a uniform and certain success on the stage. Mrs. Page's concluding words:

> Let us every one go home
> And laugh this sport o'er by a country fire,
> Sir John and all,

are in effect Shakespeare's own criticism on it—whose else can we require?—and the sufficient answer to the higher critics who have deplored in it the degradation of Falstaff: forgetting that the best of them are but shadows, and the worst no worse if imagination amend them.'[1]

Over a hundred years before Mackail, Oxberry had pointed out that it is in any case an error to concentrate on Falstaff, and the comparison with the Falstaff of the Histories, and to overlook all the other comic characters who helped, in Oxberry's opinion, to make 'this delightful comedy' 'perfect'.[2] Probably the most interesting of these are the wives, in whom Shakespeare showed conclusively, in the words of one of them, that 'wives may be merry, and yet honest too'. They are indeed 'honest' and not only in the sense of 'chaste'; equally appealing is their loyalty to, and understanding of, each other. Even that, however, is not a matter on which they can be solemn: when Ford says to Mistress Page, 'I think, if your husbands were dead, you two would marry', he receives the reply he perhaps deserves: 'Be sure of that—two other husbands'. There is no ambiguity or ambivalence in their attitude to Falstaff's letters; it is summed up in one phrase, 'What doth he think of us?' and their only other thought is 'Let's be revenged on him':

> *Mrs. Ford.* Nay, I will consent to act any villainy against him that may not sully the chariness of our honesty. O that my husband saw this letter; it would give eternal food to his jealousy.

1. *The Approach to Shakespeare* (Oxford, 1930), p. 59. The opposite view is nowhere more strongly stated than by H. B. Charlton, who, in his *Shakespearian Comedy* (London, 1938, rep. 1961), pp. 192–3, said that Shakespeare's treatment of Falstaff here was a 'crime worse than parricide—the slaughter of one's own offspring', adding 'there can be no clearer evidence of his own rejection of Falstaff' or of 'the bitterness of its author's disillusionment'.

2. *The Merry Wives of Windsor*, ed. W. Oxberry (The New English Drama, Vol. 9, London, 1820), p. i.

Mrs. Page. Why, look where he comes; and my good man too.
He's as far from jealousy as I am from giving him cause;
and that, I hope, is an unmeasurable distance.
Mrs. Ford. You are the happier woman.

The touch of pathos in that last comment should not be missed, but
of course Shakespeare will not allow himself to dwell on pathos in
such a comedy as this; the sorrow of the woman married to a
jealous husband has not been overlooked, but it has been treated
with the reserve with which a Mistress Ford would herself treat it.

Above all, the portraits of the wives are significantly unmarred
by the fulsomeness that too often accompanies portraits of domestic
virtue. Shakespeare has made the point that a woman can be
virtuous without taking herself or the world too seriously; and with
such a woman a Falstaff is hopelessly out of his element. The phrase
that perhaps best describes his predicament is Mistress Ford's
'What tempest I trow threw this whale, with so many tuns of oil in
his belly, ashore at Windsor?' A Falstaff is more in his 'natural'
environment with an Eastcheap hostess—or with Doll Tearsheet.

Page and Ford are also interestingly drawn. Page is little more
than an average decent citizen, above suspecting his wife but not
above choosing his daughter's husband; he must therefore be
taken down a peg, by discovering that the daughter is quite capable
of running off with the man she wants and so escaping the fool to
whom her father would rashly have married her. The skill with
which the dramatist portrays the jealousy of Ford, however, has
not sufficiently been noticed.

When Elizabethan dramatists did not portray jealousy as tragic,
they tended to portray it as a 'humour', dominating a man's
character and leaving no room for other aspects of temperament.
In Ford, jealousy is depicted 'in the round', and the dramatist has
shown that a man may be jealous and still not be worthless or
beneath contempt. This is achieved by revealing the way in which
Ford's mind works. There is, as it were, an intellectual basis for his
jealousy, in the sense that he convinces himself, by rationalization,
that he would be foolish not to be jealous—that jealousy is, so to
speak, a risk worth taking, since the alternative is seen as obstinate
unwillingness to acknowledge what could conceivably happen.
The line of thought, once Pistol has told him that Falstaff 'affects'
his wife—and we know already from the wives that Ford is prone
to jealousy—is: 'I do not misdoubt my wife; but I would be loath
to turn them together; a man may be too confident; I would have
nothing lie on my head; I cannot be thus satisfied' or again 'Though
Page be a secure fool, and stands so firmly on his wife's frailty, yet

I cannot put off my opinion so easily: she was in his company at Page's house; and what they made there, I know not. Well, I will look further into't, and I have a disguise to sound Falstaff. If I find her honest, I lose not my labour; if she be otherwise, 'tis labour well bestowed.' It is also perfectly 'in character' that as Brook he should continue to torture himself by hearing of Falstaff's aspirations and progress: a strain of masochism is gently hinted at (and no more than that).

Alfred Harbage has written that 'Master Ford's soliloquy when he thinks he is to be cuckolded does not express the anguish which Shakespeare would give a character actually in such danger'.[1] It may be so, but the anguish seems deep enough, and realistic enough: the difference between Ford's anguish and Othello's may be not so much in the 'tone' (to use Harbage's word) as in the audience's already established attitude to the characters. It knows that Othello's jealousy is groundless but knows also that it is dangerous, whereas in the comedy knowledge both of the stratagem being used by the wives and of the characters of all concerned removes any possibility that Ford will long continue to believe the worst. *While* he suffers, however, his suffering is acute, and certainly dramatically credible.

Of the others, Fenton is little more than the youthful romantic lead, saved from insipidity by the information that he kept company with the wild Prince and Poins and by his dignity and his willingness to do something about the difficulties that beset his wooing. By a dramatic device known from many a play, he also gains by contrast with his rivals for the hand of Anne. Anne is herself both 'sweet' and desirable; her two exchanges with Slender, at the end of I. i and in III. iv, could be played to show a gay sense of humour but in any case reveal firmness and sense ('Good Master Shallow, let him woo for himself'), as do her brief dialogue with Fenton at the beginning of III. iv and her indignant answer to the suggestion that she marry Caius: 'Alas, I had rather be set quick i' th' earth, / And bowl'd to death with turnips!' Perhaps too the imagery of that rejoinder is intended to remind us that we are dealing with a country girl.

Caius is most amusing, with his pugnacity (often expressed through his favourite oath, 'by gar') and his ability to do greater harm to the English language than he ever manages to do to his opponents; there is, however, no reason to question his courage, and his final threat 'by gar, I'll raise all Windsor' need not be seen

1. *As They Liked It* (New York, 1947), p. 135, referring to the soliloquy at the close of II. ii.

as empty. It has exactly the same effect as has Malvolio's 'I'll be revenged on the whole pack of you' at the close of *Twelfth Night*: the joy of the majority is never achieved without the unhappiness of one. In the world of comedy, fools who aspire to the hands of desirable young women must run the risk of being treated as fools and must take whatever is coming to them. Nor in *The Merry Wives* is there an Olivia to say that 'he hath been most notoriously abused' or a Duke to say 'Pursue him, and entreat him to a peace'.

No audience ever sorrowed over Slender, perhaps the finest comic portrait in the play and certainly one of the finest Shakespeare ever painted on a small canvas. It has been well said that the very name is almost too substantial for the character, and F. S. Boas has written that 'In Slender not only do we see intellect flickering with its last feeble glimmer, but the will attenuated almost to vanishing point. Palpitating on the brink of nonentity, he clings for support to the majestic personality of Shallow.'[1] As a dramatic character, however, he is no nonentity, any more than a bore (such as Jane Austen's Miss Bates would have been in real life) need be a bore as a figure in fiction; indeed he is, as Hazlitt put it, 'a very potent piece of imbecility'.[2]

Slender's knowledge is confined to bears and greyhounds; his courage is not even enough to stand up to the bluster of Pistol and Bardolph. He is completely without initiative ('I had rather than forty shillings I had my book of Songs and Sonnets here'); and although Evans tries patiently to explain to him the 'matter' of the wooing of Anne Page, 'if you be capacity of it', the capacity is quite lacking, and the enthusiasm rises only to 'Why, if it be so, I will marry her upon any reasonable demands . . . that I am freely dissolved, and dissolutely'. Yet he wanders through one scene doing nothing but sigh, quite irrelevantly, 'O sweet Anne Page'—playing the part of the love-sick swain as unsuccessfully as he played the part of the polite guest in I. i. His proposal to Anne, in III. iv, competes with Mr Collins's offer to Elizabeth Bennet in *Pride and Prejudice* for the honour of being the funniest proposal in English literature. It can end only as it does, with an immense sigh of relief at being saved from the necessity for further conversation: 'Your father and my uncle hath made motions. If it be my luck, so; if not, happy man be his dole! They can tell you how things go, better than I can. You may ask your father; here he comes.'

Conceivably the portrait of Slender, incapable of acting without the prodding of his uncle the Justice, would have even more humour if it were seen to be aimed at William Wayte, that 'certain

1. *Shakspere and his Predecessors* (London, 1896), p. 298.   2. *op. cit.*, p. 231.

loose person of no reckoning or value, being wholly under the rule and commandment of the said Gardiner', but it does not need that support. Rather, one other quality of the sketch must be praised: its superb restraint. How many dramatists, having thought up Slender, could have been content to make such sparing use of him and have refused to carry him (or Shallow's crony in *2 Henry IV*, Silence) into a second play?

Sparing use is similarly made of Justice Shallow, although the humour of this part was more varied and thus allowed repetition in a 'sequel'. Leaving aside again the possibility of personal satire, the fun of Shallow comes largely from his vanity—particularly that form of it that depends, as in *2 Henry IV*, on unreliable memories of his prowess when he was young; on his trick of repeating the most trivial of phrases ('And I thank you always with my heart, la, with my heart'; 'Sir, he's a good dog, and a fair dog: can there more be said? He is good and fair'; 'He hath wronged me, indeed he hath; at a word, he hath, believe me. Robert Shallow, Esquire, saith he is wronged'); and on his inability either to avoid platitude or to strike the right tone and give no more than the proportionate emphasis to a remark ('Though we are justices, and doctors, and churchmen, Master Page, we have some salt of our youth in us; we are the sons of women, Master Page').

The Welsh parson Evans is there mostly to 'make fritters of English' and, with his cowardice and generally over-anxious good nature, to serve as a foil to his original foe and later collaborator, Caius. He is also unforgettable in the Latin lesson. Caius' 'dry nurse', Mistress Quickly, is yet another enemy of the English language, and has even less control over her tongue: her thoughts pour out, in no semblance of order (and incidentally give headaches to editors who have to punctuate what she says). Add the jovial bluster of the Host; the less good-natured bluster of Pistol, trying to speak in the manner of the hero, or anti-hero, of Elizabethan drama, or melodrama; the 'humours' of Nym; and the blunders of young William Page—and we have one of the most astonishing galleries of perpetrators of verbal fun that even Shakespeare ever put in a play.

It is not surprising, with so many 'comics'—and particularly if the play was in fact written hurriedly—that the plotting should not be tight.[1] Nothing comes of the charge of killing deer brought by Shallow against Falstaff at the beginning of the play, and no

1. Dryden, however, found the play unique among Shakespeare's comedies for 'the mechanic beauties of the plot', 'the observation of the three Unities' ('The Grounds of Criticism in Tragedy', the preface to *Troilus and Cressida*, 1679); and George Colman and other eighteenth-century critics agreed with him.

more is heard of the rather ridiculous threat to make a Star Chamber matter of it. Unless there was indeed some special relevance in all this for purposes of personal satire, one can do no more than assume that it is one way of bringing Mr Justice Shallow up from Gloucestershire to Windsor—and even that is less likely if this play preceded *2 Henry IV.* It is probably not true, however, that nothing comes of the trick played by the Host on Caius and Evans; one must believe that they take their revenge by paying somebody to impersonate visiting German dignitaries and steal the Host's horses.[1] This part of the play nevertheless remains a sub-plot, not connected in any way with the two main 'intrigue' plots—other than that they are all variations on the tale of the biter bit and that all three involve the deflating of a character who thinks himself safe from deception. The intrigue stories—i.e. the tricks played on Falstaff by the merry wives and the outwitting of Page and his wife, Caius, and Slender, by Fenton and Anne— are most skilfully linked at the end when the revealing of Fenton's success prevents the Pages from gloating further over their exposing of Falstaff. (There is also the less important connection of Quickly's acting as go-between in both plots.)

It may be worth pointing out too that the play has been carefully composed for presentation on the most simple of stages. A disclosure space of some kind is required for the hiding of Simple from Caius in I. iv and to serve as the 'arras' behind which Falstaff stands in III. iii, and as the 'chamber' into which Falstaff steps in IV. ii; but there is no need for the audience to *see* the actors 'ascend' in III. iii or 'run up' in IV. ii, and while Falstaff could speak from a higher level in IV. v when the Host calls to him to let the 'fat woman' 'descend', it is not necessary. There is then no commitment to an 'upper stage', and even the last scene can be produced on a simple platform. The play could thus easily have been transferred from public stage to Court, or vice versa, with a minimum of bother and without the problem of transporting clumsy 'properties'.

Of the 'style' of the comedy, something has already been said in discussing the Falstaff idiom. That most of the play is in prose need not mean that prose was easier for Shakespeare (the state of the text of *Timon of Athens,* if that is indeed an unfinished play, may well suggest that it was not); nor is prose in any sense inferior for the purposes of such broad comedy as this. The effect of colloquialism is easily obtained, and sustained; and Shakespeare has

1. Daniel may still be correct in saying that conjecture whether Pistol and Nym were the men in disguise is 'somewhat idle speculation' (Introduction to the Griggs facsimile, p. xii).

no difficulty in covering the necessary range of mood, even to
Ford's jealousy. The prose also has some most subtle rhythms, and
not only when Shallow is using his characteristic repetitions, or
when Caius is piling up threats, or Evans ticking off facts on his
fingers: 'there is three umpires in this matter, as I understand; that
is, Master Page (fidelicet Master Page); and there is myself
(fidelicet myself): and the three party is (lastly and finally) mine
host of the Garter'. Falstaff, too, is fond of a singing parallelism
('she discourses, she carves, she gives the leer of invitation') and
even Quickly's meanderings often have their own kind of balance
('His worst fault is that he is given to prayer; he is something
peevish that way; but nobody but has his fault; but let that pass').
The mingling of speeches of one or two sentences with the longer
passages such as Ford's soliloquies, or his addresses (as Brook) to
Falstaff, or Falstaff's accounts of his adventures to Ford–Brook,
provides another interesting study in variation of dramatic pace.

The occasional modulating into verse is not as arbitrary as has
sometimes been maintained. It is nearly all associated either with
Fenton, to distinguish the romantic 'plot', or with the Herne the
Hunter masque, as a sign of its lesser reality. So Fenton speaks
verse, appropriately, in a serious conversation with Anne in III. iv,
and not only Anne but also Page and Mistress Page use it when
addressing him; similarly both Fenton and the Host talk in verse
in IV. vi when discussing the elopement. Ford speaks verse when
announcing his reformation, in IV. iv, and Page replies to him in
kind—the farce for the minute is over—and then Mistress Page
and company use verse when developing the plan to have Falstaff
tricked as Herne the Hunter. In the last scene, Quickly and her
allies speak verse while playing their parts in the masque, but
prose significantly returns when the characters resume their own
persons; and the entry of Fenton with his bride naturally demands
verse again. Pistol, of course, often lapses into, or imitates, verse
when he is trying to emulate Marlowe or the writers of less repu-
table heroics; and couplets may be used, as so often in Elizabethan
drama, to gain the effect of epigram or Q.E.D. at the close of a
scene or a distinctive part of one—as with Mistress Page's

> We'll leave a proof, by that which we will do,
> Wives may be merry, and yet honest too.
> We do not act that often jest and laugh;
> 'Tis old but true: 'Still swine eats all the draff'
> (IV. ii. 95–8).

The only 'problem' even worth comment is Falstaff's use of three
blank verse lines followed by a couplet, at I. iii. 76–80—and the

point here may be that he is imitating and parodying Pistol, exactly as he speaks a few lines of verse 'in King Cambyses' vein' in *1 Henry IV*, II. iv.

To search for thematic imagery in *The Merry Wives* would be folly: the play has neither the intellectual nor the emotional intensity for that. There are, however, some interesting groups of imagery that influence one's attitude to story and characters, and certainly there are some that help to establish atmosphere.[1]

The main group, not surprisingly, could be described as that arising from the typical domestic life of a family in a country town. 'Choked with a piece of toasted cheese' (and other cheese references), 'one that makes fritters of English', 'half stewed in grease like a Dutch dish', 'have my brains ta'en out and buttered', 'rain potatoes', 'bowl'd to death with turnips', 'as blue as bilberry', 'as crest-fallen as a dried pear', 'laid my brain in the sun and dried it', 'knit a knot in his fortunes with the finger of my substance', 'Welsh flannel', 'a cockscomb of frieze', 'cannot creep into a half-penny purse, nor into a pepper box', 'cooled, glowing hot, . . . like a horse-shoe', 'to the forge with it, then; shape it: I would not have things cool', 'like a barrow of butcher's offal', 'like a glover's paring knife' are representative; and, not to forget the out-of-doors, there are the delightful 'these lisping hawthorn-buds' and 'he smells April and May'. While not strictly an image, perhaps, 'plucked geese, played truant, and whipped top' gains the same effect. Amusingly some of the oaths and terms of abuse have this country flavour too: 'You Banbury cheese', for example, or 'mechanical salt-butter rogue'.

In these middle-class surroundings, the characters, not excluding Falstaff, speak most appropriately in homely proverbs or choose their allusions from the better-known parts of scripture. 'The story of the Prodigal', 'a legion of angels', 'Cain-coloured beard', 'a Herod of Jewry', 'Goliath with a weaver's beam', 'as poor as Job', 'all Eve's daughters', 'the hundred Psalms', and 'as firm as faith' are some of these. Classical allusions are correspondingly rare. Several, but by no means all, of these are used by the more highly educated Falstaff; and many are sexual in connotation, such as Actaeon, Jove and Europa, Jupiter and Leda, 'Cupid's carriers', and 'my good she-Mercury'. (The Host throws in 'bully Hercules', 'bully Hector', and 'Hector of Greece'.) If Pistol's constant attempts to be literary are put on one side, and they are all early in the play, other literary references are relatively few: the most memorable

1. 'Image' will be used in a wide sense in the following discussion, much as Caroline Spurgeon used it in *Shakespeare's Imagery* (Cambridge, 1935), to include 'imaginative picture'.

are the Marlowe song, the quotation from Sidney, the Host's 'Am I a Machiavel?', and 'like . . . three Doctor Faustuses'. As befits a play given so much to intentional and unintentional misuse of language, however, there are several linguistic images, such as 'I can construe the action of her familiar style', the 'voice of her behaviour', 'translated her will—out of honesty into English', and 'keep the terms of my honour precise'. ('Spoke the prologue of our comedy', 'puts into the press', and 'second edition' are not unrelated to these.)

A very prominent group of images belongs to the animal–bird class. 'Like rats', 'polecats', 'unkennel the fox', 'cat-a-mountain looks', 'Jack-dog priest', 'jack-an-ape', 'geminy of baboons', and 'rotten bell-wether' come to mind, not to mention 'with as little remorse as they would have drowned a blind bitch's puppies, fifteen i' the litter', 'come cut and long-tail', 'eyas-musket', and 'know turtles from jays'. The effect of these, however, is not basically to lower the world of the play to the level of the animal kingdom (as the images are alleged to lower that of *King Lear*, or as the 'dog', 'boar', and other animal images used of him influence our judgement of Richard III); they work in exactly the opposite way and make the audience smile at the idiosyncrasy of the speaker who indulges in them, as does 'the world's mine oyster, which I with sword will open'. The occasional medical image tends to have the same effect—for example, the Host's 'bully stale' and 'Mounseur Mock-water' and Falstaff's 'as cold as if I had swallowed snowballs for pills to cool the reins', and the references to Hippocrates, Galen, and Æsculapius.

The legal and financial group is not so easily explicable: that love and marriage are so often seen as arrangements to be made formally is only a partial explanation. 'Lay to pawn', 'fee-simple, with fine and recovery', 'the register' (of follies), 'fee'd every slight occasion', 'exhibit a bill in the parliament', references to (legal) 'suits' and inheriting, and, particularly, 'like a fair house built on another man's ground, so that I have lost my edifice by mistaking the place where I erected it' and 'build upon a . . . promise' may even have an autobiographical rather than a dramatic significance (although 'I will be cheaters to them both, and they shall be exchequers to me' is clear enough). Military images help to reinforce the idea that some see woman's purity as an object to be attacked and defended (e.g. 'lay an amiable siege to the honesty of this Ford's wife', 'the ward of her purity', and 'her defences which now are too too strongly embattled against me').

Some of the most vivid images have to do with ships and places and exploration. A few of these link with the previous group (e.g. 'this voyage toward my wife', 'board', 'above deck', and 'under my hatches') and those used by Falstaff reinforce the notion of his exploring for treasure ('sail like my pinnace to these golden shores', 'they shall be my East and West Indies', and 'she is a region in Guiana', for instance). The Host's, however, are far more exotic, and build up the impression of his ebullience—such as 'my Ethiopian', 'Castalian-king-Urinal', 'Anthropophaginian', and 'Bohemian-Tartar'. Falstaff's 'Pickt-hatch', 'like Bucklersbury in simple time', and 'the Countergate'—together with 'red-lattice phrases'—are distinctly English and from his own background.

Falstaff's bulk is the cause of many images, used by him and of him, mentioning oil, fat, and grease, and these, of course, add considerably to the fun as well as to the physical picture. They include 'till the wicked fire of lust have melted him in his own grease' and 'this whale, with so many tuns of oil in his belly', both from Mistress Ford, and, from Falstaff himself, 'lest the oil that's in me should set hell on fire', 'melt me out of my fat drop by drop, and liquor fishermen's boots with me', and 'stinking clothes that fretted in their own grease'. A similar effect, from the 'domestic' class, is gained by 'gross watery pumpion'.

Last but not least, there are all the images related to the horns of the cuckold, leading to a whole range of references to buck and other horned beasts—Ford fearing that he is being reduced to the level of one, and Falstaff equally erroneously thinking to make him one. These reach a deliberate crescendo in Falstaff's anticipations as, wearing horns, he awaits the arrival of his 'doe' at the beginning of the final scene; and the extravagance of 'send me a cool rut-time, Jove' makes him most laughable when it is necessary that he least be pitied.

The language, in short, is superbly adapted to the purposes of the play, and examination of it too suggests that the producers and actors who have continued to present *The Merry Wives*, and the audiences who have continued to enjoy it, may be making sounder literary judgements than those who write whole books on Shakespeare or his comedies and either neglect the play altogether or mention it only in passing.

F

ABBREVIATIONS AND REFERENCES

The following abbreviations are used in the collations and explanatory notes:

EDITIONS

Q   *A Most pleasaunt and excellent conceited Comedie, of Syr Iohn Falstaffe, and the merrie Wiues of Windsor. Entermixed with sundrie variable and pleasing humors, of Syr Hugh the Welch Knight, Iustice Shallow, and his wise Cousin M. Slender. With the swaggering vaine of Auncient Pistoll, and Corporall Nym. By William Shakespeare.* London, 1602.

Q2   *A Most Pleasant and Excellent Conceited Comedy, of Sir Iohn Falstaffe, and the Merry Wiues of Windsor. With the Swaggering Vaine of Ancient Pistoll, and Corporall Nym. Written by W. Shakespeare.* London, 1619.

Q3   *The Merry VViues of Windsor. With the humours of Sir Iohn Falstaffe, As also the swaggering vaine of Ancient Pistoll, and Corporall Nym. Written by William Shake-Speare. Newly corrected.* London, 1630.

F   *Mr. William Shakespeares Comedies, Histories, & Tragedies.* London, 1623.

F2   *Mr. William Shakespeares Comedies, Histories, and Tragedies.* London, 1632.

F3   *Mr. William Shakespear's Comedies, Histories, and Tragedies . . . The third Impression.* London, 1664.

F4   *Mr. William Shakespear's Comedies, Histories, and Tragedies . . . The Fourth Edition.* London, 1685.

Rowe   *The Works of Mr. William Shakespear . . . Revis'd and Corrected . . . By N. Rowe, Esq.* (Vol. 1) London, 1709.

Rowe2   *The Works of Mr. William Shakespear . . . Revis'd and Corrected . . . By N. Rowe Esq.* (Vol. 1) London, 1709.

Rowe3   *The Works of Mr. William Shakespear . . . With his Life, by N. Rowe Esq.* (Vol. 1) London, 1714.

Pope   *The Works of Shakespear . . . Collected and Corrected . . . by Mr. Pope.* (Vol. 1) London, 1723.

Theobald   *The Works of Shakespeare . . . Collated with the Oldest Copies, and Corrected; With Notes . . . By Mr. Theobald.* (Vol. 1) London, 1733.

Theobald2   *The Works of Shakespeare . . . Collated . . . and Corrected: With Notes . . . By Mr. Theobald. The Second Edition.* (Vol. 1) London, 1740.

Hanmer   *The Works of Shakespear . . . Carefully Revised and Corrected by the former Editions.* (Vol. 1) Oxford, 1744.

Warburton   *The Works of Shakespear. The Genuine Text . . . settled . . . By Mr. Pope and Mr. Warburton.* (Vol. 1) London, 1747.

Johnson   *The Plays of William Shakespeare . . . To which are added Notes by Sam. Johnson.* (Vol. 2) London, 1765.

Capell   *Mr William Shakespeare his Comedies, Histories, and Tragedies* [edited Edward Capell]. (Vol. 1) London, [1767].

Steevens   *The Plays of William Shakespeare . . . To which are added notes by Samuel Johnson and George Steevens.* (Vol. 1) London, 1773.

Steevens[2]   *The Plays of William Shakspeare . . . The Second Edition, Revised and Augmented.* (Vol. 1) London, 1778.

Reed   *The Plays of William Shakspeare . . . The Third Edition, revised and augmented by the Editor of Dodsley's Collection of Old Plays.* (Vol. 1) London, 1785.

Rann   *The Dramatic Works of Shakespeare . . . with notes by Joseph Rann.* (Vol. 1) Oxford, 1786.

Malone   *The Plays and Poems of William Shakspeare . . . With . . . notes . . . By Edmond Malone.* (Vol. 1 Pt 2) London, 1790.

Steevens[3]   *The Plays of William Shakspeare . . . The Fourth Edition.* (Vol. 3) London, 1793.

Reed[2]   *The Plays of William Shakspeare . . . The Fifth Edition. Revised and augmented By Isaac Reed.* (Vol. 5) London, 1803.

Reed[3]   *The Plays of William Shakspeare . . . Revised and augmented by Isaac Reed . . . The Sixth Edition.* (Vol. 5) London, 1813.

Harness   *The Dramatic Works of William Shakspeare; with notes . . . By the Rev. William Harness.* (Vol. 1) London, 1825.

Singer   *The Dramatic Works of William Shakspeare. With Notes . . . by Samuel Weller Singer.* (Vol. 1) Chiswick, 1826.

Knight   *The Pictorial Edition of the Works of Shakspere. Edited by Charles Knight. Comedies* (Vol. 1) London, [1839].

Collier   *The Works of William Shakespeare . . . with the various readings, notes . . . by J. Payne Collier.* (Vol. 1) London, 1844.

Halliwell   *The Complete Works of Shakspere, Revised . . . by J. O. Halliwell.* London and New York, [1850].

Hudson   *The Works of Shakespeare . . . with Introductions, Notes . . . by the Rev. H. N. Hudson.* (Vol. 1) Boston, 1851.

Collier[2]   *The Plays of Shakespeare: The text regulated by the old copies, and by the recently discovered Folio of 1632, containing early manuscript emendations. Edited by J. Payne Collier.* London, 1853.

Dyce   *The Works of William Shakespeare. The Text revised by the Rev. Alexander Dyce.* (Vol. 1) London, 1857.

Grant White   *The Works of William Shakespeare . . . edited . . . by Richard Grant White.* (Vol. 2) Boston, 1857.

Staunton   *The Plays of Shakespeare. Edited by Howard Staunton.* (Vol. 1) London, 1858.

Camb.   *The Works of William Shakespeare edited by William George Clark . . . and John Glover.* (Vol. 1) Cambridge and London, 1863.

Keightley   *The Plays of William Shakespeare. Carefully edited by Thomas Keightley.* (Vol. 2) London, 1864.

Dyce[2] — *The Works of William Shakespeare . . . Second edition.* (Vol. 1) London, 1866.

Hudson[2] — *The Works of Shakespeare . . . with Introductions, Notes . . . by the Rev. H. N. Hudson . . . Revised edition.* (Vol. 1) Boston, 1871.

Wheatley — *The Merry Wives of Windsor . . . edited . . . by Henry B. Wheatley.* London, 1886.

Craig — *The Complete Works of William Shakespeare. Edited . . . by W. J. Craig.* The Oxford Shakespeare. Oxford, [1892].

Hart — *The Merry Wives of Windsor. Edited by H. C. Hart.* The Arden Shakespeare. London, 1904, rep. 1932.

Chambers — *The Merry Wives of Windsor. Edited by E. K. Chambers.* The Red Letter Shakespeare. London, 1906.

New Camb. — *The Merry Wives of Windsor. Edited . . . by Sir Arthur Quiller-Couch and John Dover Wilson.* The New Shakespeare. Cambridge, 1921, rep. 1954.

Yale — *The Merry Wives of Windsor. Edited by George Van Santvoord.* The Yale Shakespeare. New Haven, 1922.

Ridley — *The Merry Wives of Windsor. Edited by M. R. Ridley.* The New Temple Shakespeare. London, 1935.

Kittredge — *The Complete Works of Shakespeare. Edited by George Lyman Kittredge.* Boston, [1936].

Alexander — *William Shakespeare The Complete Works . . . edited . . . by Peter Alexander.* The Tudor Shakespeare. London, 1951.

Sisson — *William Shakespeare The Complete Works . . . Edited by Charles Jasper Sisson.* London, [1954].

Munro — *The London Shakespeare . . . edited by . . . John Munro.* (Vol. 2) London, 1958.

Bowers — *The Merry Wives of Windsor. Edited by Fredson Bowers.* The Pelican Shakespeare. Baltimore, 1963, rep. 1969.

OTHER WORKS

Abbott — E. A. Abbott. *A Shakespearian Grammar.* Third edition, London 1873.

Ashmole — Elias Ashmole. *The Institution, Laws & Ceremonies Of the most noble Order of the Garter.* London, 1672.

Baldwin — T. W. Baldwin. *William Shakspere's 'Small Latine & Lesse Greeke'.* Urbana, Ill., 1944.

Bullough — Geoffrey Bullough. *Narrative and Dramatic Sources of Shakespeare.* (Vol. 2) London, 1958.

Capell (1783) — [Edward Capell]. *Notes and Various Readings to Shakespeare.* London, [1783].

Cartwright — Robert Cartwright. *New Readings in Shakspere.* London, 1866.

Cotgrave — Randle Cotgrave. *A Dictionarie of the French and English Tongues.* London, 1611.

Daniel — P. A. Daniel. *Notes and Conjectural Emendations Of certain Doubtful Passages in Shakespeare's Plays.* London, 1870.

Douce — Francis Douce. *Illustrations of Shakespeare.* London, 1807.

Dyce (*Remarks*) — Alexander Dyce. *Remarks on Mr. J. P. Collier's and Mr. C. Knight's editions of Shakespeare.* London, 1844.

Eliot   [John Eliot]. *Ortho-Epia Gallica. Eliots Fruits for the French.* London, 1593.

Greg   Sir Walter Greg. Private letter to J. Dover Wilson (*New Camb.*, p. 134).

Grey   Zachary Grey. *Critical, Historical and Explanatory Notes on Shakespeare.* London, 1754.

Heath   [Benjamin Heath]. *A Revisal of Shakespeare's Text.* London, 1765.

Hotson   Leslie Hotson. *Shakespeare versus Shallow.* London, 1931.

Hulme   Hilda M. Hulme. *Explorations in Shakespeare's Language.* London, 1962.

Jackson   Zachariah Jackson. *Shakespeare's Genius Justified.* London, 1819.

Jonson   *Ben Jonson*, ed. C. H. Herford, and Percy and Evelyn Simpson. Oxford, 1925–52.

Kinnear   B. G. Kinnear. *Cruces Shakespearianæ.* London, 1883.

Kökeritz   Helge Kökeritz. *Shakespeare's Pronunciation.* New Haven, 1953.

Lambrechts   Guy Lambrechts. 'Proposed New Readings in Shakespeare', *Bulletin de la Faculté des Lettres de Strasbourg*, LXIII (1965), 946–7.

Lilly   [William Lilly, John Colet, *et al.*]. *A Shorte Introduction of Grammar.* London, 1549, 1557, 1577.

Mason   J. M. Mason. *Comments on the Last Edition of Shakespeare's Plays.* Dublin, 1785.

Muir   Kenneth Muir. *Shakespeare's Sources. I. Comedies and Tragedies.* London, 1957.

Nashe   *The Works of Thomas Nashe*, Edited by Ronald B. McKerrow (1904–10) . . . With supplementary notes . . . by F. P. Wilson. Oxford, 1958.

Noble   Richmond Noble. *Shakespeare's Biblical Knowledge.* London, 1935.

O.E.D.   *The Oxford English Dictionary, being a corrected reissue of 'A New English Dictionary upon Historical Principles'.* Oxford, 1933.

Onions   C. T. Onions. *A Shakespeare Glossary.* Second edition 1919, reprinted with enlarged addenda, Oxford, 1958.

Parsons   Howard Parsons. *Emendations to Three of Shakespeare's Plays.* London, [1953].

Partridge   Eric Partridge. *Shakespeare's Bawdy.* New edition, revised, 1955; rep. London, 1961.

Ray   J. Ray. *A Compleat Collection of English Proverbs . . . To which is added A Collection of English Words Not Generally Used.* Third edition, Augmented, London, 1742.

R.E.S.   *The Review of English Studies.* Oxford.

Schmidt   Alexander Schmidt. *A Shakespeare Lexicon.* Third edition, revised Sarrazin, 1902; rep. Berlin, 1962.

Sisson *N.R.*   C. J. Sisson. *New Readings in Shakespeare.* 1956; rep. London, 1962.

Tilley   M. P. Tilley. *A Dictionary of the Proverbs in England in the Sixteenth and Seventeenth Centuries.* Ann Arbor, Michigan, 1950.

Turberville   [George Turberville]. *The Noble Arte of Venerie or Hunting.* London, [1575].

Walker   W. S. Walker. *A Critical Examination of the Text of Shakespeare.* (Vol. 3) London, 1860.

Walter   *King Henry V.* Edited by J. H. Walter. The Arden Shakespeare. Corrected edition, London, 1960.

Whiter   Walter Whiter. *A Specimen of a Commentary on Shakespeare* (1794). Ed. Alan Over and Mary Bell. London, 1967.

Wright   Joseph Wright. *The English Dialect Dictionary.* London, 1896–1905, rep. Oxford, 1961.

The conjectures of Farmer, Tollet, and Tyrwhitt are those recorded by Steevens in his second and third editions.

Abbreviations used for the titles of Shakespeare's other plays are those of C. T. Onions, *A Shakespeare Glossary*, second edition, Oxford 1919, reprinted 1958, p. x; and act, scene, and line references are to the Globe edition. *The Two Noble Kinsmen* is cited from the edition by Clifford Leech (The Signet Classic Shakespeare, New York, 1966).

THE MERRY WIVES OF WINDSOR

DRAMATIS PERSONÆ

SIR JOHN FALSTAFF.
FENTON, *a young gentleman.*
SHALLOW, *a country Justice.*
ABRAHAM SLENDER, *Shallow's kinsman.*
FRANK FORD, ⎱
GEORGE PAGE, ⎰ *citizens of Windsor.*   5
WILLIAM PAGE, *a boy, son of Page and Mistress Page.*
SIR HUGH EVANS, *a Welsh parson.*
DOCTOR CAIUS, *a French physician.*
Host of the Garter Inn.   10
BARDOLPH, ⎫
PISTOL,   ⎬ *followers of Falstaff.*
NYM,   ⎭

DRAMATIS PERSONÆ] *This ed.; not in F, Q.*   4. *Shallow's kinsman*] *This ed.;*
Cousin to Shallow *Rowe.*   5–6. *citizens of Windsor*] *Chambers; two Gentlemen,*
dwelling at Windsor *Rowe.*   11–13. *followers of Falstaff*] *As Capell; Sharpers attend-*
ing on Falstaff *Rowe.*

DRAMATIS PERSONÆ] First tabula-
ted by Rowe. Lists of names are exceptional in the Folio, and the absence of
one for this play is therefore of no
significance.

4. Shallow's kinsman] Probably
Slender is Shallow's nephew, in view
of III. iv. 36–41; but the term 'uncle' by
which Slender addresses Shallow may
have been used loosely of other rela-
tionships, as were 'cousin' and
'nephew' (cf. *Oth.*, I. i. 111–14). The
description of Slender on the Quarto's
title-page as Shallow's 'wise Cousin' is
therefore of no assistance in deter-
mining the exact relationship.

6. *GEORGE PAGE*] Page is called
'Thomas' at I. i. 42 but 'George' in
three other lines, II. i. 143 and 151 and
v. v. 199.

8. *EVANS*] The character can
hardly have been based on the Strat-
ford schoolmaster of 1575–9, Thomas
Jenkins, as is sometimes said. Jenkins
was born in London (Mark Eccles,

Shakespeare in Warwickshire, Madison,
1961, p. 56).

9. *CAIUS*] Normally pronounced
'Keys' or 'Kays', but IV. vi. 27 and the
Q spelling 'Cayus' may indicate a dis-
syllable. There can be no direct connection with the famous founder of
Gonville and Caius College in Cambridge, who was an Englishman; and
C. J. Sisson's suggestion that the real-
life original may have been Dr Peter
Chamberlain (a French gynaecologist
practising in London before 1611 and
probably by 1596) was made only in
passing and was not supported by
further evidence (*Essays and Studies*,
XIII, 1960, 10–11). Nor is it easy to see
how the presence of Caius in the play
amounts to 'satire on the fad for
foreign doctors'.

11. *BARDOLPH*] Probably to be
pronounced 'Bardle' (it is spelt
'Bardol' in the Q of *1H4*, II. iv. 329).
In *2H4* (III. ii. 235 and 244) he seems
to be addressed as a corporal, a rank

2

ROBIN, *Falstaff's page.*
PETER SIMPLE, *Slender's servant.* 15
JOHN RUGBY, *Caius' servant.*
JOHN *and* ROBERT, *Ford's servants.*
MISTRESS FORD (ALICE).
MISTRESS PAGE (MARGARET).
ANNE PAGE, *daughter of Page and Mistress Page.* 20
MISTRESS QUICKLY, *Caius' servant.*
Three or four children (dressed in the last Act as fairies).

17. *John and Robert, Ford's servants*] *As New Camb.; Servants to* Page, Ford, &c. *Rowe.*
22. *Three or four children . . . fairies*] *This ed.*

he retains in *H5*, III. ii. 3. (Nym calls him 'Lieutenant' in *H5*, II. i. 2 but perhaps ironically.) Presumably only a Falstaff could have promoted such a man to such a rank (higher in Shakespeare's day than in ours).

12. *PISTOL*] Perhaps pronounced as 'pizzle' or in such a way as to make a pun on that word possible. Cf. *2H4*, II. iv. 121–6 and 174 ('Peesell' in Q, '*Peesel*' in F). In *2H4* (e.g. II. iv. 75) and *H5* (e.g. II. i. 3) and on the title-page of Q *Wiv.* Pistol is called 'Ancient' or ensign, a rank for which he, too, hardly seems qualified. Jorgensen has pointed out the joke also on 'ancient pistol'—a very noisy and often ineffective weapon (*Redeeming Shakespeare's Words*, Berkeley and L.A., 1962, pp. 70–4).

13. *NYM*] The name is almost certainly derived from 'to nim' in the sense of 'steal' or 'pilfer', although *O.E.D. v.*[3] gives no instance earlier than 1606. In *H5* Nym and Bardolph are said to be 'sworn brothers in filching' (III. ii. 47–8). *New Cambridge* saw also a reference to 'Nym' as an alleged short form of 'Hieronimo', the hero of Kyd's *Spanish Tragedy*, and so, particularly as Nym misuses the word 'humour', interpreted him as Shakespeare's caricature of Ben Jonson, who was taunted with having played the Kyd role. (A 1597 date for *The Merry Wives* would make this suggestion less plausible still.) As in *H5* Nym's rank is that of corporal.

21. *QUICKLY*] Kökeritz sees a quibble on 'quick-lie' (cf. her colleague in *2H4*, Doll Tearsheet). In *H4* Quickly is hostess of the Boar's Head Inn in Eastcheap. See Introduction, pp. vii, lii.

THE MERRY WIVES OF WINDSOR

ACT I

SCENE I

Enter JUSTICE SHALLOW, SLENDER, *and* SIR HUGH EVANS.

Shal. Sir Hugh, persuade me not: I will make a Star
Chamber matter of it. If he were twenty Sir John
Falstaffs, he shall not abuse Robert Shallow,
Esquire.

Slen. In the county of Gloucester, Justice of Peace and 5
Coram.

ACT I

Scene 1

ACT I SCENE 1] F (*Actus primus, Scena prima*) ; . . . *The* Scene *before* Page's *House in*
Windsor. *Pope.* S.D. *Enter . . . Evans.*] *Rowe; Enter Iustice* Shallow, Slender, *Sir*
Hugh Euans, *Master* Page, Falstoffe, Bardolph, Nym, Pistoll, Anne Page,
Mistresse Ford, *Mistresse* Page, Simple. *F; Enter Iustice* Shallow, *Syr* Hugh,
Maister Page, *and* Slender. *Q.*

1. *Sir Hugh*] For 'Sir' as a normal
form of address to a clergyman (perhaps originally ironical, to one *not*
entitled to be called 'dominus' as
holding a University degree), cf. 'Sir
Oliver Martext' in *AΥL.*, III. iii. 43. Q
misunderstands when on the title-page
it refers to 'Syr *Hugh* the Welch
Knight'.

1–2. *Star Chamber matter*] The Court
of Star Chamber derived its name from
the chamber in the royal palace at
Westminster, with stars painted on the
ceiling, in which the King's Council
sat as a judicial body. It did exercise
jurisdiction over such matters as riot
(l. 32), particularly when men of title
were involved; and justices of the

peace were empowered and indeed
enjoined to use their authority to re-
press crimes of this kind. (The Elizabethan Star Chamber does not seem to
deserve the reputation the Court later
obtained as autocratic, tyrannous, and
generally not bound by law.) Shallow
is thus not exceeding his authority but
is, of course, taking himself very seriously. See also Introduction, p. xlix.

4. *Esquire*] Not, as now, a practically
meaningless title, but a title of dignity
for those one degree below knighthood. Shallow would legitimately call
himself 'Esquire', not by birth but as a
justice of the peace.

6. *Coram*] A common corruption of
'quorum', used in its original sense of

4

Shal. Ay, cousin Slender, and Custalorum.

Slen. Ay, and Ratolorum too; and a gentleman born,
Master Parson, who writes himself 'Armigero' in
any bill, warrant, quittance, or obligation—   10
'Armigero'.

Shal. Ay, that I do, and have done any time these three
hundred years.

Slen. All his successors, gone before him, hath done 't,
and all his ancestors, that come after him, may: they   15
may give the dozen white luces in their coat.

Shal. It is an old coat.

Evans. The dozen white louses do become an old coat
well; it agrees well, passant; it is a familiar beast to
man, and signifies love.   20

Shal. The luce is the fresh fish; the salt fish is an old coat.

8. Ratolorum] *F; Rotulorum Q3.*   18. louses] *F (Lowses).*   21.] *F* (The Luse
is the fresh-fish, the salt-fish, is an old Coate.) ; The luce is the fresh fish, the salt-
fish is not an old coat. *conj. Johnson;* The luce is the fresh fish—the salt fish is an old
cod. *New Camb.;* The luce is the fresh fish, the salt fish—is an old coat. *Sisson.*

those special justices of the peace at
least two of whom had to be present
before a felony could be tried.

7. *Custalorum*] A contraction of
'custos rotulorum' or keeper of the
rolls, the office of the principal justice
of the peace in each county. If Hotson
is correct in seeing satire of William
Gardiner in Shallow (see Introduction,
p. xlix), the point would seem to be that
this is an office of dignity which Gardiner could *not* have attained.

8. *Ratolorum*] Slender, not understanding that 'custalorum' means
'custos rotulorum', tries to bring that
office in, and, typically, gets it wrong.

9. *Armigero*] Steevens (1793) may be
right in suspecting that Slender mis-
takes the Latin ablative for the nominative. 'Armiger', once synonymous
with 'Esquire', originally meant one of
gentle birth who carried a knight's
shield for him, but came to mean one
entitled to a coat of arms.

10. *quittance*] formal release from a
debt or obligation.

obligation] written contract or bond.

16. *give*] In the heraldic sense: use
in a coat of arms.

luces] pike (normally, only when
fully grown)—but in ll. 18ff. there is a
pun on louses or lice. For the possible
reference to the coat of arms of William
Gardiner, or Sir Thomas Lucy, see
Introduction, pp. xlix–lii.

19. *passant*] In heraldry, the word
means 'walking, and looking towards
the dexter side, with . . . the dexter
fore-paw raised' (*O.E.D.* 4). Its use of
a fish would therefore be comically
inappropriate, but Evans is thinking
only of lice 'walking'. There may be
also a pun on an old meaning of
'passant': 'exceedingly' or 'surpassingly' (*O.E.D.* 1).

familiar] well known; 'part of the
family'; *and* intimate, sociable, perhaps even 'unduly intimate' (*O.E.D.*
A 2c). Tilley sees a connection with the
proverb 'A louse is a man's companion'
(L471). Cf. also 'familiar angel', for
guardian angel.

21.] The joke, if any, would seem to
depend on Evans's mispronunciation

Slen. I may quarter, coz.

Shal. You may, by marrying.

Evans. It is marring indeed, if he quarter it.

Shal. Not a whit. 25

Evans. Yes, per-lady: if he has a quarter of your coat,
there is but three skirts for yourself, in my simple
conjectures; but that is all one. If Sir John Falstaff
have committed disparagements unto you, I am of
the church and will be glad to do my benevolence, 30
to make atonements and compromises between you.

Shal. The Council shall hear it; it is a riot.

Evans. It is not meet the Council hear a riot: there is no
fear of Got in a riot. The Council, look you, shall
desire to hear the fear of Got, and not to hear a riot; 35
take your vizaments in that.

22. coz.] *As F*; coz? *Steevens*[3].   24. marring] *F1*; marrying *F2*.   26. per-lady]
F; py'r-lady *Capell*.   31. compromises] *F* (compremises).

of 'coat' as 'cod' or 'coad': he asserts
that luces go well with an old 'coad',
and perhaps Shallow, misunderstanding because of the mispronunciation,
'corrects' him by 'explaining' that
luces are not louses and that luces
(fresh-water fish) and cod (salt-water
fish) are quite distinct. It is difficult to
see further puns on 'cod' in the other
sense, or on 'salt' meaning 'lecherous',
as *New Cambridge* suggested, or on 'fresh
fish' in the sense of 'novice' or 'beginner' (Hart, comparing *H8*, ii. iii. 86);
but the line is certainly obscure.

22. *quarter*] add another coat of
arms to one's own (e.g. after marriage).
Evans misunderstands and takes the
word in another sense, 'dividing into
quarters'. The difficulty is in the relationship of l. 22 to the preceding line,
although any connection is obviously
through 'coat'; perhaps Slender ima-
gines that Shallow would like the salt
fish too on his coat and suggests a way
of getting it there.

coz] A contraction of 'cousin',
meaning 'kinsman'. See note on
Dramatis Personæ, l. 4, and iii. iv. 36–41
and notes.

23–4. *marrying . . . marring*] 'Marry-

ing is marring' was proverbial (Tilley
M701). Shakespeare echoes it again
in *Rom.*, i. ii. 12–13, and in *All's W.*,
ii. iii. 315.

26. *per-lady*] by our Lady. Here and
elsewhere in this edition no attempt is
made to 'regularize' or 'improve' F's
indication of Evans's Welsh speech
(most editors read 'py'r').

27. *skirts*] Evans is thinking of a
man's garment, probably a kind of
top-coat, divided at the bottom, back
and front, so that it has four 'skirts' or
tails. Cf. 'skirted page' in i. iii. 80.

31. *atonements*] agreements, reconciliation (at one + ment). Cf. *R3*,
i. iii. 36.

compromises] *New Cambridge* pointed
out that F's 'compremises' is probably
only a variant spelling, not a further
indication of Evans's confusion or mispronunciation. It compared *Mer.V.*,
i. iii. 79, 'compremyzd' ('compre-
myz'd' F).

32. *Council*] the King's Council
sitting as the Court of Star Chamber
(cf. ll. 1–2 and note)—but Evans perhaps takes it to mean a church council
or synod, as *New Cambridge* suggested.

36. *vizaments*] Evans's version of

Shal. Ha! O' my life, if I were young again, the sword
    should end it.

Evans. It is petter that friends is the sword, and end it;
    and there is also another device in my prain, which   40
    peradventure prings goot discretions with it. There
    is Anne Page, which is daughter to Master Thomas
    Page, which is pretty virginity.

Slen. Mistress Anne Page? She has brown hair, and
    speaks small like a woman.   45

Evans. It is that fery person for all the 'orld, as just as you
    will desire; and seven hundred pounds of moneys,
    and gold, and silver, is her grandsire upon his
    death's-bed (Got deliver to a joyful resurrections!)
    give, when she is able to overtake seventeen years   50
    old. It were a goot motion if we leave our pribbles
    and prabbles, and desire a marriage between
    Master Abraham and Mistress Anne Page.

Slen. Did her grandsire leave her seven hundred pound?

Evans. Ay, and her father is make her a petter penny.   55

Shal. I know the young gentlewoman; she has good gifts.

---

42. Thomas] *F; George | Theobald.*   45. woman.] *F;* woman? *conj. Lambrechts.*
54. *Slen.*] *F; Shal. Capell.*   56. *Shal.*] *Capell; Slen. F.*

'advisements'. He probably means
'take that into consideration'.

41. *discretions*] Evans prides himself
on his discretion and judgement of
what is 'discreet' or wise for others:
cf. l. 132 and IV. iv. 1.

42. *Thomas*] Elsewhere he is
'George': see note on *Dramatis Personæ*,
l. 6. 'Thomas' can hardly be a transcriber's error, as Hart suggested, and
need not imply hasty revision, as *New
Cambridge* argued: Shakespeare was
often careless with names (notably in
Tim., but not only there).

45. *small*] i.e. in a voice the opposite
of 'deep'; cf. *Tw.N.*, I. iv. 32–4, where
the Duke, commenting on the disguised Viola's un-masculine qualities,
says 'thy small pipe / Is as the maiden's
organ, shrill and sound, / And all is
semblative a woman's part' and
M.N.D., I. ii. 52.

46. *just*] exact or exactly. Cf., e.g.,
AYL., III. ii. 281.

51–2. *pribbles and prabbles*] Perhaps
Evans's improvement on mere 'brab-
bles' or quarrels. He repeats the phrase
at V. v. 160–1 (but uses 'prabbles'
alone at IV. i. 42).

54.] Most editors give this line,
as well as l. 56, to Shallow; but while
56 would sound rather odd from Slender, who has already said that he
knows Anne, l. 54 is not inappropriate
to him, and the misattribution of
56 is more easily explained if the
scribe or compositor were carelessly repeating the speech prefix of
54.

55. *a petter penny*] The phrase would
seem to have been proverbial, as
used after specified amounts to
mean 'and much more as well' (Tilley
P189).

Evans. Seven hundred pounds, and possibilities, is goot
gifts.

Shal. Well, let us see honest Master Page. Is Falstaff
there?   60

Evans. Shall I tell you a lie? I do despise a liar as I do
despise one that is false, or as I despise one that is not
true. The knight Sir John is there; and I beseech you
be ruled by your well-willers. I will peat the door for
Master Page. [*Knocks.*] What hoa? Got pless your   65
house here!

Page. [*Within*] Who's there?

[*Enter* PAGE.]

Evans. Here is Got's plessing and your friend, and
Justice Shallow, and here young Master Slender,
that peradventures shall tell you another tale, if   70
matters grow to your likings.

Page. I am glad to see your worships well. I thank you
for my venison, Master Shallow.

Shal. Master Page, I am glad to see you: much good do
it your good heart! I wished your venison better; it   75
was ill killed. How doth good Mistress Page? And I
thank you always with my heart, la, with my heart.

59, 65. Master] F (M^r).   65. Knocks] *Rowe* (before 'for', *l. 64*); not in F.
67. Within] *Dyce*; not in F; Above, at the window *Collier*^{2}.   Enter Page] As *Rowe*
(after l. 66); not in F; Scene II. Enter Mr. Page *Pope* (*Pope's scene divisions not listed
hereafter*); after l. 71 *Collier*^{2}.   69. here] F$_I$ (heere); here's F$_2$.   72. worships]
F; Worship's *Rowe*.

64. *well-willers*] those who wish you
well. Hart was able to cite several
other uses (in Holland's *Plinie*,
Greene's *Mamillia*, and Howell's *Arbor
of Amitie*) to refute the allegation that
the word is another of Evans's errors.

70. *tell you another tale*] A folk-saying
or 'proverb' (Tilley T49).

71. *likings*] Again, not Evans's error
but a recognized form: cf. *Oth.*, III. i.
51.

72. *worships*] The F plural is justified
by ll. 244 and 254, where Anne addresses Slender as 'your worship'.

74-5. *much . . . heart!*] A common
polite greeting, used again e.g., in a

slightly corrupted form, in *Tim.*,
I. ii. 73.

76. *ill killed*] A technical phrase, of a
deer killed in such a way as to make the
meat less good (e.g. by draining too
much blood too soon). Probably
Shallow also means that Falstaff had
done the killing (and been caught in
the act).

77. *la*] Slender is fond of this intensive, which has been thought effemi-
nate. Biron's use of it in *LLL.*, v. ii. 414
(where it is made to rhyme, perhaps
badly, with 'flaw'), and Whit's in
Jonson's *Bartholomew Fair*, IV. v. 30,
do both seem to imply some criti-

Page. Sir, I thank you.

Shal. Sir, I thank you; by yea and no I do.

Page. I am glad to see you, good Master Slender.   80

Slen. How does your fallow greyhound, sir? I heard say
    he was outrun on Cotsall.

Page. It could not be judged, sir.

Slen. You'll not confess, you'll not confess.

Shal. That he will not. 'Tis your fault, 'tis your fault;   85
    'tis a good dog.

Page. A cur, sir.

Shal. Sir, he's a good dog, and a fair dog: can there be
    more said? He is good and fair. Is Sir John Falstaff
    here?   90

Page. Sir, he is within; and I would I could do a good
    office between you.

Evans. It is spoke as a Christians ought to speak.

Shal. He hath wronged me, Master Page.

Page. Sir, he doth in some sort confess it.   95

Shal. If it be confessed, it is not redressed: is not that
    so, Master Page? He hath wronged me, indeed he
    hath; at a word, he hath, believe me. Robert
    Shallow, Esquire, saith he is wronged.

98. hath; at] *F* (hath, at).   hath, believe me.] *As Dyce²;* hath: beleeue me, *F.*

cism of the speaker; cf. also *Tim.,*
III. i. 22.

79. *by yea and no*] Such phrases as this
and 'la' and 'much good do it your
good heart' are used to emphasize
Shallow's effusive desire to be pleasant.
Perhaps this one also is comically inappropriate in his mouth; cf. Falstaff's
use of it in his letter to Prince Hal in
2H4, II. ii. 142. Quickly uses a similar
phrase in *Wiv.,* I. iv. 88.

81. *fallow*] light brown.

82. *Cotsall*] the Cotswold hills (a
local pronunciation). It seems unnecessary to see a reference to some
regular Cotswold Games, such as those
later established in James I's time.

85. *your fault*] the normal check
caused when the dog loses the scent
(*O.E.D.* 'fault' *sb.* 8; 'your' as in *Ant.,*
II. vii. 46, 'What manner o' thing is

your crocodile?'). This explanation,
first given by *New Cambridge,* is more
satisfactory than taking 'your fault' as
'your own misfortune' and comparing
III. iii. 202.

88, 89. *good . . . and . . . fair*] Shallow
is apparently again airing his knowledge of coursing terms. *New Cambridge*
aptly cites, from Turberville's *Book of
Hunting,* ch. 6, 'the tokens whereby a
man may knowe a good and fayre
Hounde'.

96. *If . . . redressed*] The allusion is to
the proverb 'A fault confessed is half
redressed' (D. C. Browning, *Everyman's
Dictionary of Quotations and Proverbs,*
1951, No. 6453) rather than to 'Confession of a fault pardons it', as Tilley
suggests (C590). Ray and Tilley also
record 'Confession of a fault is half
amends' (C589).

Page. Here comes Sir John.   100

Enter SIR JOHN FALSTAFF, BARDOLPH, NYM, *and* PISTOL.

Fal. Now, Master Shallow, you'll complain of me to the
    King?

Shal. Knight, you have beaten my men, killed my deer,
    and broke open my lodge.

Fal. But not kissed your keeper's daughter?   105

Shal. Tut, a pin; this shall be answered.

Fal. I will answer it straight: I have done all this. That
    is now answered.

Shal. The Council shall know this.

Fal. 'Twere better for you if it were known in counsel: 110
    you'll be laughed at.

Evans. *Pauca verba*; Sir John, good worts.

Fal. Good worts? Good cabbage! Slender, I broke your
    head: what matter have you against me?

Slen. Marry, sir, I have matter in my head against you,   115
    and against your cony-catching rascals, Bardolph,
    Nym, and Pistol.

100. S.D.] *As Q; not in F.*   102. King] *F;* Councell *Q.*   109. Council] *F*
(Councell).   110. counsel] *F* (councell); counsell *Q;* Council *Rowe.*   116–17.
Bardolph, Nym, and Pistol.] *As F; Pistoll and Nym. They carried mee to the*
Tauerne and made mee drunke, and afterward picked my pocket. Q.

102. *King*] Since elsewhere in the
play there are attempts to place the
action in the reign of Henry IV or
Henry V, this certainly need not imply
revision of the play after the death of
Elizabeth. Cf. 1. iv. 5 and note.

103. *my men*] Hart assumes from
ll. 113–14 that Slender was one of them,
but Shakespeare does not say so; it
would be no more rash to infer that
113–14 are to be connected with the
stealing of Slender's purse, since—
unless words are imported from Q at
l. 117—Falstaff shows a perhaps incriminating knowledge of that episode
at l. 137.

105.] As earlier editors have suggested, this seems to be a quotation
from some lost deer-stealing ballad.

106. *a pin*] a trifle, 'nothing to do
with the question'.

110. *in counsel*] in secret, in confidence (*O.E.D. sb.* 5. c). Emendations
such as Pope's 'if it were not known in
council' are thus unnecessary.

112. Pauca verba] few words. Cf.
Holofernes in *LLL.*, IV. ii. 172; Pistol's
use of 'pauca' in the same sense in *H5*,
II. i. 83; and Nym's 'pauca, pauca' in
l. 122.

113. *Good . . . cabbage!*] 'Wort',
common as the second element in
words like 'colewort', also meant
specifically a plant of the cabbage
family: hence Falstaff's pun on Evans's
mispronunciation of 'words'.

114. *matter*] cause of complaint (but
Slender probably misunderstands).

116. *cony-catching*] Literally 'rabbit-
catching', metaphorically 'cheating',
as in Robert Greene's exposure of
underworld techniques in his 'Cony-

Bard. You Banbury cheese!

Slen. Ay, it is no matter.

Pist. How now, Mephostophilus?   120

Slen. Ay, it is no matter.

Nym. Slice, I say; *pauca, pauca*; slice, that's my humour!

Slen. Where's Simple, my man? Can you tell, cousin?

Evans. Peace, I pray you. Now let us understand: there
    is three umpires in this matter, as I understand;   125
    that is, Master Page (fidelicet Master Page); and
    there is myself (fidelicet myself); and the three
    party is (lastly and finally) mine host of the Garter.

Page. We three to hear it and end it between them.

Evans. Fery goot; I will make a prief of it in my note-   130
    book, and we will afterwards 'ork upon the cause
    with as great discreetly as we can.

Fal. Pistol!

Pist. He hears with ears.

127. three] *F;* third *Pope.*   128. Garter] *Q3;* Gater *F.*

catching' pamphlets. Cf. the modern
idiom 'to be the bunny'. Falstaff uses
the phrase again at I. iii. 31; and cf.
Shr., v. i. 102.

117. *Pistol*] Most editors add here
the sentence from Q given in the
collations. It is not necessary—see
ll. 137–66 and the note on l. 103—and
may be only the spelling-out of the
obvious often found in reported texts.
Sisson, *N.R.*, p. 64, on similar grounds
argued against inclusion of the Q line
(he had originally adopted it in his
1954 text).

118. *Banbury cheese*] The town later
more famous for its cakes was renowned then for another reason also:
'as thin as Banbury cheese' was proverbial (Tilley C268). (Tewkesbury
provided the corresponding simile for
thickness: Falstaff tells Doll in *2H4*,
II. iv. 262, that Poins's wit is 'as thick as
Tewksbury mustard'.)

120. *Mephostophilus*] Lucifer's fellow-
devil, probably best known from
Marlowe's *Dr Faustus* (which, although
not published until 1604, was already
most successful on the stage). As Leslie

Hotson has shown, Pistol sees himself
as 'a player King' (*Yale Review*, 38,
1948, 51–68); and in this play as in
both parts of *H4*, his head is full of
phrases, quotations, and misquotations
from the popular drama of the day,
not all of which have been traced. See
also IV. v. 65.

122. *Slice*] Probably Nym is carrying
on the 'cheese' metaphor and suggesting that Slender be sliced up.

humour] For the topical interest in
the word, and Nym's characteristic
abuse of it, see Introduction, p. lxiii.
Here it means apparently either
'mood' or 'temperament'.

126, 127. *fidelicet*] Evans's mispronunciation, and misuse, of the Latin
videlicet, 'namely'.

128. *Garter*] There was apparently
a real Garter Inn at Windsor in the
sixteenth century.

134.] Pistol may be alluding to the
Bible (e.g. Psalms 44:1: 'We have
heard with our ears') and so, as Noble
points out (p. 181), the joke may be on
the Parson, who does not recognize the
source.

Evans. The tevil and his tam! What phrase is this, 'He   135
hears with ear'? Why, it is affectations.

Fal. Pistol, did you pick Master Slender's purse?

Slen. Ay, by these gloves, did he, or I would I might
never come in mine own great chamber again else,
of seven groats in mill-sixpences, and two Edward   140
shovel-boards that cost me two shilling and two-
pence apiece of Yead Miller, by these gloves.

Fal. Is this true, Pistol?

Evans. No, it is false, if it is a pick-purse.

Pist. Ha, thou mountain foreigner! Sir John and master
mine,   145
I combat challenge of this latten bilbo.
Word of denial in thy labras here!
Word of denial: froth and scum, thou liest!

Slen. [*Pointing at Nym*] By these gloves, then, 'twas he.

---

137. Master] F (M.).   145–8.] *Verse as Pope; prose F.*   149. S.D.] *As New Camb.; not in F.*

135. *The tevil and his tam!*] Proverbial for 'the devil and worse' (Tilley D225). Cf. iv. v. 101.

139. *great chamber*] Apparently, main living room ('bedchamber' and 'reception room' have also been suggested).

140. *seven groats in mill-sixpences*] Probably the phrase is not meant to make perfect sense: 'groats' were small four-penny coins (Fluellen insults Pistol by offering him one 'to heal' his broken head in *H5*, v. i. 61–7); mill- (or milled-) sixpences were silver sixpences stamped in the 'mill' and in time came to have more than their nominal value.

140–1. *Edward shovel-boards*] shillings minted in the reign of Edward VI and afterwards used for the game of shovel-board—which is presumably why Slender was foolish enough to pay more than twice their face-value for them.

142. *Yead*] A familiar or jocular form of 'Ed' or 'Ned' (Falstaff once calls Poins 'Yedward' in *1H4*, i. ii. 149).

145. *mountain foreigner*] foreigner

from the (wild) Welsh mountains.

145–6. Either with 'Sir John and master mine' or the following words, Pistol apparently breaks into verse, perhaps quoting from plays again. It is almost impossible to decide whether some of his lines are meant as verse or prose.

146. *combat challenge*] A 'poetic' reversal of verb and object: challenge combat, demand the ancient right of trial by combat (Pistol is showing off his knowledge of the technical language of chivalry).

latten bilbo] (person who has only a) brass sword. 'Latten' may not even have been 'brass'; it came to mean tin-plate. Bilbao became known in England as 'Bilboa' and gave its name not only to its own good swords but also to swords generally, as did Toledo.

147. *labras*] Pistol apparently thinks the Latin *labra* ('lips') is a singular and makes the same error as those who speak nowadays of 'stratas'. The confusion may also arise from false analogy with the Spanish *palabras* ('words'), frequent in Elizabethan drama.

Nym. Be advised, sir, and pass good humours: I will say   150
    'marry trap with you', if you run the nuthook's
    humour on me; that is the very note of it.

Slen. By this hat, then he in the red face had it; for
    though I cannot remember what I did when you
    made me drunk, yet I am not altogether an ass.   155

Fal. What say you, Scarlet and John?

Bard. Why, sir, for my part, I say the gentleman had
    drunk himself out of his five sentences.

Evans. It is his 'five senses'. Fie, what the ignorance is!

Bard. And being fap, sir, was, as they say, cashiered;   160
    and so conclusions passed the careers.

---

151. 'marry trap with you'] *This ed.; marry trap with you F; marry trap* with you *Johnson.*   160. fap] *F;* sap *Parsons.*   160–1. cashiered; and so] *As F;* cashiered. *Nym.* And so *Kittredge.*   161. careers] *F* (Car-eires).

150. *Be avised*] Either 'think carefully' (cf. *O.E.D.* 'advise' *v.* 5 and French *s'aviser*; and *Tw.N.*, IV. ii. 102, Feste to the incarcerated Malvolio, 'Advise you what you say') or 'take my advice', 'be counselled' (*O.E.D.* 'advised' *ppl. a.* 6, citing *1H4*, IV. iii. 5).

pass good humours] Here (and in l. 152) 'humour' becomes almost meaningless, as Shakespeare ridicules the over-use of it: presumably, 'put a good face on it'. Cf. l. 161 and note.

151. *marry trap with you*] Not satisfactorily explained. 'Marry' (a corruption of 'By Mary') is a common asseveration, and often harmless. Johnson, suspecting a once-familiar saying, explained the full phrase as an 'exclamation of insult', 'when a man was caught in his own stratagem'. Alternatively a later proverb listed by Tilley (T469) may be relevant: 'to understand trap', deriving from the slang use of 'trap' for 'fraud' or 'sharp practice', meant 'to know one's own interest'; hence, Nym may be saying 'mind your own business'. If 'trap' were also used as slang for a thief-taker earlier than *O.E.D.* records, the transition to 'nuthook' in l. 151 would be even easier.

151–2. *nuthook's humour*] 'Nuthook', originally a hooked stick for pulling down nuts, became a nickname for a beadle or constable. Thus, 'the game of trying to capture thieves'.

152. *note*] Kökeritz sees a kind of jingling pun on 'nut' and 'note'.

156. *Scarlet and John*] Will Scarlet and Little John (Robin Hood's companions). Bardolph is apparently addressed by both names, the first being suggested by his red nose, of which so much fun is made in *2H4* and *H5*. The allusion may be specifically to the old ballad 'Robin Hood and the Jolly Pinder of Wakefield', one line of which Silence sings in *2H4*, V. iii. 107.

158. *sentences*] Bardolph's blunder for 'senses', as Evans points out—but it has meaning of a sort, since 'sentences' may be paraphrased as 'moral precepts'. (Indeed, Baldwin, I. 708, thinks that Bardolph *means* that.)

160. *fap*] Although *O.E.D.* listed no other instance of the word, meaning 'drunk', before the nineteenth century, Sisson, *N.R.*, p. 64, records that Hilda Hulme has since found it in seventeenth-century West Midlands churchwardens' accounts. Emendation (e.g. Parsons's 'sap', as in 'sap-money',

Slen. Ay, you spake in Latin then too; but 'tis no
    matter. I'll ne'er be drunk whilst I live again, but
    in honest, civil, godly company, for this trick: if I
    be drunk, I'll be drunk with those that have the fear   165
    of God, and not with drunken knaves.
Evans. So Got 'udge me, that is a virtuous mind.
Fal. You hear all these matters denied, gentlemen; you
    hear it.

Enter ANNE PAGE, [*with wine; then*] MISTRESS FORD *and*
    MISTRESS PAGE.

Page. Nay, daughter, carry the wine in; we'll drink   170
    within.   [*Exit Anne Page.*]
Slen. O heaven, this is Mistress Anne Page.
Page. How now, Mistress Ford?
Fal. Mistress Ford, by my troth, you are very well met:
    by your leave, good mistress.   *Kisses her.*   175
Page. Wife, bid these gentlemen welcome. Come, we
    have a hot venison pasty to dinner; come, gentle-
    men, I hope we shall drink down all unkindness.
                                    Exeunt all except Slender.

---

169. S.D.] *As Capell; not in F; Enter Mistresse* Foord, *Mistresse* Page, *and her daughter*
Anne *Q; Enter Mistress* Anne Page, *with Wine Rowe.*   171. S.D.] *Theobald; not
in F or Q.*   172.] *Rowe adds* 'Enter Mistress Ford *and Mistress* Page'.   175. S.D.]
Q; not in F.   178. S.D.] *As New Camb.; not in F; Exit all, but* Slender *and mistresse*
Anne. *Q; Ex.* Fal. Page, *&c. Manent* Shallow, Evans *and* Slender. *Rowe.*

money allowed to servants for liquor)
is therefore unnecessary.

cashiered] As R. H. Case pointed out
in an appendix to Hart's edition, this
cannot mean 'robbed' unless Bardolph
means 'robbed by others'—or unless
Falstaff is guilty of deliberate misunderstanding in l. 168. The normal
meaning (*O.E.D.*) was 'dismissed' or
'discarded', as in I. iii. 6. (It is some
slight consolation that Bardolph's
words make no sense to Slender.)

161. *passed the careers*] got out of hand.
It is a technical term from horseman-
ship (strictly, a short gallop, perhaps
with quick turns, at speed), and a good
parallel is *H5*, II. i. 131–3, where Nym

comments, of the King's alleged responsibility for Falstaff's death, 'The
king is a good king; but it must be as it
may; he passes some humours and
careers', i.e. he sometimes does odd
things or lets events run away with
him.

172, 173. *Mistress*] 'Mistress' was applied to both married and unmarried
women until at least the eighteenth
century, as was the written 'Mrs'.

175 and S.D.] That the kiss was no
more than a polite salutation is shown
by, e.g., *H8*, I. iv. 94–6.

178. *drink ... unkindness*] In accordance with the maxim 'Drink and be
friends' (Tilley F732).

Slen. I had rather than forty shillings I had my book of
Songs and Sonnets here.   180

[*Enter* SIMPLE.]

How now, Simple, where have you been? I must
wait on myself, must I? You have not the book of
Riddles about you, have you?

Sim. Book of Riddles? Why, did you not lend it to Alice
Shortcake upon All-hallowmas last, a fortnight   185
afore Michaelmas?

[*Enter* SHALLOW *and* EVANS.]

Shal. Come, coz; come, coz; we stay for you. A word
with you, coz. Marry, this, coz: there is, as 'twere,
a tender, a kind of tender, made afar off by Sir
Hugh here. Do you understand me?   190

Slen. Ay, sir, you shall find me reasonable; if it be so, I
shall do that that is reason.

Shal. Nay, but understand me.

Slen. So I do, sir.

Evans. Give ear to his motions. Master Slender, I will   195
description the matter to you, if you be capacity of
it.

Slen. Nay, I will do as my cousin Shallow says. I pray

180. S.D.] *Rowe; not in F.*   186. Michaelmas] *F; Martlemas Theobald.*   S.D.]
As New Camb.; not in F.   195. motions. Master Slender, I] *F* (motions; (Mʳ.
Slender) I); Motions, Mr. Slender: I Rowe.

179–80. *book of Songs and Sonnets*]
Probably the *Songs and Sonnets* of
Henry Howard, Earl of Surrey, and
others ('Tottel's *Miscellany*'), published in 1557 and at least eight times
in the next thirty years. Slender needs
some such volume, or his book of
Riddles, either as reading matter because he cannot entertain himself even
for a minute or as a source of quotations and small talk.

182–3. *book of Riddles*] Not necessarily any identifiable volume: there
may have been two or three such collections available.

185–6. *All-hallowmas . . . Michael-*

mas] Simple's knowledge is appropriately as slender as his master's: All-
hallowmas (1 November) is not a fortnight before Michaelmas (29 September).

187. *stay*] wait.

189. *afar off*] not directly, only as an
intermediary.

195. *motions*] proposals; but for the
probable pun, not intended by Evans,
cf. III. i. 95.

198. *Nay . . . says*] Perhaps Slender
does not understand at all but thinks
Evans is trying to make peace between
him and Falstaff's retainers (*New
Cambridge*).

you pardon me; he's a Justice of Peace in his
country, simple though I stand here.   200

Evans. But that is not the question: the question is concerning your marriage.

Shal. Ay, there's the point, sir.

Evans. Marry, is it; the very point of it—to Mistress
Anne Page.   205

Slen. Why, if it be so, I will marry her upon any reasonable demands.

Evans. But can you affection the 'oman? Let us command to know that of your mouth or of your lips;
for divers philosophers hold that the lips is parcel of   210
the mouth. Therefore, precisely, can you carry your
good will to the maid?

Shal. Cousin Abraham Slender, can you love her?

Slen. I hope, sir, I will do as it shall become one that
would do reason.   215

Evans. Nay, Got's lords, and His ladies! You must speak
possitable, if you can carry her your desires towards her.

Shal. That you must. Will you, upon good dowry,
marry her?   220

Slen. I will do a greater thing than that, upon your
request, cousin, in any reason.

Shal. Nay, conceive me, conceive me, sweet coz: what
I do is to pleasure you, coz. Can you love the maid?

Slen. I will marry her, sir, at your request; but if there   225
be no great love in the beginning, yet heaven may
decrease it upon better acquaintance, when we are
married and have more occasion to know one

211. mouth] *F; mind Pope.*   carry] *F1; marry F2.*   219–20.] *Prose as Pope;*
That you must: / Will . . . *F.*

200. *simple . . . here*] A common mild
asseveration: 'as sure as I stand
here'.

216. *Got's . . . ladies*] It is true that F
has 'got's' but it does not follow, *pace*
Hart, that Jupiter is meant. The Q
gives some reason for believing that
other oaths in the original text of the
play were also not mild. See Introduction, p. xxxv.

217. *possitable*] A blunder for 'posi-
tively'.

carry her] Apparently, 'convince her
of'. Cf. ll. 211–12; cf. also III. ii. 63 and
note.

223. *conceive me*] understand me
(*O.E.D.* 'conceive' II. 9).

225–9.] This is Slender's version of
the popular saying, 'Marry first and
love will come after' (Tilley L534).

another. I hope upon familiarity will grow more
content: but if you say 'Marry her', I will marry   230
her; that I am freely dissolved, and dissolutely.
Evans. It is a fery discretion answer; save the fall is in
the 'ord 'dissolutely': the 'ort is, according to our
meaning, 'resolutely'. His meaning is good.
Shal. Ay, I think my cousin meant well.   235
Slen. Ay, or else I would I might be hanged, la!
Shal. Here comes fair Mistress Anne.

[*Enter* ANNE PAGE.]

Would I were young for your sake, Mistress Anne!
Anne. The dinner is on the table; my father desires your
worships' company.   240
Shal. I will wait on him, fair Mistress Anne.
Evans. Od's plessed will, I will not be absence at the
grace.   [*Exeunt Shallow and Evans.*]
Anne. Will't please your worship to come in, sir?
Slen. No, I thank you, forsooth, heartily; I am very well.   245
Anne. The dinner attends you, sir.
Slen. I am not a-hungry, I thank you, forsooth. [*To
Simple*] Go, sirrah, for all you are my man, go wait
upon my cousin Shallow. [*Exit Simple.*] A Justice of

230. content] *F*; contempt *Theobald.*   232. fall] *F*; faul' *Hanmer*; fault *Collier.*
233. 'ord] *F*; 'Ort *Rowe³.*   237. S.D.] *Rowe (after l. 236)*; not in *F.*   240.
worships'] *Capell*; worships *F1*; Worship's *F4.*   243. S.D.] *As Rowe*; not in *F.*
247–8. *To Simple*] *New Camb. (as Steevens²)*; not in *F.*   249. S.D.] *Theobald*; not
in *F.*

230. *content*] An editor is not entitled, with Theobald, to write jokes
for Shakespeare, by supplying the
proverb (Tilley F47) '(too much)
familiarity breeds contempt'. It is, of
course, quite possible that Shakespeare
meant Slender to try to quote another
proverb and get it wrong, as he certainly gets 'resolved' and 'resolutely'
wrong in the following lines. He thereby catches for the minute Evans's
disease, and Quickly's—for the sake
of the laugh.
232. *fall*] mistake. *O.E.D.* does not

seem to list this sense, but cf. modern
'slip'. Other editors suppose an
elision ('faul''), a mispronunciation,
or a compositor's misreading of
'falt'.
238.] Shallow's greeting, of course,
is a cliché (Tilley S68).
245.] Slender's answer does make
sense: there was a proverb 'Fresh air
is ill for the diseased or wounded man'
(Tilley A93) and he is thus denying
the (unintended) implication that he
ought to 'come in' because he is not
well.

Peace sometime may be beholding to his friend for   250
a man. I keep but three men and a boy yet, till my
mother be dead: but what though, yet I live like a
poor gentleman born.

Anne. I may not go in without your worship: they will
not sit till you come.   255

Slen. I' faith, I'll eat nothing; I thank you as much as
though I did.

Anne. I pray you, sir, walk in.

Slen. I had rather walk here, I thank you. I bruised my
shin th' other day with playing at sword and dagger   260
with a master of fence—three veneys for a dish of
stewed prunes—and, by my troth, I cannot abide
the smell of hot meat since. Why do your dogs bark
so? Be there bears i' th' town?

Anne. I think there are, sir; I heard them talked of.   265

Slen. I love the sport well, but I shall as soon quarrel at
it as any man in England. You are afraid if you see
the bear loose, are you not?

Anne. Ay, indeed, sir.

252. though,] *F;* though? *Capell.*   264.] *Collier*[2] *adds* 'Dogs bark'.

252. *what though*] no matter; what
if I do (frequent in Shakespeare).

260. *sword and dagger*] Hart, citing
Two Angry Women of Abingdon and
Harington's *Metamorphosis of Ajax*,
shows that this method of fighting, or
duelling, would seem to have been
common among retainers rather than
among gentlemen, so that once again
Slender is giving himself away.

261. *master of fence*] proved and
recognized master or 'professor' of
fencing.

three veneys] i.e. the best of three
bouts (French *venue*).

262. *stewed prunes*] A most inappropriate wager or trophy, for a dish of
stewed prunes in the window was the
sign or badge of a brothel (they seem
to have been served inside the house as
an aphrodisiac) and so came to be a
synonym for a prostitute—as did 'hot
meat'. Cf. *1H4*, iii. iii. 127–8, *2H4*,

ii. iv. 156–9; this is also the innuendo
in *Meas.*, ii. i. 91 ff. Slender seems un-
aware of it.

262–3.] The connection between the
hurt shin and hot meat may be only
the smell of blood or rawness of flesh—
sufficient for Slender's 'mind'. Q
hardly improves matters with a feeble
pun on 'hot': 'I cannot abide the
smell of hot meate / Nere since I broke
my shin. Ile tel you how it came / By
my troth. A Fencer and I plaid three
venies / For a dish of stewd prunes and
I with my ward / Defending my head
he hot [hit, or hurt] my shin. Yes
faith.' *New Cambridge*, e.g., incorpor-
ates in its text the words 'and I . . .
shin', after 'prunes'. Sisson, *N.R.*, p.65,
argues that, in a speech by Slender on
such an occasion, 'no intelligibility is
necessary or even desirable'.

266. *the sport*] the popular sport of
bear-baiting.

Slen. That's meat and drink to me, now. I have seen   270
Sackerson loose twenty times, and have taken him
by the chain; but, I warrant you, the women have
so cried and shrieked at it that it passed: but
women, indeed, cannot abide 'em; they are very
ill-favoured rough things.   275

Enter PAGE.

Page. Come, gentle Master Slender, come: we stay for
you.
Slen. I'll eat nothing, I thank you, sir.
Page. By cock and pie, you shall not choose, sir: come,
come.   280
Slen. Nay, pray you lead the way.
Page. Come on, sir.
Slen. Mistress Anne, yourself shall go first.
Anne. Not I, sir; pray you keep on.
Slen. Truly, I will not go first; truly, la, I will not do you   285
that wrong.
Anne. I pray you, sir.
Slen. I'll rather be unmannerly than troublesome. You
do yourself wrong, indeed, la!   *Exeunt.*

275. S.D.] *Q; not in F.*

270. *That's . . . me*] Proverbial (Tilley M842); cf. *AYL.*, v. i. 11–12, 'It is meat and drink to me to see a clown'. In ll. 271–2 Slender may similarly be trying to adapt the proverbial boast of strength, that one could 'bind bears' (B134).

271. *Sackerson*] One of the most famous of the bears used for bear-baiting in Shakespeare's day.

273. *passed*] surpassed, was truly remarkable. Cf. l. 19 and IV. ii. 113 and notes.

275. *ill-favoured*] ugly.

279. *By cock and pie*] A euphemistic oath: 'cock' (*O.E.D. sb.*[8]) is a perversion of 'God' (via 'gock'); 'pie' (*O.E.D. sb.*[3]) 'a collection of rules, adopted in the pre-Reformation Church, to show how to deal . . . with the concurrence of more than one office on the same day'. Shallow uses the same oath in *2H4*, v. i. 1.

288.] Again Slender is only quoting a proverb (Tilley U15).

SCENE II

Enter EVANS *and* SIMPLE.

Evans. Go your ways, and ask of Doctor Caius' house
    which is the way; and there dwells one Mistress
    Quickly, which is in the manner of his nurse; or his
    dry nurse; or his cook; or his laundry; his washer,
    and his wringer.   5
Sim. Well, sir.
Evans. Nay, it is petter yet. Give her this letter; for it is a
    'oman that altogether's acquaintance with Mistress
    Anne Page; and the letter is to desire and require her
    to solicit your master's desires, to Mistress Anne   10
    Page. I pray you be gone. I will make an end of my
    dinner; there's pippins and cheese to come.   *Exeunt.*

SCENE III

Enter FALSTAFF, HOST, BARDOLPH, NYM, PISTOL, *and* ROBIN.

Fal. Mine host of the Garter!
Host. What says my bully rook? Speak scholarly and
    wisely.

Scene II

SCENE II] *F; Scene II. The lobby in* Page's *house Halliwell.*   S.D.] *F; Enter sir*
Hugh *and* Simple, *from dinner. Q.*   5. wringer] *Theobald;* Ringer *F.*   8.
altogether's] *Steevens², conj. Tyrwhitt;* altogeathers *F.*   10. desires,] *F1;* desires
F3.   12. cheese] *F;* seese *Dyce.*

Scene III

SCENE III] *F;* Scene VII. *Changes to the Garter-Inn. Pope; Scene III. A Room in the*
garter Inn. *Capell.*   S.D. Robin] *Rowe;* Page *F.*   2. rook] *As F; Rock Rowe¹⁻²*
(throughout play) ; Rooke *Rowe³.*

Scene II

3–4. *nurse . . . dry nurse*] Not Evans's
error but apparently means house-
keeper, for Caius also applies the word
to Quickly at III. ii. 58.
    4. *laundry*] i.e. laundress.
    12. *pippins*] apples, as dessert.
    cheese] The Welsh were traditionally
very fond of cheese. Falstaff, in v. v.

82–3, fears that the 'Welsh fairy' will
turn him into cheese and eat him. Cf.
also II. ii. 292.

Scene III

    2. *bully rook*] For 'bully' as a half-
affectionate form of address (*O.E.D.*
sb.¹ 1) cf. *MND.*, IV. ii. 19, 'O sweet
bully Bottom!' (spoken by Flute) and

Fal. Truly, mine host, I must turn away some of my
    followers.   5
Host. Discard, bully Hercules, cashier: let them wag;
    trot, trot.
Fal. I sit at ten pounds a week.
Host. Thou'rt an emperor, Caesar, Keiser, and Pheazar.
    I will entertain Bardolph; he shall draw, he shall   10
    tap. Said I well, bully Hector?
Fal. Do so, good mine host.
Host. I have spoke; let him follow. [*To Bard.*] Let me see
    thee froth and lime. I am at a word; follow.   *Exit.*
Fal. Bardolph, follow him. A tapster is a good trade; an   15
    old cloak makes a new jerkin; a withered serving-
    man a fresh tapster. Go; adieu.

9. Keiser] *F1 ; Kesar Q ; Keisar F2.*   Pheazar] *F ; Phesser Q ;* Pheazar *Steevens².*
13. *To Bard.] Camb. ; not in F.*   14. lime] *Q* (lyme) *; liue F1 ;* live *F2.*   S.D.] *Q ;
not in F.*

Tp., v. i. 258, 'Coragio, bully-monster,
coragio!' (Stephano to Caliban). Its
use is a distinguishing mannerism of
the Host, who repeats it in ll. 6 and 11.
'Rook', on the other hand, is better
known as a term of disparagement but
may be used by the Host with jocular
irony (as is, probably, 'bully Hector'
in l. 11. Others have seen a reference
to the rook or castle in chess; and *New
Cambridge* even suggested that it goes
back to Falstaff's original name in the
Henry IV plays, Oldcastle.
    scholarly] Such references to Fal-
staff's learning are further evidence to
New Cambridge of a source or earlier
play in which the hero was a scholar;
but they too may all be ironical or
simply part of Ford's flattery, for example (cf. II. ii. 174).
    6. *cashier*] See I. i. 160 and note.
    wag] move, depart (*O.E.D. v.* 7).
    8. *sit*] dwell here, have my lodging
(*O.E.D. v.* 8).
    9. *Keiser*] emperor (the regular, ME,
form, until the language adopted the
German 'Kaiser'; it is derived from
'Caesar'). Cf. *George-a-Greene the Pinner
of Wakefield* (attributed to Robert
Greene), v. i. (ed. Dickinson), where a

shoemaker proclaims 'King or Kaisar,
none shall pass this way, / Except King
Edward'.
    Pheazar] Q 'Phesser' is no help and
may suggest that the reporter also did
not know what it meant. Malone and
Dyce explained it as 'one who pheezes',
i.e. beats or frightens; most editors now
accept Hart's conjecture that the Host
means 'vizier' (Turkish viceroy).
There may even be a quibble involving
both.
    10. *entertain*] employ, hire (*O.E.D.
v.* II. 5. b). Cf. l. 51 and note.
    10, 11. *draw, tap*] draw liquor (from
the cask), serve as a tapster.
    14. *froth and lime*] 'Froth' clearly
means 'make the beer go further by
serving it with plenty of froth on it';
and 'lime' (if the Q reading is correct)
refers to a method of adulterating
wine, by adding lime to remove any
taste of sourness (cf. *1H4,* II. iv. 136–9).
F 'liue' ('live'), however, also makes
good sense: earn your living, by cheating the customers with the froth.
    at a word] not inclined to waste
words. Cf. I. i. 98 and *2H4,* III. ii. 319,
'I have spoke at a word'.
    15–16. *an old . . . jerkin*] One of many

Bard. It is a life that I have desired: I will thrive.

Pist. O base Hungarian wight, wilt thou the spigot
   wield?   *Exit Bardolph.*   20

Nym. He was gotten in drink: is not the humour conceited?

Fal. I am glad I am so acquit of this tinder-box: his
   thefts were too open; his filching was like an unskil-
   ful singer, he kept not time.   25

Nym. The good humour is to steal at a minute's rest.

Pist. 'Convey', the wise it call. 'Steal'! Foh, a fico for the
   phrase!

Fal. Well, sirs, I am almost out at heels.

Pist. Why, then, let kibes ensue.   30

---

19. Hungarian] *F;* gongarian *Q.*   20. S.D.] *As* Q (*before l. 19*); *not in* F.
26. minute's] *F, Q;* minim's *Collier*², *conj. Bennet Langton.*

---

forms of an old proverb (Tilley B607).
A jerkin was a close-fitting short coat
or jacket.

16–17. *a withered . . . tapster*] Falstaff
completes his sentence by deliberately
varying, or misquoting, another proverb, 'an old servingman a young
beggar' (Tilley S255).

19–20.] 'Hungarian' seems to have
been a term of general abuse. Tilley
quotes a proverb (from the seventeenth
century) 'He is hidebound, he is an
Hungarian' (H810) and cites from
Ray's *Collection of English Proverbs,*
1670, 'To be hide-bound, an Hungarian, a Curmudgeon'. Hart also
gives good evidence for associating the
word with the needy discarded
soldiers returned from wars in Hun-
gary; and there is sure to be a pun on
'hungry', as recorded elsewhere at
this time in *O.E.D.*, with the implication that hunger often leads to theft.
Steevens said he remembered a line in
an old play, 'O base *Gongarian*, wilt
thou the distaff wield?' but it has
never been traced (Q reads 'O bace
gongarian wight, wilt thou the spicket
willd?'). The words may be one original verse line, or, as elsewhere, Pistol
may be combining phrases from
different sources.

21. *gotten in drink*] begotten while his
parents were drunk—and therefore
not a real man. Falstaff spells out this
belief in *2H4*, IV. iii. 98–101. Some
editors insert the line which replaces
this in Q—'His minde is not heroick.
And theres the humour of it'—
which once again only labours the
obvious.

21–2. *is . . . conceited?*] i.e. (presumably) is that not an ingenious appli-
cation of the facts, or interpretation?

23. *tinder-box*] Bardolph—because
of his red nose, but also, as the remainder of the speech makes clear, because
he is inflammable, likely to cause
trouble.

26. *minute's*] Since the phrase was,
and is, common to indicate the shortest
possible time, emendation to 'minim's',
with *Rom.*, II. iv. 23, as the alleged
parallel, is gratuitous, particularly as
Q confirms the reading of F.

27. *fico*] fig (Spanish). Pistol uses it
again ('figo') in *H5*, III. vi. 59, and
indeed 'a fig for it' was a standard
phrase (Tilley F210), often with an
obscene gesture.

29. *out at heels*] with shoes worn
through, and so poverty-stricken,
penniless (Tilley H389).

30. *kibes*] *O.E.D.* explains 'kibe' as

Fal. There is no remedy: I must cony-catch; I must shift.

Pist. Young ravens must have food.

Fal. Which of you know Ford of this town?

Pist. I ken the wight: he is of substance good.   35

Fal. My honest lads, I will tell you what I am about.

Pist. Two yards, and more.

Fal. No quips now, Pistol. Indeed, I am in the waist two yards about, but I am now about no waste: I am about thrift. Briefly, I do mean to make love to   40 Ford's wife. I spy entertainment in her: she discourses, she carves, she gives the leer of invitation; I can construe the action of her familiar style, and the

42. carves] *F;* craues *Q3.*

'a chapped or ulcerated chilblain, *esp.* one on the heel'; but Hart argues convincingly that most Elizabethans distinguished between chilblains and the sore heels, caused by inadequate covering, referred to here. (The three other uses of the word in Shakespeare do not decide the question.)

32. *shift*] Not necessarily 'cheat' but 'improvise', 'live on my wits': cf. *Ven.,* 690, 'Danger deviseth shifts; wit waits on fear', or *AYL.,* iv. i. 76–8, 'for lovers lacking—God warn us!—matter, the cleanliest shift is to kiss'.

33.] The line is at one and the same time a variation on a proverb—'small birds must have meat' (Tilley B397); a Biblical allusion—Job 38:41 and Psalms 147:9; and a reference to the reputation of the raven as an unprincipled bird of prey.

35. *ken the wight*] know the man (cf. l. 19). The words would probably have sounded archaic to the Elizabethan audience also; and again Pistol may be quoting from some old melodrama or poem.

41. *entertainment*] Not only, surely, willingness to listen but also pleasure, of various kinds. (Similarly, there must be a double meaning in 'familiar' in l. 43.)

42. *carves*] Most of the notes written

on this word are misleading and cite imaginary or unhelpful parallels, such as *Err.,* II. ii. 119–20, and *LLL.,* v. ii. 323 (Biron's complaint, of Boyet, that ''A can carve too, and lisp; why, this is he / That kiss'd his hand away in courtesy'). It is debatable whether Vittoria's 'I did nothing to displease him [her husband], I carved to him at supper-time' (Webster's *White Devil,* I. ii. 123) means, as F. L. Lucas claims, that she made 'advances by signalling with the fingers—a sort of digitary ogle'; and there is doubtful support in the passage cited from Overbury's Character of 'A very very Woman' (*A Wife,* 1614): 'Her lightnesse gets her to swim at top of the Table, where her wry little finger, bewrayes *caruing*; her neighbours at the latter end, know they are welcome, and for that purpose shee quencheth her thirst' which Lucas takes to mean 'a sort of motion of the little finger backwards and forwards, not unlike carving, as the wineglass was raised to the lips'. That there is some kind of association between carving at table and making guests feel, properly or improperly, at home —and that it goes beyond the allotting of the choicest cuts—does seem certain. Cf. also *The Two Noble Kinsmen,* IV. iii. 90.

    hardest voice of her behaviour, to be Englished
    rightly, is, 'I am Sir John Falstaff's'.   45
Pist. He hath studied her will, and translated her will—
    out of honesty into English.
Nym. The anchor is deep: will that humour pass?
Fal. Now, the report goes she has all the rule of her
    husband's purse; he hath a legion of angels.   50
Pist. As many devils entertain; and to her, boy, say I.

---

46. studied her will, and translated her will] *F*; studied her well, *Q*; study'd her well, and translated her well *Pope*; studied her will, and translated her well *Collier²*; studied her well and translated her will *Grant White*; studied her well and translated her ill *conj. Camb.*   48. anchor] *F*; authour *conj. Johnson*; angle *conj. Kinnear.*   50. he] *F*; She *Q*.   a legion] *Rowe³*; a legend *F*; legians *Q*.   51. entertain] *F*; attend her *Q*.

---

44. *voice*] Baldwin (1. 569) sees a pun on the 'voices' (active and passive) of the verb 'to love' and also suggests 'a glancing pun' on 'action'–'active' in the previous line.

46. *will*] Emendation seems unnecessary although Whiter (p. 83) and Farmer noted that 'well'–'deep' (as in l. 48) was a Shakespearian image-link. Pistol surely means 'will', her intention or desire, possibly with a quibble on 'will' meaning 'carnal desire' and certainly with a pun on the legal will that has to be 'translated' into ordinary English to be understood.

47. *honesty*] chastity (a normal Elizabethan meaning).

48. *The anchor is deep*] Explanations of this crux are unconvincing, from Hart's suggestion of a pun on 'anchor', in the sense of 'anchoret' or 'hermit', to Kökeritz's argument (*R.E.S.*, 23, 1947) that the word meant is 'anker', a wine keg—a meaning that adds little (and the word is not found elsewhere before 1673). The natural interpretation is that just as a deep anchor normally holds firmly, so Falstaff's ideas are firm. There would be further point in Nym's phrase if it refers to the proverb (Tilley A240) 'An anchor that is ever in the water never learns to swim'—i.e. Falstaff may have had a long association with women but has

learnt little about them (which would be a good follow-up to Pistol's comment).

50. *legion*] F's 'legend' may be right, if there was in fact confusion between the two words as *O.E.D.* implies (citing also 'a Legend of his Divels' from Mrs Behn's *Roundheads*, 1682). 'Legend' could mean e.g. a list (*O.E.D. sb.* 4), and a collection of saints' lives. 'Legion', however, seems preferable: not only was it commonly used in the sense of 'great number' (*O.E.D.* 3), derived from Mark 5:9, but also Falstaff is probably quoting Matthew 26:53 ('Thinkest thou that I cannot now pray to my Father, and he shall presently give me more than twelve legions of angels?'). Hence the pun on 'angels', gold coins stamped with the device of the archangel Michael and worth about ten shillings. The pun is repeated by Quickly, almost in reverse, at II. ii. 68–9; cf. also *Ado*, II. iii. 35.

51. *As many devils entertain*] Hart explains 'many bad people have many, or have the use of many, angels (i.e. money)'—which does some violence to the syntax; Schmidt, more convincingly, glosses 'entertain' as 'to take or keep in service'—a common meaning of the word (cf. l. 10 of this scene) and relevant if (as Warburton sup-

Nym. The humour rises; it is good. Humour me the
    angels.

Fal. I have writ me here a letter to her; and here another
    to Page's wife, who even now gave me good eyes too,   55
    examined my parts with most judicious œillades:
    sometimes the beam of her view gilded my foot,
    sometimes my portly belly.

Pist. Then did the sun on dunghill shine.

Nym. I thank thee for that humour.   60

Fal. O, she did so course o'er my exteriors with such a
    greedy intention that the appetite of her eye did
    seem to scorch me up like a burning-glass! Here's
    another letter to her; she bears the purse too: she is
    a region in Guiana, all gold and bounty. I will be   65
    cheaters to them both, and they shall be exchequers
    to me: they shall be my East and West Indies, and I
    will trade to them both. Go bear thou this letter to
    Mistress Page; and thou this to Mistress Ford: we
    will thrive, lads, we will thrive.   70

Pist. Shall I Sir Pandarus of Troy become,

56. œillades] *Hanmer, conj. Pope;* illiads *F;* eyliads *Johnson.*   59. *Pist.*] *F; Pist*
[*Aside*] *Theobald.*   66. cheaters] *F;* cheater *Theobald.*

posed) Pistol is advising Falstaff to
have as many devils on his side as Ford
(or Mrs Ford) has angels on his (or
hers).

    to her, boy] The whole phrase is
probably a hunting cry; certainly 'to
her' is a regular expression of encouragement. Cf. III. iv. 36.

    52, 54. *me*] Good examples of the
'ethic dative', which seems to be un-
usually frequent in Falstaff's speech in
all three plays.

    56. *œillades*] a significant look, espe-
cially an amorous one (French *œil* +
ade). Regan tells Oswald that Goneril
'gave strong œillades and most speaking looks / To noble Edmund' (*Lr.*,
IV. v. 25–6). Dennis, in *The Comical
Gallant*, rendered it as 'Eye-lids'!

    57. *gilded*] Falstaff is carrying on the
metaphor of Mrs Page's eyes being like
the rays ('beam') of the sun.

    59.] Pistol is alluding to the proverb

'The sun is never the worse for shining
on a dunghill' (Tilley S982).

    62. *intention*] Perhaps a pun (1) im-
port or aim; (2) intentness or thorough-
ness (*O.E.D.* 7b, 8—and cf. 'inten-
tively', *Oth.*, I. iii. 155).

    65. *Guiana*] Like the East and West
Indies of l. 67, Guiana was to be the
source of untold wealth to those who
could exploit it. Shakespeare may well
be thinking of Ralegh's 1595 voyage to
find Eldorado.

    66. *cheaters*] Yet another pun:
'cheater' was a common shorter form
of 'escheater', an official of the Ex-
chequer who supervised the 'escheats'
or forfeited estates that came to the
king. The same pun is in *Tit.*, v. i. 111.

    71–2.] The lines are printed as
verse in F and may well be a quotation.
The meaning is: 'If I, who wear a
sword and ought therefore to be a
soldier, descend to being a mere pro-

H

And by my side wear steel? Then Lucifer take all!
Nym. I will run no base humour. Here, take the humour-
    letter; I will keep the haviour of reputation.
Fal. [*To Robin*] Hold, sirrah, bear you these letters tightly;
    Sail like my pinnace to these golden shores.   76
    Rogues, hence, avaunt, vanish like hailstones; go;
    Trudge; plod away i' th' hoof; seek shelter, pack!
    Falstaff will learn the honour of the age;
    French thrift, you rogues—myself and skirted page.   80
                                    Exeunt Falstaff and Robin.
Pist. Let vultures gripe thy guts, for gourd and fullam
    holds,
    And high and low beguiles the rich and poor;

75. *To Robin*] Theobald (*after l. 76*); *not in* F.   tightly] F; rightly Q3.   76.
these] F; the Q.   78. i' th'] F1 (ith'); oth' F2.   79. honour] F; humor Q.
80. S.D.] Q (*Exit Falstaffe, and the Boy.*); *not in* F.   81–2.] *Verse as Pope; prose* F.

curer, like Pandarus of Troy (who
acted as go-between for Troilus and
Cressida), then the devil may as well
take charge of everything'.

74. *haviour*] deportment (*O.E.D.*
'haviour' or 'havour' 2). Cf. *Cym.*,
III. iv. 9.

75. *sirrah*] Not used ironically,
meaning 'Sir', but correctly used to the
page as one over whom Falstaff has
authority.

tightly] skilfully, carefully. This
meaning of the word is common (cf.
Ant., IV. iv. 15), and the reading is
confirmed by Q.

76–80.] Falstaff's transition to
verse here is unexpected but not inexplicable. Again half-seriously speaking of his plan as if it were the equivalent of a romantic voyage in search
of Eldorado, he adopts for the minute
the manner of Pistol.

76. *pinnace*] a small light vessel often
used as a tender, scout, or message-
ship—whence perhaps its common
figurative meanings (*O.E.D.* 3) of
'mistress' or 'prostitute' or (as Hart
shows) 'bawd'.

78.] Tilley records a slightly later
'proverb' (H587) 'to beat it on the
hoof' (travel the hard way) and this

colloquial use of 'hoof' is still not rare—
nor is 'pack' in the sense of 'be off' (cf.
the far commoner 'send someone
packing'). F2's 'oth' is tempting but
not necessary.

79. *honour*] Editors who accept Q's
'humor' assume that F's 'honour' is a
misreading.

80. *French thrift*] Perhaps being
waited on by fewer servants was—or
was thought to be—the French custom
(this has been argued with dubious
success); or perhaps 'French thrift'
was the equivalent of the modern
'Scottish thrift'.

skirted] Cf. I. i. 27 and note.

81. *Let . . . guts*] Perhaps, as Halliwell suggested, Pistol is parodying (or
unintentionally ruining) Marlowe's
Tamburlaine, II. vii. 48–50 (ed. U. M.
Ellis-Fermor).

gourd and fullam] Each is explained
by *O.E.D.* as a kind of false, or loaded,
dice. Similarly 'high and low' in l. 82
are dice loaded to throw high or low
numbers.

holds] wins the day, prevails.

82.] Pistol is now ringing the
changes on the second verse of Psalm
49 (or perhaps a metrical version of it).
Compare II. i. 110. Muir (pp. 14–15)

Tester I'll have in pouch when thou shalt lack,
Base Phrygian Turk!

Nym. I have operations which be humours of revenge.   85

Pist. Wilt thou revenge?

Nym. By welkin and her star!

Pist. With wit or steel?

Nym. With both the humours, I: I will discuss the
humour of this love to Ford.   90

Pist.   And I to Page shall eke unfold
How Falstaff, varlet vile,
His dove will prove, his gold will hold,
And his soft couch defile.

Nym. My humour shall not cool: I will incense Ford to   95
deal with poison; I will possess him with yellowness,
for the revolt of mine is dangerous. That is my true
humour.

85.] *As one line, Pope;* I ... opperations, / Which ... reuenge *F.*   operations] *F;*
operations in my head *Q.*   87. star] *F;* stars *Collier*[2].   89. discuss] *F;* disclose
Q.   90. Ford] *F;* Page *Q.*   91. Page] *F;* Foord *Q.*   97. the] *F;* this *Pope.*
mine] *F;* Mien *Theobald;* men *conj. Johnson;* mine anger *conj. Camb.;* mind *conj.*
Jackson.

thinks that ll. 91–4 may similarly
have begun from the metrical version
of Psalm 50.

83. *Tester*] a small coin, originally a
shilling, but by Shakespeare's day
equal to sixpence.

84. *Phrygian Turk*] There are many
parallels for 'Turk' as a term of abuse
(originally as 'infidel' or 'savage').
Perhaps 'Phrygian' is attached as an
intensive because the Phrygians were
particularly war-like (cf. 'Phrygian
mode' in music); or perhaps Pistol
thinks of it because Pandarus is still in
his mind (cf. 'Lord Pandarus of
Phrygia', *Tw.N.*, III. i. 58).

85. *operations*] (Presumably) plans
for action.

86–9. *Wilt ... humours, I:*] Again it
is possible that these should be printed
as two verse lines.

89. *both the humours*] i.e. *my* wit and
Ford's steel (sword).

discuss] make known, disclose
(*O.E.D. v.* 5). Cf. IV. v. 2; the word

is also used thus four times in *H5*.

90, 95. *Ford*] In fact, in II. i, Nym
goes to Page, and Pistol goes to Ford;
some editors therefore alter 'Ford' to
'Page' in both l. 90 and l. 95 and
alter 'Page' in l. 91 to 'Ford'. But
apparently Shakespeare changed his
mind, for, as *New Cambridge* noted,
Nym's speech (ll. 95–8) is more appropriate when spoken, as in F, about
Ford; and presumably Pistol replies
to Falstaff in l. 71 (before Nym does)
because he is addressed first, being the
intended messenger to Page.

93. *prove*] put to the test. Cf. *1H6*,
II. ii. 58.

96. *yellowness*] jealousy (probably so
called because the liver was thought to
be the seat of the passions, and yellowness is the symptom of the known
disease of the liver, jaundice).

97. *the revolt of mine*] (Presumably)
this rebellion of mine against Falstaff;
but *New Cambridge*, accepting the
emendation 'mind', well compares

Pist. Thou art the Mars of Malcontents. I second thee;
  troop on.   *Exeunt.* 100

SCENE IV

Enter MISTRESS QUICKLY *and* SIMPLE.

Quick. What, John Rugby! [*Enter* RUGBY.] I pray thee
  go to the casement and see if you can see my master,
  Master Doctor Caius, coming. If he do, i' faith, and
  find anybody in the house, here will be an old abus-
  ing of God's patience and the King's English.   5
Rug. I'll go watch.
Quick. Go; and we'll have a posset for 't soon at night, in
  faith, at the latter end of a sea-coal fire. [*Exit Rugby.*]
  An honest, willing, kind fellow, as ever servant shall
  come in house withal; and, I warrant you, no tell-   10

Scene IV

SCENE IV] *F;* Scene IX. *Changes to Dr.* Caius's *house. Pope; Scene IV. A Room in
Doctor* Caius' *House. Capell.*   S.D.] *Q ; Enter Mistris Quickly, Simple, Iohn Rugby,
Doctor, Caius, Fenton. F; Enter Mistress* Quickly, Simple *and* John Rugby. *Rowe.*
1. S.D.] *Wheatley; not in* F.   8. S.D.] *Rowe (after l. 6) ; not in* F*; Rugby goes to the
window New Camb.*

Gent., III. ii. 58–9, 'You are already
Love's firm votary / And cannot soon
revolt and change your mind'.
  99. *Mars of Malcontents*] Although
'Malcontents' were most in theatrical
fashion at the time of Marston's *Malcontent* (1600 or, more probably, 1604),
the word was known much earlier.
O.E.D. first finds it as a noun in 1581;
and Nashe uses it often and as early as
1589 (e.g. in *The Anatomy of Absurdity,* I.
22). Shakespeare elsewhere applies it to
a malcontent in love; but here it may
have rather the significance of 'rebel'
or 'dissentient from accepted opinion'
(of which there are other instances).
Mars is mentioned, of course, as the
God of war.

Scene IV
  4. *old*] excessive, great (*O.E.D. a.*
I. 6).

  5. *King's English*] A standard phrase
(even in the days of the second
Elizabeth) and therefore not a 'proof'
that the play was revised in the reign
of James I. In any case, there is a half-
hearted attempt elsewhere to put the
action of the play in the reign of
Henry IV or Henry V: Fenton 'kept
company with the wild Prince and
Poins' (III. ii. 66–7)—even if certain
references in v. v are inconsistent with
this (see v. v. 47 and note).
  7. *posset*] a drink, often used as a
restorative, normally made by curd-
ling hot milk with wine or ale, and
sometimes spiced. In many ways it
was the equivalent of the modern egg-
flip 'laced' with brandy.
  8. *sea-coal*] better-class coal brought
by sea, most often from Newcastle on
Tyne.
  10. *withal*] This is the normal use of

tale nor no breed-bate. His worst fault is that he is
given to prayer; he is something peevish that way;
but nobody but has his fault; but let that pass. Peter
Simple, you say your name is?

Sim. Ay, for fault of a better.   15

Quick. And Master Slender's your master?

Sim. Ay, forsooth.

Quick. Does he not wear a great round beard, like a
glover's paring-knife?

Sim. No, forsooth: he hath but a little wee face, with a   20
little yellow beard—a Cain-coloured beard.

Quick. A softly-sprighted man, is he not?

Sim. Ay, forsooth, but he is as tall a man of his hands
as any is between this and his head: he hath fought
with a warrener.   25

---

20. wee] F (wee-); whey- *Capell.*   21. Cain-coloured] F (Caine colourd); kane
colored *Q;* Cane-colour'd *Rowe*[3].

the word as a substitute for 'with' 'esp.
at the end of a relative clause or its
equivalent' (*O.E.D.*); cf. II. i. 83.

11. *breed-bate*] maker of discord,
mischief-maker. Poins is similarly
allowed by Falstaff in *2H4*, II. iv. 273-
4, to be one who 'breeds no bate with
telling of discreet stories'.

12. *peevish*] silly, as in *1H6*, v. iii. 185,
rather than 'obstinate', as often elsewhere.

13. *nobody . . .fault*] A popular saying
(Tilley M116)—as is Simple's reply to
her query (F106).

19. *glover's paring-knife*] The simile
is rather startling, but Shakespeare
should have known what such a knife
looked like, for his father was a glover
(one who worked in leather, not only
to make gloves).

20. *wee*] Many editors print 'whey',
under the influence of Q's version of
Quickly's previous speech: 'I take it
hee is somewhat a weakly man: / And
he has as it were a whay coloured
beard', and Kökeritz assumes that
'wee' is a dialectal pronunciation of
'whey'. Q's 'whay', however, is as
likely as not a confused remembrance

of the 'Cain-coloured beard' (which is
also duly preserved in Q in Simple's
reply). *Pace* Hart, *O.E.D.* has one
example of 'wee' as an adjective meaning 'tiny' *c.* 1450; and Steevens cites
two others from Elizabethan drama.

21. *Cain-coloured*] of the traditional
colour of Cain's beard (red or reddish-
yellow according to *O.E.D.*); similarly
'Judas-coloured' (red) is frequent (cf.
AYL., III. iv. 7-10).

22. *softly-sprighted*] 'soft' or meek in
spirit.

23. *tall . . . hands*] 'Tall' meant
valiant, but was often used ironically;
'of his hands', with his hands. For the
complete phrase, cf. *Wint.*, v. ii. 177-8,
'I'll swear to the prince thou art a tall
fellow of thy hands'.

24. *between . . . head*] Hart shows that
the phrase was a cliché.

25. *warrener*] Simple, meaning to
praise Slender, succeeds only in revealing that he was caught stealing
rabbits. Keats preserved the full irony
of the phrase when he wrote to Haydon
on 8 April 1818 about Wordsworth,
who had allegedly left town in a dis-
gruntled mood: 'O that he had not fit

Quick. How say you?—O, I should remember him: does
    he not hold up his head, as it were, and strut in his
    gait?

Sim. Yes, indeed, does he.

Quick. Well, heaven send Anne Page no worse fortune!   30
    Tell Master Parson Evans I will do what I can for
    your master: Anne is a good girl, and I wish—

[*Enter* RUGBY.]

Rug. Out, alas, here comes my master.

Quick. We shall all be shent. Run in here, good young
    man; go into this closet; he will not stay long. (*Simple*   35
    steps into the closet.) What, John Rugby! John! What,
    John, I say! Go, John, go enquire for my master: I
    doubt he be not well, that he comes not home.
    [*Singing*] And down, down, adown-a, etc.

[*Enter* DOCTOR CAIUS.]

Caius. Vat is you sing? I do not like des toys. Pray you go   40
    and vetch me in my closet *une boitine verde*—a box, a

---

32. S.D.] *Rowe; not in F.*   33. *Rug.*] *F; Rugby* [*calls from the window*] *New Camb.*
Out, alas,] *F* (Out alas:).   34. shent] *F;* shent. [*Exit Rugby*] *Wheatley.*   35–6.
S.D.] *Q* (*He steps into the Counting-house*); *not in F; Shuts Simple in the closet Rowe*
(*before* 'he').   39. *Singing*] *As Theobald; not in F.*   *Enter Doctor Caius.*] *Rowe;*
not in F.   40. des toys] *F* (des-toyes); *dese toys Capell.*   41. *une boitine verde*]
Craig; vnboyteene verd *F; un boitier verd Rowe;* un boitier vert *Camb.;* une boite
en verde *Hart.*

---

with a Warrener that is din'd at
Kingston's' (*Letters*, ed. Hyder E.
Rollins, 1958, I. 265–6).

33. *Out, alas*] Cf. IV. v. 60. 'Out' is
merely an intensifier in such phrases.

34. *shent*] Past participle of the verb
'shend', to reprove or scold; now only
dialectal.

38. *doubt*] fear.

39. *And down . . .*] The refrain seems
to have been used in more songs than
one, but perhaps there was one favourite version and tune. Cf. *Ham.*, IV. v.
170–1.

40. *toys*] Either 'whims', 'caprices',
or 'absurdities' (cf. *R3*, I. i. 60).

41. *boitine verde*] small green box.
There are many difficulties in inter-
preting Caius' French as printed in F.
Presumably Shakespeare would not
have intended the Frenchman to speak
unidiomatically, but Shakespeare himself may not have progressed beyond
'schoolboy French' (see l. 49 and note).
Apparently too some of the F spelling
is phonetic rather than 'standard'. An
editor can but leave it much as it is,
'correcting' only what he assumes to be
scribal or compositorial error (as
clearly in l. 46). 'Boitine', if it is what
Shakespeare intended, is perfectly in-
telligible but may have been his own

green-a box. Do intend vat I speak? A green-a box.

Quick. Ay, forsooth; I'll fetch it you. [*Aside*] I am glad
he went not in himself: if he had found the young
man, he would have been horn-mad.   45

*Caius. Fe, fe, fe, fe, ma foi, il fait fort chaud. Je m'en vais voir
à la court la grande affaire.*

Quick. Is it this, sir?

Caius. Oui, mette le au mon pocket: dépêche, quickly. Vere is
dat knave Rugby?   50

Quick. What, John Rugby! John!

Rug. Here, sir!

Caius. You are John Rugby, and you are Jack Rugby.
Come, take-a your rapier, and come after my heel to
the court.   55

---

43. Ay . . . I] *Prose as Capell;* I . . . you: / I . . . F.   *Aside*] *Pope; not in* F.
46–7. *ma foi . . . affaire*] *This ed.; mai foy, il fait for ehando, Ie man voi a le Court la grand
affaires* F; *ma foi, Il fait fort chaud, je m'en va a la Cour—la grande Affaire Rowe*[1]; *ma
foi Il fait fort chaud, je m'en vais à la Cour—la grande Affaire Rowe*[3].   49–50.] *Prose
as Pope; Ouy . . . quickly: /* Vere . . . F.   49. *mette*] F; *mettez Theobald.   dépêche*]
Rowe (Depêch); de-peech F; *depêchez Theobald.*   51.] *Wheatley adds* 'Re-enter
Rugby'.

---

invention (*boîte* + the diminutive *ine*
regularly attached to nouns and adjectives).

42. *intend*] Caius must mean 'attend',
unless, as Bowers suggests, he is
anglicizing the French *entendre*, to
hear.

45. *horn-mad*] beside himself with
anger, like a horned beast in the breed-
ing season, ready to attack anything.
The phrase is proverbial (Tilley H628)
Cf. III. v. 140–2 (where even more
clearly the phrase takes on the other
association, of a cuckolded husband
mad with jealousy) and *Err.*, II. i. 57–9:
'*Dromio.* Why, mistress, sure my
master is horn-mad. / *Adriana.* Horn-
mad, thou villain! *Dromio.* I mean not
cuckold-mad; / But sure, he is stark
mad.'

46. *chaud*] F1 prints Caius' French
in italic, presumably because the
words were written in the 'Italian'
hand; and *ehando*, followed by Ff 2–4,

is probably a misreading of *chaude* in
that script (indeed the word in F1 can
easily be misread as *chaudo*).

46–7. *m'en vais voir . . . affaire*] This
reading, postulating a F omission because of the similarity in appearance
of 'vais' and 'voir', seems more likely
than Rowe's ellipsis, which has been
generally adopted. F's 'Court' is supported by Eliot's *Ortho-Epia Gallica*,
which has 'Venez à la Court' (though
elsewhere 'cour'); and J. W. Lever
(*Shakespeare Survey* 6, 1953, 79–90) has
suggested that Eliot left his mark
on Shakespeare's French in other
places.

49. *pocket*] If Shakespeare intended
Caius to lapse into English, as he does
with 'quickly', then strictly the word
should be printed in roman. (Both are
italic in F.) Possibly, however, Shakespeare's own French failed, as it
seems to have failed again in ll. 57–8.

53. *Jack*] See note on l. 102.

Rug. 'Tis ready, sir, here in the porch.

Caius. By my trot, I tarry too long. Od's me, *que ai je
     oublié*? Dere is some simples in my closet dat I vill not
     for the varld I shall leave behind.

Quick. Ay me, he'll find the young man there, and be   60
     mad!

Caius. O *diable, diable*! Vat is in my closet? Villainy,
     larron! [*Pulling Simple out*] Rugby, my rapier!

Quick. Good master, be content.

Caius. Wherefore shall I be content-a?   65

Quick. The young man is an honest man.

Caius. What shall de honest man do in my closet? Dere
     is no honest man dat shall come in my closet.

Quick. I beseech you, be not so phlegmatic. Hear the
     truth of it: he came of an errand to me from Parson   70
     Hugh.

Caius. Vell?

Sim. Ay, forsooth; to desire her to—

Quick. Peace, I pray you.

Caius. Peace-a your tongue. [*To Simple*] Speak-a your   75
     tale.

Sim. To desire this honest gentlewoman, your maid, to
     speak a good word to Mistress Anne Page for my
     master in the way of marriage.

Quick. This is all, indeed, la, but I'll ne'er put my finger   80
     in the fire, and need not.

57–8. *que . . . oublié?*] F (*que ay ie oublie:*); *Qu'ay je oublié? Warburton; Qu'ay
j'oublié? Johnson.*   62–3.] *Prose as Pope;* O . . . Closset? / Villanie . . . *F.*   62.
Villainy] *F;* Villaine *Q3.*   63. *larron*] *Rowe;* La-roone *F.*   S.D.] *As Theobald;
not in F.*   75. *To Simple*] *This ed., as Steevens; not in F.*

57. *Od's me*] Another elliptical oath,
formed (probably) from 'God save
me'.

58. *simples*] medicines made from
single ingredients, especially herbs or
plants—but the audience, of course,
knows of another kind of Simple in the
closet.

63. *larron*] French for thief (though
O.E.D. cites one earlier example suggesting that French *larron* may already
have been anglicized). By 'villainy'

Caius possibly means 'villain'; cf.
II. iii. 15.

69. *phlegmatic*] No doubt Quickly
means the opposite, choleric, for pre-
dominant phlegm was supposed to
make for coldness or dullness.

80–1. *I'll . . . need not*] Quickly is
citing a proverb (Tilley F230) that
may be paraphrased 'there's no sense
in getting one's fingers burnt if one
doesn't have to'. Her theory hardly
corresponds with her practice.

Caius. Sir Hugh send-a you? Rugby, ballow me some
    paper. Tarry you a little-a while.   *Writes.*

Quick. [*Aside to Simple*] I am glad he is so quiet: if he had
    been throughly moved, you should have heard him   85
    so loud and so melancholy. But notwithstanding,
    man, I'll do you your master what good I can; and
    the very yea and the no is, the French doctor, my
    master—I may call him my master, look you, for I
    keep his house; and I wash, wring, brew, bake,   90
    scour, dress meat and drink, make the beds, and do
    all myself—

Sim. [*Aside to Quickly*] 'Tis a great charge to come under
    one body's hand.

Quick. [*Aside to Simple*] Are you avised o' that? You   95
    shall find it a great charge; and to be up early and
    down late; but notwithstanding—to tell you in
    your ear; I would have no words of it—my master
    himself is in love with Mistress Anne Page; but
    notwithstanding that, I know Anne's mind—that's   100
    neither here nor there.

Caius. You jack'nape, give-a this letter to Sir Hugh; by

82. ballow] *F; baillez Theobald;* baille *Camb.*   83. S.D.] *Q* (*The Doctor writes*);
not in F.   84, 93, 95. S.D.] *Camb.; not in F.*   87. you] *F1* (yoe); for *F2*; omitted
by Capell.   90. wring] *Rowe³;* ring *F.*   100. that,] *Rowe;* that *F.*

82. *ballow*] The emendations 'baillez' and 'baille' are implausible: a
scribe or compositor could hardly have
misread thus in either script. 'Ballow'
must be an anglicized form of French
bailler, to bring (Eliot, c1ᵛ, has 'Baille
moy vne chemise blanche', translated
as 'Giue me a cleane shirt'; cf. *O.E.D.*
'bail' *v.*¹) or Caius' attempt to find an
equivalent. (The only other occurrence
of 'ballow' in Shakespeare and, probably, in Elizabethan literature is in F
Lr., IV. vi. 247, and would seem to be
irrelevant: Edgar, speaking in dialect
as a 'peasant', uses it as a noun to
mean, apparently, cudgel.)
    86. *melancholy*] Quickly doesn't mean
'melancholy'; and when she does mean
it (in l. 147) the best she can do is
'allicholy'.

87. *you*] Another example of the
construction described by Abbott
(220) as 'representing the old dative'.
It may even be paraphrased as 'since
you ask me'.
    93. *charge*] Sometimes explained as
'responsibility' (*O.E.D. sb.* II. 8²) but
also, obviously, 'burden' in the sense of
'weight' (*sb.* I. 1). This and the following line form the first *double entendre* of
a series; and the Q reporter, remembering the trend but not the detail,
invented his own indecencies.
    95. *avised*] aware, informed—though
O.E.D. cites this line under 'advised'
ppl.a. 1. 'having considered' (cf. I. i.
150 and note).
    100-1. *that's . . . there*] Yet another
ready-made phrase (Tilley H438).
    102. *jack'nape*] The regular form is

gar, it is a shallenge. I will cut his troat in de Park,
and I will teach a scurvy jack-a-nape priest to
meddle or make. You may be gone; it is not good   105
you tarry here. By gar, I will cut all his two stones;
by gar, he shall not have a stone to throw at his
dog.   [*Exit Simple.*]

Quick. Alas, he speaks but for his friend.

Caius. It is no matter-a ver dat: do not you tell-a me dat   110
I shall have Anne Page for myself? By gar, I vill
kill de Jack-priest; and I have appointed mine host
of de Jarteer to measure our weapon. By gar, I will
myself have Anne Page.

Quick. Sir, the maid loves you, and all shall be well. We   115
must give folks leave to prate: what the good year!

Caius. Rugby, come to the court with me.—[*To
Quickly*] By gar, if I have not Anne Page, I shall turn
your head out of my door.—Follow my heels,
Rugby.   120

Quick. You shall have An—[*Exeunt Caius and Rugby*]—

---

108. S.D.] *Rowe; not in F.*   113. Jarteer] *F1; Garter F4; Jartere Rowe; Jarterre
Theobald; Jarretière Collier.*   116. good year] *Capell;* good-ier *F;* goujeres
Hanmer; goujere *Johnson.*   117–18. *To Quickly*] *As Wheatley; not in F.*   121.
S.D.] *Chambers, as conj. Daniel; not in F; after l. 120 Rowe.*

'jackanapes', meaning 'monkey' and
so 'fool', 'idiot'. (Cf. iv. iv. 67 and note.)
O.E.D. suggests that the original term
was Jack Napes, perhaps a playful
name for a tame ape. 'Jack' was a
general term of abuse, for a male, as in
l. 53 and in 'Jack priest' in l. 112, with
the further point that 'Sir John' was
the traditional name for a priest in
popular tales.

105. *meddle or make*] The proverb 'I
will neither meddle nor make' (Tilley
M852) is alluded to several times in
Shakespeare.

107–8.] This, of course, is another
proverb (Tilley S880); and the pun on
'stone'–'testicle' is obvious enough.

113.] *Jarteer*] Garter: Caius is possibly conflating the Fr. *jarretière.*

to measure our weapon] i.e. to act as
my second. (The seconds in a duel

measured the weapons to make sure
that there was no unfair advantage.)

115.] Once again Quickly is relying
on folk wisdom: 'All shall be well and
Jack shall have Jill' (Tilley A164); and
her next phrase is another cliché.

116. *what the good year*] Another more
or less meaningless asseveration.
(Quickly uses it again in *2H4*, ii. iv.
64.) It was apparently equivalent to
'what the devil'.

121.] F makes the jest clear by
italicizing 'An' and printing with a
hyphen or dash ('*An*—fooles head')
and spelling 'An' throughout the
speech, exceptionally. Caius goes out
believing that Quickly has said 'You
shall have Anne'; then she adds the
proverbial 'fool's head of your own'
(Tilley F519).

fool's head of your own. No, I know Anne's mind for
that; never a woman in Windsor knows more of
Anne's mind than I do, nor can do more than I do
with her, I thank heaven.   125

Fent. [*Within*] Who's within there, hoa?

Quick. Who's there, I trow? Come near the house, I
pray you.

[*Enter* FENTON.]

Fent. How now, good woman, how dost thou?

Quick. The better that it pleases your good worship to   130
ask.

Fent. What news? How does pretty Mistress Anne?

Quick. In truth, sir, and she is pretty, and honest, and
gentle, and one that is your friend—I can tell you
that by the way, I praise heaven for it.   135

Fent. Shall I do any good, think'st thou? Shall I not lose
my suit?

Quick. Troth, sir, all is in His hands above; but notwith-
standing, Master Fenton, I'll be sworn on a book
she loves you. Have not your worship a wart above   140
your eye?

Fent. Yes, marry, have I; what of that?

Quick. Well, thereby hangs a tale. Good faith, it is such
another Nan; but, I detest, an honest maid as ever
broke bread; we had an hour's talk of that wart—   145
I shall never laugh but in that maid's company!—

---

126. *Within*] *Rowe; not in F.*   127. I trow] *F (I troa); trow conj. Hart.*   128.
S.D.] *As Rowe; not in F.*

126–7. *hoa . . . trow*] Perhaps
Quickly completes a rhyme here (F
spells 'hoa', 'troa'). 'I trow' (rather
than 'trow') is unusual in the sense of
'I wonder' rather than 'I believe', but
it is used again in II. i. 61.

127. *near*] Hart gives good reason for
believing that 'near' often meant 'in'
or 'into', citing, e.g., III. iii. 138.

133. *honest*] virtuous.

140. *Have*] The verb takes the second
person according to the general sense
('you') rather than strict syntax

(the third person, 'your worship').

143. *thereby hangs a tale*] Another
'proverb' (Tilley T48) or cliché, still
in popular use.

143–4. *such another Nan*] so remarkable a Nan. The comparable modern
idiom would probably be 'such a Nan'
or 'such a one' (cf. *Troil.*, I. ii. 282,
where Pandarus says to Cressida 'You
are such a woman!').

144. *detest*] Quickly means 'protest'.

144–5. *an honest . . . bread*] Yet another 'proverb' (Tilley M68).

but, indeed, she is given too much to allicholy and
musing; but for you—well—go to.

Fent. Well, I shall see her to-day. Hold, there's money
for thee: let me have thy voice in my behalf; if thou   150
seest her before me, commend me.

Quick. Will I? I' faith, that we will; and I will tell your
worship more of the wart the next time we have
confidence; and of other wooers.

Fent. Well, farewell; I am in great haste now.   155

Quick. Farewell to your worship. [*Exit Fenton.*] Truly,
an honest gentleman—but Anne loves him not; for
I know Anne's mind as well as another does.—Out
upon't, what have I forgot?   *Exit.*

152. we] F (wee); I *Hanmer.*   156. S.D.] *Rowe (after l. 155); not in F.*

147. *allicholy*] i.e. melancholy.   153–4. *have confidence*] confer *or* con-
148. *go to*] An expression of im-   fide in each other.
patience (here feigned).

ACT II

SCENE I

Enter MISTRESS PAGE, *with a letter.*

Mrs. Page. What, have I scaped love-letters in the holiday-time of my beauty, and am I now a subject for
them? Let me see.   [*Reads.*]
    'Ask me no reason why I love you, for though Love
use Reason for his precisian, he admits him not for   5
his counsellor. You are not young, no more am I; go
to, then, there's sympathy. You are merry, so am I;
ha, ha, then, there's more sympathy. You love sack,
and so do I; would you desire better sympathy? Let
it suffice thee, Mistress Page—at the least, if the love   10
of soldier can suffice—that I love thee. I will not say
pity me—'tis not a soldier-like phrase—but I say,
love me. By me,
            Thine own true knight,

ACT II

Scene i

Act II Scene i] *F; Act II. Scene i. Before* Page's *house. Pope.*   S.D.] *Rowe;*
Enter Mistris Page, *Mistris* Ford, *Master* Page, *Master* Ford, Pistoll, Nim, Quickly,
Host, Shallow. *F; Enter Mistresse* Page, *reading of a Letter. Q.*   1. I] *Q3; not in F.*
3. *Reads*] *Capell; not in F.*   5. precisian] *F;* physician *Collier², conj. Johnson.*
11. soldier] *F1;* a soldier *F3.*   13–19. By me . . . FALSTAFF.] *As Capell; By me*
. . . night: | Or . . . might, | For . . . Falstaffe. F; By . . . Knight, | By . . . night, | Or . . .
light, | With . . . might, | For . . . Falstaff. *Johnson.*

1–2. *holiday-time*] hey-day. 'Holiday'
seems to have had the happiest associations for Shakespeare: cf. III. ii. 62
and note.

    5. *precisian*] puritanical (or puritan)
guide in religious or spiritual matters
—as opposed to a sympathetic
'counsellor'. Proverb lore had it
that 'Love is without reason' (Tilley
L517).

    6. *counsellor*] confidant, one who can

be trusted not to take a merely formal
view of a problem. Falstaff is thus
telling Mrs Page not to be concerned
that Reason might puritanically be
against their liaison, and he proceeds
to enumerate such arguments for that
liaison as the more sympathetic con-
fidant could give.

    8. *sack*] wine from Spain or the
Canaries, often but not always white;
sometimes equated with sherry.

37

By day or night,   15
Or any kind of light,
With all his might
For thee to fight,
JOHN FALSTAFF.'

What a Herod of Jewry is this? O wicked, wicked   20
world: one that is well-nigh worn to pieces with age
to show himself a young gallant! What an unweighed
behaviour hath this Flemish drunkard picked—
with the devil's name—out of my conversation, that
he dares in this manner assay me? Why, he hath not   25
been thrice in my company! What should I say to
him? I was then frugal of my mirth. Heaven forgive
me! Why, I'll exhibit a bill in the parliament for the
putting down of men. How shall I be revenged on

20–31.] *Prose as Pope;* What . . . world: / One . . . age / To . . . F *(thereafter as prose
but beginning each line with a capital letter until* 'of men') *;* What . . . World! / One . . .
Age, / To . . . unwayed / Behaviour . . . pickt, / *then prose. Rowe.*   22. an un-
weighed] *F1* (an vnwaied)*;* unwayed *F3;* one unweigh'd *Capell.*   24. with] *F1;*
I' th' *F3.*   27–8. mirth. Heaven forgive me!] *Kittredge;* mirth: (heauen forgiue
mee:) *F;* mirth—heav'n forgive me— *Johnson.*   29. men] *F;* fat men *Theobald;*
Mum *Hanmer.*

20–31.] The setting-out of these lines in F is quite likely to be the fault of the transcriber, Ralph Crane, who in *Demetrius and Enanthe* and *The Witch* sometimes writes prose out thus in separate lines. The compositor would think that verse was indicated and would start setting them accordingly, until he decided, after 'putting down' (l. 29), that the divisions into lines were meaningless. *New Cambridge*'s early theory that 'at this point the "copy" was written in short lengths, which suggests players' parts' is both implausible and unnecessary.

20. *Herod*] The allusion is probably to the miracle plays, in which Herod was traditionally loud-mouthed and thus absurd as well as evil.

Jewry] Judaea, 'the form . . . in the Liturgy and all the Bibles except the Genevan' (Noble, p. 271).

22. *unweighed*] Either 'unconsidered', 'unbalanced' (*O.E.D.* 'weigh' *v.*[1] II. 11)

or 'light' (III). This is the only time Shakespeare uses the word, but cf. Lucio's description of the Duke in *Meas.,* III. ii. 147–8, as 'a very superficial, ignorant, unweighing fellow'.

23. *Flemish*] The inhabitants of the Low Countries—and, of course, the Danes—were alleged to be often drunk.

24. *with the devil's name*] Presumably, 'with the help of the devil' or (as F3 took it, printing 'i' th'') 'acting in the name of the devil'.

conversation] conduct, or, perhaps, 'social relationship with him' (Coriolanus, in North's Plutarch, was 'churlishe, unciuill, and unfit for any mans conuersation'—Bullough, v. 506).

26–7. *What should I say to him?*] What did he expect me to say to him?

28. *exhibit*] submit, introduce (*O.E.D.* 'exhibit' *v.* II. 5. a).

29. *putting down*] suppression (but

him? For revenged I will be, as sure as his guts are   30
made of puddings.

Enter MISTRESS FORD.

Mrs. Ford. Mistress Page! Trust me, I was going to your
house.

Mrs. Page. And, trust me, I was coming to you. You look
very ill.   35

Mrs. Ford. Nay, I'll ne'er believe that; I have to show to
the contrary.

Mrs. Page. Faith, but you do, in my mind.

Mrs. Ford. Well, I do, then; yet, I say, I could show you
to the contrary. O Mistress Page, give me some   40
counsel!

Mrs. Page. What's the matter, woman?

Mrs. Ford. O woman, if it were not for one trifling respect,
I could come to such honour!

Mrs. Page. Hang the trifle, woman, take the honour.   45
What is it? Dispense with trifles—what is it?

Mrs. Ford. If I would but go to hell for an eternal
moment or so, I could be knighted.

Mrs. Page. What? Thou liest! Sir Alice Ford? These
knights will hack; and so thou shouldst not alter the   50
article of thy gentry.

---

31. S.D.] *Q; not in F.*   50. will hack] *F;* will lack *Warburton;* we'll hack *conj.*
Johnson.

---

there may be a *double entendre*—which
would make Theobald's emendation
even sillier).

30–1. *guts . . . puddings*] Close to
tautology: 'pudding' is defined by
O.E.D. (*sb.* 1. 1) as 'the stomach or one
of the entrails of a pig, sheep, or other
animal, stuffed with . . . minced
meat . . . , etc. . . . ; a kind of sausage',
and the plural 'puddings' normally
meant 'guts'.

36. *have*] have something (i.e. the
letter).

48. *moment*] Hart argued that
'moment' could mean any period of
time—and thereby spoilt the joke.

50. *hack*] No clear explanation of the
word has ever been given, although
from IV. i. 57, in a scene where nearly
every phrase spoken by Quickly involves a *double entendre*, it would seem
to mean 'associate with loose women'.
Cf. *O.E.D.* 'hack' *v.*[3] 1 *trans*, 'to put to
indiscriminate or promiscuous use';
and *LLL.*, III. i. 33, where 'hackney'—
of which 'hack' is often used as
an abbreviation—apparently means
'whore' (*O.E.D. sb.* 4). Mistress Page
(who has just read a letter from Sir
John) is thus saying that knights can
be expected to behave promiscuously.
The argument that there is some

Mrs. Ford. We burn daylight. Here, read, read; perceive
   how I might be knighted. I shall think the worse of
   fat men as long as I have an eye to make difference of
   men's liking; and yet he would not swear, praised   55
   women's modesty, and gave such orderly and well-
   behaved reproof to all uncomeliness that I would
   have sworn his disposition would have gone to the
   truth of his words; but they do no more adhere and
   keep place together than the hundred Psalms to the   60
   tune of 'Greensleeves'. What tempest, I trow, threw
   this whale, with so many tuns of oil in his belly,
   ashore at Windsor? How shall I be revenged on
   him? I think the best way were to entertain him with
   hope till the wicked fire of lust have melted him in   65
   his own grease. Did you ever hear the like?

Mrs. Page. Letter for letter, but that the name of Page
   and Ford differs! To thy great comfort in this

55. praised] *Theobald;* praise *F.*   60. place] *F;* pace *Rann, conj. Mason.*
hundred Psalms] *F;* hundredth Psalm *Rowe.*   61. trow] *Rowe;* troa *F.*

reference to Essex's lavish conferring
of knighthoods during the Cadiz
voyage is far-fetched.

51. *article of thy gentry*] matter of your
rank (*O.E.D.* 'article' *sb.* IV. 10. b, and
'gentry' 1).

52. *burn daylight*] Proverbial for
'waste time' (Tilley D123), as in *Rom.,*
I. iv. 43.

55. *liking*] bodily condition (*O.E.D.*
6), as in *1H4,* III. iii. 6.

55–9. *and yet . . . words*] Hart and
New Cambridge suspect the passage to
be a 'fossil' from an old play, since the
description hardly fits the normal
Falstaff. It would not be the only time,
however, that Falstaff has pretended
to admire virtue.

57. *uncomeliness*] improper behaviour
(cf. *O.E.D.* 'comeliness' 2).

58. *gone to*] gone along with, accord-
ed with.

59. *adhere*] agree, go together
(*O.E.D.* 4).

60. *hundred*] Rowe's emendation
'hundredth' has won general acceptance, and *New Cambridge* defends it

on the ground that 'hundred' was a
common sixteenth-century spelling of
'hundredth'. But the emendation
partly spoils the joke, for—as Hart
pointed out—the hundredth psalm
is in fact one of praise, 'Make a joyful
noise unto the Lord, all ye lands'.
There is even less likelihood of all
hundred (or so) psalms being sung or
fitted to the lively tune of 'Greensleeves'.

61. *'Greensleeves'*] A popular love
song, to the tune of which many words
were later set. It is in 6/8 time. The
music is given, with words written to
it by Sir Philip Sidney, in Bruce
Pattison's *Music and Poetry of the English
Renaissance,* 1948, p. 175.

trow] wonder. Cf. I. iv. 127 and
note.

62. *tuns*] casks (not necessarily of
fixed capacity, 252 old wine-gallons).

65–6. *the wicked fire . . . grease*] An
adaptation of a proverb ('frying or
stewing in one's own grease', Tilley
G433) that also lies behind the very
different III. v. 105.

mystery of ill opinions, here's the twin-brother of
thy letter; but let thine inherit first, for I protest mine   70
never shall. I warrant he hath a thousand of these
letters, writ with blank space for different names—
sure, more—and these are of the second edition. He
will print them, out of doubt; for he cares not what
he puts into the press, when he would put us two: 75
I had rather be a giantess, and lie under Mount
Pelion. Well, I will find you twenty lascivious
turtles ere one chaste man.

Mrs. Ford. Why, this is the very same: the very hand, the
very words. What doth he think of us?   80

Mrs. Page. Nay, I know not: it makes me almost ready
to wrangle with mine own honesty. I'll entertain
myself like one that I am not acquainted withal; for,
sure, unless he know some strain in me that I know
not myself, he would never have boarded me in this   85
fury.

Mrs. Ford. 'Boarding' call you it? I'll be sure to keep him
above deck.

Mrs. Page. So will I: if he come under my hatches, I'll
never to sea again. Let's be revenged on him: let's   90
appoint him a meeting, give him a show of comfort
in his suit, and lead him on with a fine-baited delay

84. strain] *F;* stain *Pope.*

69. *ill opinions*] i.e. the bad opinion
of her that Falstaff seems to have
formed for no apparent reason.

70. *inherit*] come into possession (of
a legacy or gift—here Falstaff's offer
of the 'knighthood'). Mrs Page is
jocularly resigning any claim that her
letter may be the older of 'twins' and
thus entitled to the 'inheritance'.

77. *Pelion*] The giants Otus and
Ephialtes, in an attempt to climb to
heaven and defeat the gods, tried to
pile Mt Ossa on Mt Olympus, and
Mt Pelion on top of Ossa. Legend also
said that the Titans were buried under
these mountains. The fate of Falstaff's
mistress would be comparable.

78. *turtles*] turtledoves, proverbial
for their faithfulness.

82. *wrangle . . . honesty*] quarrel with,
or act in a way contrary to, my own
virtue. 'Honesty' is used again, in the
same sense, in l. 96.

entertain] treat *or* think of.

84. *strain*] quality or tendency (a
sense not unknown today).

85. *boarded*] accosted, approached.
It is a nautical metaphor, from the
original sense of coming alongside
another ship (not necessarily to attack
it). Mrs Ford and Mrs Page then carry
on the metaphor in its other common,
sexual, senses.

92. *fine-baited delay*] delay during
which tempting bait will be dangled
in front of him—an admirable description of the tactics they do
adopt.

I

till he hath pawned his horses to mine host of the
Garter.

Mrs. Ford. Nay, I will consent to act any villainy against   95
him that may not sully the chariness of our honesty.
O that my husband saw this letter; it would give
eternal food to his jealousy.

Mrs. Page. Why, look where he comes; and my good
man too. He's as far from jealousy as I am from   100
giving him cause; and that, I hope, is an unmeasurable distance.

Mrs. Ford. You are the happier woman.

Mrs. Page. Let's consult together against this greasy
knight. Come hither.   [*They stand back.*]   105

Enter FORD, [*with*] PISTOL, *and* PAGE, [*with*] NYM.

Ford. Well, I hope it be not so.

Pist. Hope is a curtal dog in some affairs:
Sir John affects thy wife.

Ford. Why, sir, my wife is not young.

Pist. He woos both high and low, both rich and poor,   110
Both young and old, one with another, Ford;
He loves the gallimaufry: Ford, perpend.

99–100. good man] *F; goodman Bowers.*   105. *They stand back*] *Theobald (They
retire); not in F.   Enter ... Nym*] *Rowe (as Q); not in F.   110–12.] Verse as Pope;
prose F.*   112. the] *F1; thy F2.*

93–4. *pawned . . . Garter*] This first
mention of horses, and of the Host's
concern with them, presumably as
post-horses, has received much comment because of loose ends later in the
play (see Introduction, pp. xlvii ff.). In
themselves, however, the words create
no problem. Falstaff is known to be in
need of money; the wives will lead him
on till he has even less and has to pawn
his horses to pay for his food and
lodging. In the long run the horses are
'arrested' because of his debt to Ford–
Brook (v. v. 115–16).

96. *chariness*] scrupulous integrity
(*O.E.D.* 2; cf. 'chary' 4, 5), often
applied as here to a woman's honour.

99–100. *good man*] So F; but the

word 'goodman' (husband) may be
intended, as in III. ii. 22.

107–8.] Again it is difficult to know
whether Pistol's first words are a
complete verse line from some lost
play. He is bound to be quoting single
phrases, at least.

107. *curtal*] with docked tail (and
therefore less good for hunting, because of loss of balance).

108. *affects*] aims at or (less probably)
loves.

110.] Another Biblical quotation
(Psalms 49:2).

112. *gallimaufry*] Strictly a cooking
term, meaning hotchpotch; thus
'variety', 'mixture'. Cf. *Wint.*, IV. iv.
335–6.

perpend] consider (cf. 'perpend, my

Ford. Love my wife?

Pist. With liver burning hot. Prevent,
          Or go thou, like Sir Actæon he,   115
          With Ringwood at thy heels.
          O, odious is the name!

Ford. What name, sir?

Pist. The horn, I say. Farewell.   119
          Take heed; have open eye; for thieves do foot by night:
          Take heed, ere summer comes, or cuckoo-birds do sing.
          —Away, Sir Corporal Nym!—Believe it, Page, he
          speaks sense.   *Exit.*

114–17.] *This ed.*; With . . . preuent: / Or . . . with / Ring-wood . . . name. *F;*
as prose, Pope; With . . . go thou / Like . . . heels: / O . . . name! *Capell.*   121. do
sing] *F;* affright *Theobald.*   122–3.] *As Theobald;* Away sir Corporall *Nim:* /
Beleeue it (*Page*) he speakes sence. *F; Page* belieue him what he ses. Away sir
Corporall Nym. *Q;* Away, Sir corporal. / *Nym.* Believe . . . sense. *conj. Johnson;*
Away, sir corporal Nym. / *Nym.* Believe . . . sense. *Collier.*   123. E*x*it] *Q;*
not in F.

---

princess, and give ear', *Tw.N.*, v. i.
307–8).

114–16.] Again, the status and
division of Pistol's lines are doubtful.
The division adopted in the text perhaps makes better verse of them than
does the usual setting out.

114. *liver burning hot*] Another allusion to the liver as the supposed seat of
the passions.

114–15. *prevent, Or*] anticipate (the
danger), and get in first lest.

115–16. *Sir Actæon . . . heels*] Perhaps
'Sir' is used by Pistol because he is
quoting from some old play or poem,
or because he is implying his own
familiarity with the characters of
mythology (cf. 'Sir Corporal Nym' in
l. 122). (It was not uncommon, however, to add 'Sir' to the names of
characters from classical myth and
legend. Cf. 'Sir Diomed' in *Troil.*,
iv. v. 88.) Actæon, either because he
happened to see the naked Diana
bathing or because he boasted that he
was a better hunter than the goddess,
was chased and killed by his own
hunting dogs. 'Ringwood' was a
popular name for a hound, and one of

Actæon's dogs had already been
called 'Ringwood' not only in Gold-
ing's translation of Ovid but also in the
song 'New Mad Tom of Bedlam'. (See
Baldwin II. 430–2.) Since as a stag
Actæon had horns, the Elizabethans
seem to have turned him also into a
symbol of cuckoldry: hence his name
is 'odious' (l. 117). Cf. III. ii. 38–9,
where both self-satisfied rashness and
cuckoldry are involved in the allusion.

121. *ere . . . sing*] The cuckoo is
associated with warm weather (there
is still 'competition' each year in
England to report the first cuckoo of
spring) and because of its habit of
leaving other birds to hatch its eggs, it
gave its name to the cuckold, the
deceived husband, on whom, so to
speak, the cuckoo's trick has been
played.

122–3.] The Q version of Pistol's
words lends support to the F reading
and tells against most emendations.
Pistol cannot go without assuring Page
that what Nym has already told him or
has still to tell him is just as true as what
he, Pistol, has told Ford.

Ford. [*Aside*] I will be patient; I will find out this.

Nym. [*To Page*] And this is true; I like not the humour   125
of lying. He hath wronged me in some humours. I
should have borne the humoured letter to her; but
I have a sword, and it shall bite upon my necessity.
He loves your wife; there's the short and the long.
My name is Corporal Nym; I speak, and I avouch;   130
'tis true: my name is Nym, and Falstaff loves your
wife. Adieu. I love not the humour of bread and
cheese. Adieu.   *Exit.*

Page. The 'humour' of it, quoth 'a! Here's a fellow
frights English out of his wits.   135

Ford. I will seek out Falstaff.

Page. I never heard such a drawling, affecting rogue.

124. *Aside*] *As Capell; not in F.*   125. *To Page*] *As Hanmer; not in F.*   130–2.
My . . . wife] *Prose as F;* My . . . avouch; / 'Tis . . . wife *New Camb.*   130.
avouch; 'tis] *F;* auouch tis *Q.*   133. cheese. Adieu.] *F;* cheese: / And theres
the humor of it. *Q;* cheese; and there's the humour of it. Adieu. *Capell.*   *Exit*]
Q; not in F.   134. The 'humour' of it] *This ed.;* The humour of it *F;* *The humour
of it Capell;* (*aside*) 'The humour of it' *Dyce.*   135. English] *F;* humor *Q.*
136, 138, 141.] *As asides, Capell.*   137. *Page*] *F; Page* (*aside*) *Dyce.*   drawling,
affecting] *F* (drawling-affecting).

128. *bite*] For 'bite' used of the
stroke of a sword reaching its mark, cf.
Lr., v. iii. 276–7, 'I have seen the day,
with my good biting falchion / I
would have made them skip'.

  upon my necessity] when I need it.

129. *the short and the long*] Hart shows
that this is the normal earlier form of
our 'the long and the short of it'. Cf.
ii. ii. 56. (Tilley's citations, L419, give
further evidence.)

132–3. *bread and cheese*] Earlier
editors explained this, on good authority, as the proverbial description of
the hard fare Nym had been forced
to accept as Falstaff's retainer. *New
Cambridge*, however, citing *O.E.D.*'s
other mention of bread and cheese 'as
a child's name for the young leaves of
the cuckoo-bread plant', sees an allusion to Page's fate as the eating of
cuckoo-bread if he does not take Nym's
advice. Perhaps both meanings are
there.

133.] Editors who include the Q

phrase 'And theres the humor of it' do
so because they think it necessary if
sense is to be made of Page's next line.
They themselves are assuming, however, that Page quotes four of Nym's
words, whereas he may be quoting
only one. 'There's the humour of it'
does not occur anywhere in F *Wiv.*; it
is Nym's favourite phrase in *H5* and
probably gets into Q *Wiv.* by confusion of memory. See Introduction,
pp. xxi–xxii.

134–41.] These lines are not necessarily 'asides' in the ordinary sense, but
neither Ford nor Page listens to what
the other is saying.

135. *his*] its.

137. *drawling, affecting*] Shakespeare
does not use 'drawling' elsewhere, and
O.E.D., taking it to refer to the
lengthening of sounds 'in an indolent
or affected manner' and so to 'speaking slowly', cites no earlier example.
'Affecting', however, is common in
the sense of trying to be impressive,

Ford. If I do find it—well.

Page. I will not believe such a Cataian, though the
    priest o' th' town commended him for a true man.   140

Ford. 'Twas a good sensible fellow—well.

Page. How now, Meg?

      [*Mistress Page and Mistress Ford come forward.*]

Mrs. Page. Whither go you, George? Hark you.

Mrs. Ford. How now, sweet Frank, why art thou
    melancholy?   145

Ford. I melancholy? I am not melancholy. Get you
    home, go.

Mrs. Ford. Faith, thou hast some crotchets in thy head
    now. Will you go, Mistress Page?

Mrs. Page. Have with you. You'll come to dinner,   150
    George? [*Aside to Mistress Ford*] Look who comes
    yonder: she shall be our messenger to this paltry
    knight.

Mrs. Ford. [*Aside to Mistress Page*] Trust me, I thought
    on her: she'll fit it.   155

        [*Enter* MISTRESS QUICKLY.]

Mrs. Page. You are come to see my daughter Anne?

Quick. Ay, forsooth; and, I pray, how does good
    Mistress Anne?

---

139. *Page*] F; *Page (aside)* Dyce.   142. S.D.] *Theobald (after l. 141); not in F;*
Page *and* Ford *meeting their wives.* Pope.   146–7.] *Prose as Pope;* I . . . not
melancholy: / Get . . . *F.*   148–9. head now. Will] *Hanmer;* head, / Now: will
F1; head. Now: will *F3.*   151. *Aside . . . Ford*] *Johnson; not in F.*   154. *Aside . . .*
Page] *As Capell; not in F.*   155. S.D.] *Rowe (after l. 153); not in F.*

'putting on airs', affected. There is a
close parallel to the thought of the
whole line in Mercutio's disgust with
Tybalt in *Rom.*, II. iv. 30–1, 'The pox
of such antic, lisping, affecting fan-
tasticoes; these new tuners of accents'.

  139. *Cataian*] Cathaian or Chinese—
apparently noted for boasting and
falsehood (Hart cites a relevant passage from William Watreman's translation *The Fardle of Facions*, 1555). Sir

Toby, however, is not thinking of
either boasting or lying when he applies the term to Olivia (not in her
presence) in *Tw.N.*, II. iii. 80.

  140. *priest o' th' town*] The modern
idiom would be 'parish priest'.

  148. *crotchets . . . head*] absurd ideas.
The phrase is proverbial (Tilley
C843).

  150. *Have with you*] I am coming
(used again in ll. 210 and 220).

Mrs. Page. Go in with us and see; we have an hour's talk
    with you.   160
      Exeunt Mistress Page, Mistress Ford, and Mistress Quickly.

Page. How now, Master Ford?

Ford. You heard what this knave told me, did you not?

Page. Yes; and you heard what the other told me?

Ford. Do you think there is truth in them?

Page. Hang 'em, slaves: I do not think the knight   165
    would offer it. But these that accuse him in his in-
    tent towards our wives are a yoke of his discarded
    men: very rogues, now they be out of service.

Ford. Were they his men?

Page. Marry, were they.   170

Ford. I like it never the better for that. Does he lie at the
    Garter?

Page. Ay, marry, does he. If he should intend this
    voyage toward my wife, I would turn her loose to
    him, and what he gets more of her than sharp   175
    words, let it lie on my head.

Ford. I do not misdoubt my wife; but I would be loath to
    turn them together; a man may be too confident;
    I would have nothing lie on my head; I cannot be
    thus satisfied.   180

Page. Look where my ranting host of the Garter comes;
    there is either liquor in his pate or money in his
    purse when he looks so merrily.

Enter HOST.

---

159. we have] *F;* we would have *Hudson²*, *conj. Walker;* we'd have *Craig.*   160.
S.D.] *Q; not in F.*   171–2.] *Prose as Pope;* I . . . that, / Do's . . . *F.*   181.
ranting] *F;* ramping *Q.*   183. Enter Host] *Dyce; not in F; after l. 184, Collier;*
Enter Host and Shallow Q (before l. 181); *Enter Host, Shallow, and Slender Harness*
(after l. 184).

166. *offer it*] attempt it, presume so
far. Cf. *Troil.*, II. iii. 67–8, 'Agamemnon
is a fool to offer to command Achilles'.

167. *yoke*] pair, brace.

174. *voyage*] The image is used again,
of an attempt to seduce, in *Cym.*,
I. iv. 171–3: Posthumus, making his
wager on Imogen's virtue, says to

Iachimo, 'If you make your voyage
upon her and give me directly to
understand you have prevailed, I am
no further your enemy'.

176. *lie on my head*] be my responsibility or blame—but Ford in l. 179
twists it to mean 'wear the horns of
cuckoldry'.

How now, mine host?

Host. How now, bully rook? Thou'rt a gentleman.—   185
Cavaliero Justice, I say!

Enter SHALLOW.

Shal. I follow, mine host, I follow. Good even and
twenty, good Master Page! Master Page, will you
go with us? We have sport in hand.

Host. Tell him, Cavaliero Justice; tell him, bully rook.   190

Shal. Sir, there is a fray to be fought between Sir Hugh
the Welsh priest and Caius the French doctor.

Ford. Good mine host o' th' Garter, a word with you.

Drawing him aside.

Host. What say'st thou, my bully rook?

Shal. [*To Page*] Will you go with us to behold it? My   195
merry host hath had the measuring of their
weapons, and, I think, hath appointed them
contrary places; for, believe me, I hear the parson
is no jester. Hark, I will tell you what our sport
shall be.   [*They converse apart.*]   200

Host. Hast thou no suit against my knight, my guest
cavalier?

---

186. S.D. *Enter Shallow*] Collier[2]; *not in* F.   193. S.D.] *Capell; not in F;* Ford *and
the Host talkes.* Q; *They go a little aside. Johnson (after l. 194).*   195. *To Page*]
Johnson; not in F.   200. S.D.] *Capell; not in* F.   202. cavalier] F (-Caualeire);
-cavaleiro *Kittredge.*

---

186. *Cavaliero*] From the earlier
meaning of '(Spanish) knight on
horseback', it came to mean, in Dr
Johnson's dictionary definition, 'a gay
sprightly military man' or 'gallant'
and is used ironically in that sense here
and at II. iii. 70 and in *2H4*, v. iii. 62.

187–8. *Good even and twenty*] Good
afternoon, many times over. 'Twenty'
seems to have been used to indicate
any reasonably large number; 'even'
meant any time after noon. The time
of the action, however, must be early
morning, because the Host and his
party are on the way to the 'duel' from
which they all return to interrupt
Falstaff's first assignation with Mrs

Ford, between ten and eleven (a.m.).
The 'error' here gives ammunition to
those who argue that Shakespeare was
carelessly taking over unaltered some
parts of the 'earlier' play he was
'revising'; but there is an identical
problem in *Measure for Measure* where
Lucio, at IV. iii. 154, says 'Good even'
to the Duke and Isabella only thirty-
eight lines after the Duke has said
'Good morning' to Isabella. One
wonders whether 'good even' may not
have meant 'good day'. In any case,
there are other instances of time confusion in Shakespeare.

195–7. *My merry host . . . weapons*] See
I. iv. 113 and note.

Ford. None, I protest; but I'll give you a pottle of burnt
sack to give me recourse to him, and tell him my
name is Brook—only for a jest.   205
Host. My hand, bully; thou shalt have egress and
regress—said I well?—and thy name shall be
Brook. It is a merry knight. —Will you go,
Anheers?
Shal. Have with you, mine host.   210
Page. I have heard the Frenchman hath good skill in his
rapier.

203. *Ford*] *Q; Shal. (Shallow) F.*   205. *Brook*] *Q (Brooke, throughout play; here
misprinted 'Rrooke') ; Broome F (throughout play).*   209. *Anheers*] *As F; myn-heers
Hanmer, conj. Theobald; on here Collier, conj. Theobald; on, heris Warburton; on,
hearts Steevens³, conj. Heath; on, heers Knight; on, sirs Halliwell; Minheers Grant
White; Ameers New Camb., conj. Hart.*

203. **Ford**] The F attribution of the
speech to Shallow must be wrong, in
view of the subsequent action involving Ford in disguise. *New Cambridge*
claims that the Host's previous question is 'pointless as addressed to Ford'
—but it would certainly be pointless
addressed to Shallow, for the Host has
already been appointed 'umpire' to
hear the dispute between him and
Falstaff (I. i. 124–8). It is far simpler
to assume that the Host is replying to
Ford's opening remarks to him, asking
for his help in approaching Falstaff
(and Falstaff must be the Host's
'knight', his 'guest cavalier').

pottle] half a gallon, or a vessel containing half a gallon.

203–4. *burnt sack*] Generally explained as heated or mulled wine, but
one wonders whether, in view of the
Elizabethan fondness for sugaring
liquor, it may not mean rather wine
to which burnt sugar has been added.

205. *Brook*] For this name, following
Q, as against F's 'Broome', see Introduction, pp. xxxiv–xxxv.

206–7. *egress and regress*] Legal terms,
not used strictly but meaning 'the free-
dom or opportunity to come and go'.

209. *Anheers*] No fully satisfactory
emendation or explanation has been
proposed. That the F reading ('An-

heires') is a form of a non-extant but
then understood word is suggested
both by the fact that the later seventeenth-century Folios did not attempt
to emend (except in the spelling) and
by the occurrence in *1H4*, II. i. 85, of
what may well be the same word:
Gadshill asserts that he keeps company
not with 'sixpennie strikers' and such
riff-raff, 'but with nobilitie, & tranqui-
litie, Burgomasters & great Oneyres'
(Q0 and, subst., Q1; the later Qq
and F1 read 'Oneyers'). The required
word, because of the association with
'Burgomasters', is thus probably an
anglicization of the Dutch *heer* (or
possibly German *herr*). 'Minheers' (for
'mynheers') would fit if one could
believe not only (with Grant White
and Sisson) that it could have been
misread as 'An-heires' but also (which
is far less likely) that it could have been
misread as 'Oneyres' ('mynheers' is
found by Dyce as early as the 1647
Fletcher Folio, in *The Beggar's Bush*).
Indeed 'Myne Heire' occurs, as a term
of address, in the Crane manuscript of
Sir John Van Olden Barnavelt (B.M.
Add. MS. 18653) and does not look in
the least like 'An-Heire', 'On-Heire',
or 'Oneyre'. 'Amheeres' (for 'ameers'
or 'emirs', the Turkish title) is more
likely to have been misread as 'an-

Shal. Tut, sir, I could have told you more. In these
       times you stand on distance, your passes, stocca–
       does, and I know not what. 'Tis the heart, Master   215
       Page, 'tis here, 'tis here. I have seen the time, with
       my long sword I would have made you four tall
       fellows skip like rats.
Host. Here, boys, here, here; shall we wag?
Page. Have with you. I had rather hear them scold than   220
       fight.   [*Exeunt Host, Shallow, and Page.*]
Ford. Though Page be a secure fool, and stands so firmly
       on his wife's frailty, yet I cannot put off my opinion
       so easily: she was in his company at Page's house;
       and what they made there, I know not. Well, I   225
       will look further into 't, and I have a disguise to
       sound Falstaff. If I find her honest, I lose not my
       labour; if she be otherwise, 'tis labour well be-
       stowed.   *Exit.*

220. hear] *F;* have *Hanmer.*   than] *F* (then); than see them *Collier²*.   221.
S.D.] *Rowe; not in F.*   223. frailty] *F;* fealty *Theobald², conj. Theobald¹;* fidelity
Collier².   229. *Exit] Rowe; Exeunt F.*

heires' but perhaps fits less easily into
the *1H4* context.

214. *stand on*] rely on, abide by the
accepted practice concerning.

distance] the distance between the
duellists (which would determine the
'passes' or thrusts used).

214–15. *stoccadoes*] Another technical term for thrusts in fencing. The
whole sentence is like Mercutio's
scornful account of Tybalt's text-book
fencing, in *Rom.*, II. iv. 21–9: 'He fights
as you sing prick-song, keeps time,
distance, and proportion . . . ah, the
immortal passado! the punto reverso!
the hai!'

216–17. *I have seen the time . . . I*] The
phrase seems to have been a favourite
with Shakespeare, as given to old men
recalling their alleged youthful prowess; cf. Capulet, in *Rom.*, I. v. 23–4,
and *Lr.*, v. iii. 276–7. A great part of
the comedy of Shallow in *2H4* (III. ii)
comes from such 'memories' of his
'mad' youth.

217. *long sword*] Shallow is probably

contrasting the heavier sword of his
day (Q reads 'two hand sword') with
the lighter modern rapier of l. 212.

you] Almost equivalent to 'for you'.
Cf. I. iv. 87 and note. (Harness, misunderstanding the phrase, brought
Slender on stage that Shallow might
have four men to address.)

tall] (allegedly) valiant.

219. *wag*] go, as in I. iii. 6.

222. *secure*] rashly over-confident.
So York calls to Bolingbroke, whom he
thinks in danger, 'Open the door,
secure, fool-hardy king' (*R2*, v. iii. 43)
and the Ghost tells Hamlet how he
was murdered when 'Upon my secure
hour thy uncle stole' (*Ham.*, I. v. 61).

222–3. *stands . . . frailty*] relies so
much on what is really his wife's frailty,
believing it to be otherwise. Theobald's
emendation 'fealty' is quite unnecessary.

225. *made*] did (or created).

227. *lose*] waste (*O.E.D. v.¹* 6). 'To
lose one's labour' is a common idiom
—as in *Love's Labour's Lost*.

SCENE II

Enter FALSTAFF *and* PISTOL.

Fal. I will not lend thee a penny.

Pist. Why, then the world's mine oyster, which I with
sword will open.

Fal. Not a penny. I have been content, sir, you should
lay my countenance to pawn; I have grated upon   5
my good friends for three reprieves for you and your
coach-fellow Nym—or else you had looked through
the grate, like a geminy of baboons; I am damned
in hell for swearing to gentlemen my friends you
were good soldiers and tall fellows; and when   10
Mistress Bridget lost the handle of her fan, I took 't
upon mine honour thou hadst it not.

Pist. Didst not thou share? Hadst thou not fifteen pence?

Fal. Reason, you rogue, reason: think'st thou I'll en-

Scene II

Scene II] *F;* Scene VII. *The* Garter-Inn. *Pope; Scene II. A Room in the garter Inn.*
Capell.   S.D.] *Q; Enter* Falstaffe, Pistoll, Robin, Quickly, Bardolffe, Ford. *F.*
2–3.] *Prose as F;* Why . . . oyster, / Which . . . *Steevens³;* I will retort the sum in
equipage *Q.*   7. coach-fellow] *F;* couch-fellow *Theobald.*

2–3.] It is difficult to find any justification for tacking on to this speech,
as some editors do, the line that replaces it in Q and is presumably the
best the reporter could do to recall the
original. (*New Cambridge* even uses the
Q line to *open* the scene.) There is no
difficulty in the F text: Pistol replies
that if Falstaff will lend him nothing
he will have to use his sword to extract
money from an unwilling—and rotten—world; he is adapting the proverbial 'open an oyster with a dagger'
(Tilley M777), where the dagger implies keeping one's distance because of
the smell.

5. *countenance*] reputation, position,
standing (*O.E.D. sb.* III. 9, 10). Falstaff has, in short, allowed Pistol to
trade on his, Falstaff's, name.

grated upon] The metaphor was
common and is self-explanatory; it

corresponds to the modern colloquial
'made myself a nuisance to'.

7. *coach-fellow*] a horse yoked with
another to draw a carriage; hence, a
companion. Shakespeare uses 'yoke-
fellow' in the same sense in *Lr.*, III. vi.
39, and 'yoke-fellows' in *H5*, II. iii. 56.

8. *the grate*] i.e. prison-bars.

geminy] pair, of twins; Latin *gemini*,
plural of *geminus*, the name also given
to the constellation Castor and Pollux.

10. *tall*] brave.

11. *handle of her fan*] Such handles
were often made of precious metal,
pearl, or ivory.

11–12. *took 't upon mine honour*] gave
my word of honour (that).

14. *Reason . . . reason*] i.e. and it is
reasonable enough (that I should have
shared in the spoils, since I risked
damnation by lying about the matter).

danger my soul gratis? At a word, hang no more   15
about me; I am no gibbet for you. Go—a short knife
and a throng!—to your manor of Pickt-hatch, go!
You'll not bear a letter for me, you rogue? You stand
upon your honour? Why, thou unconfinable base-
ness, it is as much as I can do to keep the terms of my   20
honour precise: I, I, I myself sometimes, leaving the
fear of heaven on the left hand, and hiding mine
honour in my necessity, am fain to shuffle, to hedge,
and to lurch; and yet you, rogue, will ensconce your
rags, your cat-a-mountain looks, your red-lattice   25
phrases, and your bold beating oaths, under the
shelter of your honour! You will not do it, you?
Pist. I do relent: what would thou more of man?

17. throng!] *F* (throng,); thong, *Pope*.   21. I, I, I] *F*; I *Pope*; I, ay, I *Grant White*; Ay, ay, I *New Camb*.   22. heaven] *F*; God *Q*.   26. bold beating] *F* (bold-beating-); bold-bearing *conj. Warburton*; bull-baiting *Hanmer*; bowl-beating *conj. New Camb*.   28. relent] *F*; recant *Q*.

15–16. *hang no more about me*] It is not clear whether the verb is used intransitively, 'be an encumbrance on me no longer' (*O.E.D. v.* II. 14. e and 15), with a pun on the other sense (Pistol is destined for a gibbet, but Falstaff is not it), or transitively, 'fasten no more crimes or responsibility on me', as one hangs a felon on a gibbet.

16–17. *a short knife and a throng*] Presumably, using your short knife for cutting purses in a convenient crowd—and no doubt there is a linking of the idea of *picking* purses and '*Pickt*-hatch', a disreputable part of London where there would certainly be no 'manors'.

19. *unconfinable*] limitless, infinite.

23–4. *shuffle . . . hedge . . . lurch*] All three words are used colloquially or as thieves' jargon and they are more or less synonymous: 'shuffle', cheat; 'hedge', use devious methods (as in *Troil.*, III. iii. 158, where to 'hedge aside from the direct forthright' is to abandon honour, which 'travels in a strait so narrow, / Where one but goes

abreast'); 'lurch', pilfer, steal (*O.E.D. v.*[1] 3) rather than 'remain in or about a place furtively' (*O.E.D. v.*[1] 1, citing this line).

24. *ensconce*] hide, shelter, or protect (particularly within or behind a fortification). Cf. III. iii. 82.

25. *cat-a-mountain*] Variously used of the leopard, panther, tiger-cat, or wild cat, and probably applied to Pistol because of his lawlessness and (perhaps) his moustaches, which remind Falstaff of the feline's whiskers.

red-lattice] i.e. tavern or ale-house, which normally had red-painted lattice instead of glass windows. Cf. *2H4*, II. ii. 85–9.

26. *bold beating*] The phrase has caused difficulty, probably only because of the F hyphens (which may be easily explained as the responsibility of Ralph Crane, who often thus linked adjectives, and adjectives and nouns). Johnson well compared 'beating' with 'thwacking' or 'swinging' as intensives.

28. *relent*] give way (*O.E.D. v.*[1] 2. b).

[*Enter* ROBIN.]

Rob. Sir, here's a woman would speak with you.
Fal. Let her approach.   30

Enter MISTRESS QUICKLY.

Quick. Give your worship good morrow.
Fal. Good morrow, goodwife.
Quick. Not so, and't please your worship.
Fal. Good maid, then.
Quick. I'll be sworn—as my mother was, the first hour I   35
    was born.
Fal. I do believe the swearer. What with me?
Quick. Shall I vouchsafe your worship a word or two?
Fal. Two thousand, fair woman, and I'll vouchsafe thee
    the hearing.   40
Quick. There is one Mistress Ford, sir—I pray come a
    little nearer this ways—I myself dwell with Master
    Doctor Caius—
Fal. Well, on; Mistress Ford, you say—
Quick. Your worship says very true.—I pray your wor-   45
    ship come a little nearer this ways.
Fal. I warrant thee, nobody hears. Mine own people,
    mine own people.
Quick. Are they so? Heaven bless them, and make them
    his servants!   50
Fal. Well, Mistress Ford—what of her?

28. *Enter Robin*] *Rowe; not in F.*   30. S.D.] *Q; not in F.*   32. goodwife] *F1*
(good-wife); good wife *F4*.   35–6.] *Prose as Pope;* Ile be sworne, / As . . . borne.
F.   44. on; Mistress] *F;* one Mistress *Halliwell, conj. Douce.*   49. Heaven] *F;*
God *Q.*

32. *goodwife*] A civil form of address
to the mistress of a house. Cf. 'goodman', III. ii. 22.
    33. *and't*] if it.
    35. *I'll be sworn*] I'll swear to that (as
in III. iii. 25)—and Quickly proceeds
with a delightful 'Freudian' conflation
of the proverbs 'as good a maid as her
mother' and 'as innocent as a new-born
babe' (Tilley M14, B4). Hudson must
be the only reader of the play to deduce

that Quickly is 'a maiden' (p. 212).
    38. *vouchsafe*] grant to, or bestow
on—obviously not the word Quickly
means, for she is asking for the favour.
    42. *ways*] This is the genitive of
'way', used in such adverbial expres-
sions as 'come this ways' and 'go thy
ways' (l. 133).
    49–50. *Heaven . . . servants*] An ex-
ample of expurgation. See Introduction, pp. xxxv–xxxvi.

Quick. Why, sir, she's a good creature.—Lord, Lord,
your worship's a wanton! Well, heaven forgive you
and all of us, I pray!
Fal. Mistress Ford; come, Mistress Ford.   55
Quick. Marry, this is the short and the long of it; you have
brought her into such a canaries as 'tis wonderful.
The best courtier of them all, when the court lay at
Windsor, could never have brought her to such a
canary. Yet there has been knights, and lords, and   60
gentlemen, with their coaches—I warrant you,
coach after coach, letter after letter, gift after gift—
smelling so sweetly, all musk, and so rushling, I
warrant you, in silk and gold, and in such alligant
terms, and in such wine and sugar of the best and the   65
fairest, that would have won any woman's heart;
and, I warrant you, they could never get an eye-
wink of her; I had myself twenty angels given me
this morning; but I defy all angels—in any such sort,
as they say—but in the way of honesty; and, I war-   70
rant you, they could never get her so much as sip on
a cup with the proudest of them all, and yet there
has been earls, nay, which is more, pensioners, but,
I warrant you, all is one with her.

---

65. in such wine] *F;* such wine *Hanmer.*   69. this] *F;* of a *Collier².*

---

57. *canaries*] Presumably, quandary
(Steevens, 1778). Quickly perhaps
associates such a state of confusion
either with the dance called a canary
or with canary wine (see III. ii. 81–3
and notes).
58–9. *when the court lay at Windsor*]
The phrase may be no more than an
attempt to add local colour. The notes
of Hart and *New Cambridge*, e.g., see
difficulty or topical reference when
probably none exists.
60. *has*] Quickly is always likely to
be muddled, but this use of the 'quasi-
singular' before the plural subject is
normal (Abbott 335).
63. *rushling*] Quickly's version of
'rustling', perhaps by conflation with
rushes moving in the wind.

64. *alligant*] An attempt at either
'elegant' or 'eloquent'.
69. *defy*] deny, reject.
angels] gold coins. See I. iii. 50 and
note.
73. *pensioners*] gentlemen of the royal
bodyguard within the palace, noted
for their colourful uniforms (cf. *MND.*,
II. i. 8–11)—but of course they would
not be superior to earls. There were
also royal 'pensioners', 'Knights of
Windsor', who in return for £18 per
annum and clothes were required to
attend the Chapel twice a day and
pray for the monarch (see a note in
McKerrow's edition of Nashe, III.
348). If perchance Quickly is thinking of them, she is even more confused.

Fal. But what says she to me? Be brief, my good she-   75
    Mercury.

Quick. Marry, she hath received your letter; for the
    which she thanks you a thousand times; and she
    gives you to notify that her husband will be absence
    from his house between ten and eleven.   80

Fal. Ten and eleven.

Quick. Ay, forsooth; and then you may come and see the
    picture, she says, that you wot of; Master Ford, her
    husband, will be from home. Alas, the sweet woman
    leads an ill life with him: he's a very jealousy man;   85
    she leads a very frampold life with him, good heart.

Fal. Ten and eleven. Woman, commend me to her; I
    will not fail her.

Quick. Why, you say well. But I have another messenger
    to your worship: Mistress Page hath her hearty   90
    commendations to you too; and let me tell you in
    your ear, she's as fartuous a civil modest wife, and
    one, I tell you, that will not miss you morning nor
    evening prayer, as any is in Windsor, whoe'er be the
    other; and she bade me tell your worship that her   95
    husband is seldom from home, but she hopes there
    will come a time. I never knew a woman so dote
    upon a man; surely, I think you have charms, la;
    yes, in truth.

Fal. Not I, I assure thee; setting the attraction of my   100
    good parts aside, I have no other charms.

Quick. Blessing on your heart for 't!

Fal. But I pray thee tell me this: has Ford's wife and

75–6. *she-Mercury*] Mercury (Hermes) was the messenger of the gods.

79. *gives you to notify*] Perhaps further confusion, between 'notifies' and 'gives you notice'; but 'notify' could mean 'take note of' or 'observe' (*O.E.D.* 1).

83. *wot*] know—a (false) new formation from the preterite of 'wit'. Not archaic then, and used often by Shakespeare.

86. *frampold*] disagreeable because of his ill-temper, peevish. The deriva-

tion is unknown but Wright (under 'frampald') records forms of the word in many dialects.

92. *fartuous*] Quickly's unfortunate version of 'virtuous'.

93. *miss you*] Another example of the 'ethic dative' (Abbott 220).

98, 101. *charms*] enchantments—meaning magic charms.

101. *parts*] qualities (and often used also for appearance, good looks).

102. *Blessing . . . for 't*] i.e. God's blessing (Tilley G266).

Page's wife acquainted each other how they love
        me?   105
Quick. That were a jest indeed! They have not so little
        grace, I hope; that were a trick indeed! But
        Mistress Page would desire you to send her your
        little page, of all loves: her husband has a mar-
        vellous infection to the little page; and, truly,   110
        Master Page is an honest man. Never a wife in
        Windsor leads a better life than she does; do what
        she will, say what she will, take all, pay all, go to
        bed when she list, rise when she list, all is as she will;
        and, truly, she deserves it; for if there be a kind   115
        woman in Windsor, she is one. You must send her
        your page, no remedy.
Fal. Why, I will.
Quick. Nay, but do so, then, and, look you, he may
        come and go between you both; and in any case   120
        have a nay-word, that you may know one another's
        mind, and the boy never need to understand any-
        thing; for 'tis not good that children should know
        any wickedness: old folks, you know, have discre-
        tion, as they say, and know the world.   125
Fal. Fare thee well; commend me to them both. There's
        my purse; I am yet thy debtor. Boy, go along with
        this woman. [*Exeunt Mistress Quickly and Robin.*] This
        news distracts me.
Pist. This punk is one of Cupid's carriers.   130

---

128. S.D.] *As Rowe (after 'distracts me'); not in F.*   130. *Pist.*] F; *Pist.* [*aside*]
Kittredge.   punk] F (Puncke); pink *Warburton.*

---

109. *of all loves*] The nearest equivalent is 'for love's sake' but the
Elizabethan phrase is more emphatic.
Hermia uses it in *MND.*, II. ii. 154,
when calling in alarm to Lysander
whom she had thought to be near her:
'Speak, of all loves! I swoon almost
with fear'.

110. *infection to*] Quickly's attempt at
'affection for' or 'attraction to'.

113. *take all, pay all*] Another ready-
made phrase (Tilley A203).

117. *no remedy*] A common phrase, of

the same meaning as the modern 'it
can't be helped'.

121. *nay-word*] password (as also in
v. ii. 5).

130–2.] There is no corresponding
speech in Q; and Hart and *New
Cambridge* regard the lines as an addition or afterthought, to make a connection with *H5*, where Pistol is
married to Quickly. *New Cambridge*
has to add, however, that 'Pistol
would hardly call his future wife a
"punk" '—and therefore accepts the

Clap on more sails, pursue; up with your fights;
Give fire; she is my prize, or ocean whelm them all!
                                                    [*Exit.*]

Fal. Say'st thou so, old Jack? Go thy ways; I'll make
more of thy old body than I have done. Will they
yet look after thee? Wilt thou, after the expense of   135
so much money, be now a gainer? Good body, I
thank thee. Let them say 'tis grossly done; so it be
fairly done, no matter.

Enter BARDOLPH.

Bard. Sir John, there's one Master Brook below would
fain speak with you, and be acquainted with you;   140
and hath sent your worship a morning's draught of
sack.

Fal. Brook is his name?

Bard. Ay, sir.

Fal. Call him in. [*Exit Bardolph.*] Such Brooks are   145
welcome to me, that o'erflows such liquor. Ah, ha,
Mistress Ford and Mistress Page, have I encompassed you? Go to; via!

---

132. *Exit*] *Rowe; not in F.*   138. S.D.] *Q; not in F.*   145. S.D.] *Theobald; not in F.*   146. o'erflows] *F;* o'erflow with *Pope;* o'er-flow *Capell.*

emendation 'pink'. There need be no connection with *H5* at all; and the Pistol of *H4* was quite capable of chasing any punk.

130. *punk*] Walter Whiter pointed out (p. 224) that women (good or bad)—sailing ships formed a Shakespearian image-link, as in *Troil.*, I. i. 103–7 and three passages in *Rom.* This neither supports nor rules out the emendation: 'pink', if accepted, would be the word used for a small sailing ship.

carriers] go-betweens.

131. *fights*] protective screens used on warships going into battle.

132. *whelm*] overturn, or submerge (*O.E.D. v.* 2, 4).

133. *Say'st thou so?*] Falstaff is ruminating, not commenting on Pistol's words, to which he pays no attention.

Go thy ways] See l. 42 and note.

133–4. *make more of*] think more highly of.

145–6. *Such Brooks . . . liquor*] These lines afford evidence that when Shakespeare wrote the play Ford's pseudonym was 'Brook'; 'Such Broomes . . .' is meaningless.

146. *o'erflows*] The third person plural in -s (Abbot 333).

147–8. *encompassed*] Explained by *O.E.D.* (*v.* 5), citing only this line, as 'got round' (which is plausible); by Schmidt as 'come by' (comparing 'compass' in such uses as 'Things out of hope are compass'd oft with venturing', *Ven.*, 567; cf. also *Gent.*, II. iv. 214).

148. *Go to*] Normally an exclamation of impatience and therefore perhaps means here 'hurry up! on with it!'.

via] An exclamation of encourage-

Enter [BARDOLPH, *and*] FORD *in disguise.*

Ford. Bless you, sir.

Fal. And you, sir. Would you speak with me?   150

Ford. I make bold to press with so little preparation
    upon you.

Fal. You're welcome. What's your will?—Give us
    leave, drawer.   [*Exit Bardolph.*]

Ford. Sir, I am a gentleman that have spent much; my   155
    name is Brook.

Fal. Good Master Brook, I desire more acquaintance
    of you.

Ford. Good Sir John, I sue for yours: not to charge you,
    for I must let you understand I think myself in   160
    better plight for a lender than you are—the which
    hath something emboldened me to this unseasoned
    intrusion; for they say, if money go before, all ways
    do lie open.

Fal. Money is a good soldier, sir, and will on.   165

Ford. Troth, and I have a bag of money here troubles
    me; if you will help to bear it, Sir John, take all, or
    half, for easing me of the carriage.

Fal. Sir, I know not how I may deserve to be your
    porter.   170

Ford. I will tell you, sir, if you will give me the hearing.

Fal. Speak, good Master Brook, I shall be glad to be
    your servant.

Ford. Sir, I hear you are a scholar—I will be brief with
    you—and you have been a man long known to me,   175
    though I had never so good means as desire to make
    myself acquainted with you. I shall discover a thing
    to you, wherein I must very much lay open mine

---

148. S.D.] *As Theobald; not in F; Enter* Foord *disguised like* Brooke. *Q.*   154. S.D.]
Theobald; not in F.   167–8. all, or half,] *F;* half, or all, *Collier²*.

ment (from the Italian but used as
'French' by the Dauphin in *H5*, IV. ii.
4). Cf. *3H6*, II. i. 182.

153–4. *Give us leave*] please leave us to
ourselves.

159. *charge*] put a load upon, and so,
figuratively, put to expense.

162. *unseasoned*] unseasonable.

163–4. *if money . . . open*] As Ford
indicates, a popular maxim (Tilley
M1050).

174. *scholar*] See I. iii. 2 note.

177. *discover*] reveal (a normal
Elizabethan meaning).

K

own imperfection; but, good Sir John, as you have
one eye upon my follies, as you hear them unfolded,   180
turn another into the register of your own, that I
may pass with a reproof the easier, sith you yourself
know how easy it is to be such an offender.

Fal. Very well, sir; proceed.

Ford. There is a gentlewoman in this town—her hus-   185
band's name is Ford.

Fal. Well, sir.

Ford. I have long loved her and, I protest to you, bestowed much on her; followed her with a doting
observance; engrossed opportunities to meet her;   190
fee'd every slight occasion that could but niggardly
give me sight of her; not only bought many presents
to give her, but have given largely to many to know
what she would have given: briefly, I have pursued
her as love hath pursued me; which hath been on   195
the wing of all occasions. But whatsoever I have
merited, either in my mind or in my means, meed
I am sure I have received none, unless experience
be a jewel, that I have purchased at an infinite rate
and that hath taught me to say this: 200

Love like a shadow flies when substance love pursues;
Pursuing that that flies, and flying what pursues.

199. jewel, that] *F1;* Jewel that *F4;* Jewel *Rowe;* jewel. That *New Camb.*

181. *register*] In the sense (still
familiar) of catalogue. Ford is perhaps
adapting the proverb 'He that speaks
ill of another let him first think of himself' (Tilley I27).

182. *sith*] since (OE *siððan*). The
word was going out of use and is
probably meant to add to the quaint
formality of Ford's manner of speech
in his role as Brook.

190. *observance*] deference, dutiful
attention (as in *AYL.*, v. ii. 102, 104;
and *Troil.*, I. iii. 31).

engrossed] Probably 'collected' (as
in *Ant.*, III. vii. 37) rather than 'mono-
polized' (as explained by Onions,
comparing *Rom.*, v. iii. 115, 'engross-
ing death').

191. *fee'd*] paid for, purchased.

194. *would have given*] would wish to
be given.

197. *meed*] recompense or reward.

201–2. Love . . . pursues] The in-
verted commas preceding each of these
lines in F are a regular Elizabethan
method of drawing attention to an epigrammatic or proverbial pronouncement. (Tilley lists this proverb in the
form 'Love, like a shadow, flies one
following and pursues one fleeing'—
L518.)

201. substance] i.e. money—with,
of course, a quibble based on the wider
meaning of 'substance' in the proverbial 'shadow and substance' antithesis.

Fal. Have you received no promise of satisfaction at her
    hands?

Ford. Never.   205

Fal. Have you importuned her to such a purpose?

Ford. Never.

Fal. Of what quality was your love, then?

Ford. Like a fair house built on another man's ground,
    so that I have lost my edifice by mistaking the place   210
    where I erected it.

Fal. To what purpose have you unfolded this to me?

Ford. When I have told you that, I have told you all.
    Some say that though she appear honest to me, yet
    in other places she enlargeth her mirth so far that   215
    there is shrewd construction made of her. Now, Sir
    John, here is the heart of my purpose: you are a
    gentleman of excellent breeding, admirable dis-
    course, of great admittance, authentic in your place
    and person, generally allowed for your many war-   220
    like, court-like, and learned preparations.

Fal. O sir!

Ford. Believe it, for you know it. There is money; spend
    it, spend it, spend more; spend all I have, only give

209–11.] In law, any building erected on ground that was not one's own
property belonged to the owner of the
ground and this was recognized in the
proverb (Tilley G470) 'Who builds
upon another's ground loses both
mortar and stones'. This makes less
convincing, though it does not rule out,
Roy F. Montgomery's theory that
there is a reference here to the problem
of Burbage's Theatre, which stood on
ground the lease of which expired in
April 1597. (Later, in 1598–9, it was
surreptitiously pulled down and the
timbers used to build the Globe on the
Bankside.—*Shakespeare Quarterly*, v,
1954, 207–8.) Whiter (p. 224) found
the comparison of love to a mansion
that was (but was not necessarily
thought to be) in danger of destruction
in, e.g., *Troil.*, IV. ii. 109–11; *Rom.*,

III. ii. 26–7; and *Gent.*, v. iv. 7–12.

215. *enlargeth her mirth*] gives free
rein to her natural love of merri-
ment.

216. *shrewd*] malicious (a frequent
Shakespearian use).

219. *admittance*] Almost equivalent
to 'admissibility' (*O.E.D.* 2): Falstaff
is readily admitted to the best of
homes.

authentic] entitled to respect (*O.E.D.*
1).

220. *generally allowed*] universally
accepted or approved.

221. *preparations*] Presumably a
stilted use of the word to mean equipment, in the sense of natural endow-
ments, or, as *O.E.D.* suggests (*sb.* 4), 'a
personal capacity gained by previous
instruction or training; an accomplish-
ment'.

me so much of your time in exchange of it as to lay   225
an amiable siege to the honesty of this Ford's wife.
Use your art of wooing; win her to consent to you;
if any man may, you may as soon as any.

Fal. Would it apply well to the vehemency of your
affection that I should win what you would enjoy?   230
Methinks you prescribe to yourself very pre-
posterously.

Ford. O, understand my drift: she dwells so securely on
the excellency of her honour that the folly of my
soul dares not present itself; she is too bright to be   235
looked against. Now, could I come to her with any
detection in my hand, my desires had instance and
argument to commend themselves; I could drive
her then from the ward of her purity, her reputation, her marriage-vow, and a thousand other her   240
defences which now are too too strongly embattled
against me. What say you to 't, Sir John?

Fal. Master Brook, I will first make bold with your
money; next, give me your hand; and last, as I am a
gentleman, you shall, if you will, enjoy Ford's wife.   245

Ford. O good sir!

Fal. I say you shall.

Ford. Want no money, Sir John; you shall want none.

Fal. Want no Mistress Ford, Master Brook; you shall
want none. I shall be with her, I may tell you, by   250
her own appointment; even as you came in to me,
her assistant, or go-between, parted from me: I say

225. exchange] *F* (enchange).   235. soul] *F; suit Collier²*.   252. assistant] *F;*
spokes mate *Q.*

226. *amiable*] of love, amorous.
229. *apply well to*] be consistent with.
233. *dwells so securely*] relies so confidently (but again in 'securely' there is the suggestion of false confidence; cf. II. i. 222).
234. *folly*] wantonness—as often in Shakespeare; cf. III. ii. 31.
236. *looked against*] looked at or into—as one is unable to look directly at the sun.

237. *had*] would have (a subjunctive).
instance] evidence.
239. *ward*] Generally explained as 'posture of defence in fencing' but is also often used of a fortress or stronghold, or parts of them.
240. *other her*] An example of the transposition of the unemphatic possessive pronoun (Abbott 13).
241. *too too*] The repetition lends emphasis; cf. *Ham.*, I. ii. 129.

I shall be with her between ten and eleven; for at
that time the jealous rascally knave her husband
will be forth. Come you to me at night, you shall   255
know how I speed.

Ford. I am blest in your acquaintance. Do you know
Ford, sir?

Fal. Hang him, poor cuckoldly knave, I know him not.
Yet I wrong him to call him poor: they say the   260
jealous wittolly knave hath masses of money, for the
which his wife seems to me well-favoured. I will use
her as the key of the cuckoldly rogue's coffer, and
there's my harvest-home.

Ford. I would you knew Ford, sir, that you might avoid   265
him if you saw him.

Fal. Hang him, mechanical salt-butter rogue! I will
stare him out of his wits; I will awe him with my
cudgel: it shall hang like a meteor o'er the cuckold's
horns. Master Brook, thou shalt know I will pre-   270
dominate over the peasant, and thou shalt lie with
his wife. Come to me soon at night. Ford's a knave,
and I will aggravate his style; thou, Master Brook,

---

259. cuckoldly] *F;* cuckally *Q1;* cuckoldy *Q3.*   263. cuckoldly] *F1;* cuckally
Q; Cuckold- *F2.*

---

255. *at night*] A natural enough instruction, which would not be worthy
of comment except that it again gives
ammunition to those who postulate
'revision', since Brook in fact returns
the following morning.

256. *speed*] fare.

261. *wittolly*] The adjective—not
used elsewhere by Shakespeare—is
formed from 'wittol', a husband who
is complaisant about being cuckolded
(and it too is found in Shakespeare
only in this scene, l. 288).

262. *well-favoured*] good-looking,
and so, more generally, attractive.

264. *harvest-home*] A splendid image:
the festival to celebrate the bringing
home of the corn.

267. *mechanical*] vulgar—a secondary
or derived meaning from the original
one of 'engaged in manual or other

inferior labour' (as Bottom and his
friends in *MND.,* III. ii. 9–10, are to
Puck 'rude mechanicals, / That work
for bread upon Athenian stalls').

salt-butter] The best explanation is
Hart's: salt-butter, particularly that
imported from Flanders, was considered inferior and would be eaten
only if one could afford no better. He
quotes from Nashe's *Pierce Penniless*
(1592) a contemptuous reference to
one who pretends to social standing
though in fact living all year with only
'salt butter and Holland cheese in his
chamber'.

268. *stare*] For a possible second
meaning, see note on v. v. 160.

273. *aggravate his style*] 'Aggravate'
had both its modern meaning of 'make
worse' and that of 'increase' ('to aggravate thy store' in *Sonn.,* cxlvi. 10). Fal-

shalt know him for knave and cuckold. Come to me
soon at night.   *Exit.*   275
Ford. What a damned Epicurean rascal is this? My
heart is ready to crack with impatience. Who says
this is improvident jealousy? My wife hath sent to
him, the hour is fixed, the match is made. Would
any man have thought this? See the hell of having   280
a false woman: my bed shall be abused, my coffers
ransacked, my reputation gnawn at, and I shall not
only receive this villainous wrong, but stand under
the adoption of abominable terms, and by him that
does me this wrong. Terms! Names! Amaimon   285
sounds well; Lucifer, well; Barbason, well: yet they
are devils' additions, the names of fiends. But
cuckold? Wittol? Cuckold! The devil himself hath
not such a name. Page is an ass, a secure ass: he will
trust his wife, he will not be jealous. I will rather   290
trust a Fleming with my butter, Parson Hugh the
Welshman with my cheese, an Irishman with my
aqua-vitæ bottle, or a thief to walk my ambling

275. S.D.] *Q; not in F.*   285. this] *F;* the *Rowe².*   288. cuckold? Wittol?
Cuckold!] *This ed.;* Cuckold, Wittoll, Cuckold? *F;* Cuckold, Wittol-Cuckold!
Rowe¹; Cuckold, Wittol, Cuckold! *Rowe³.*

staff probably means both, and is
thinking of the horns which he will
add to Ford's attainments or title.

276. *Epicurean*] pleasure-loving, and
so, sensual.

283. *stand under*] run the risk of, or
have to submit to.

284. *the adoption of*] being 'christened'
with (*O.E.D.* 'adopt' 7).

abominable] exciting disgust (probably a stronger adjective then).

285–6. *Amaimon . . . Lucifer . . .
Barbason*] All these 'additions' or
names of devils are recorded elsewhere, the first two, notably, in *1H4*,
II. iv. 370–3 (where Falstaff is ridiculing Glendower) and the third in *H5*,
II. i. 57–8 (where Nym defies Pistol:
'I am not Barbason; you cannot conjure me'). J. H. Walter has suggested,
however, that 'Barbason' may be
Shakespeare's conflation of the demon

Barbas with the French knight Barbason whom he had read about in
Holinshed.

288. *Wittol*] See note on l. 261.

290–1. *I will . . . butter*] As in l. 267,
the reference derives from the scorn
directed at those who live on a weak
diet of butter (instead of meat), in the
alleged manner of the inhabitants of
the Low Countries.

292. *Welshman . . . cheese*] The
Welshman's proverbial fondness for
cheese is ridiculed also at I. ii. 11–12
and v. v. 82–3.

293. *aqua-vitæ*] Lit. water of life and
since 1547, at the latest, commonly
applied to strong spirits. The Irish
were said to be too fond of these—
particularly of their own whisky,
usquebaugh (the name of which also
means 'water of life').

293–4. *ambling gelding*] Properly

gelding, than my wife with herself. Then she plots,
then she ruminates, then she devises; and what   295
they think in their hearts they may effect, they will
break their hearts but they will effect. Heaven be
praised for my jealousy!—Eleven o'clock the hour:
I will prevent this, detect my wife, be revenged on
Falstaff, and laugh at Page. I will about it; better   300
three hours too soon than a minute too late. Fie,
fie, fie; cuckold, cuckold, cuckold!   *Exit.*

SCENE III

Enter CAIUS *and* RUGBY.

Caius. Jack Rugby!
Rug. Sir?
Caius. Vat is the clock, Jack?
Rug. 'Tis past the hour, sir, that Sir Hugh promised to
    meet.   5
Caius. By gar, he has save his soul, dat he is no come; he
    has pray his Pible well, dat he is no come; by gar,
    Jack Rugby, he is dead already, if he be come.
Rug. He is wise, sir: he knew your worship would kill him
    if he came.   10
Caius. By gar, de herring is no dead so as I vill kill him.

297. Heaven] *F;* God *Q.*

Scene III

SCENE III] *F;* Scene XI. *Windsor-Park. Pope; Scene III. Field near Windsor. Knight.*
S.D.] *Rowe (as Q); Enter Caius, Rugby, Page, Shallow, Slender, Host. F.*   11. is . . .
him] *F;* be not so dead as I shall make him *Q.*

a gelding with a comfortable trot
or canter but it seems to have become the standard term for a riding
horse.
  298. *Eleven . . . hour*] Ford is not, of
course, stating the time, but saying
over to himself the (approximate) time
of Falstaff's appointment with Mistress
Ford—nor is his 'better *three* hours too

soon' a statement of how early he
intends to be.
  300–1. *better . . . late*] Proverbial
(Tilley H745).

Scene III

  11. *no dead so as*] not as dead as he
will be when. 'Dead as a herring' was
a stock phrase even then (Tilley H446).

Take your rapier, Jack; I vill tell you how I vill kill
him.

Rug. Alas, sir, I cannot fence.

Caius. Villainy, take your rapier.   15

Rug. Forbear; here's company.

Enter HOST, SHALLOW, SLENDER, *and* PAGE.

Host. Bless thee, bully Doctor.

Shal. Save you, Master Doctor Caius.

Page. Now, good Master Doctor.

Slen. Give you good morrow, sir.   20

Caius. Vat be all you, one, two, tree, four, come for?

Host. To see thee fight, to see thee foin, to see thee
traverse, to see thee here, to see thee there, to see
thee pass thy punto, thy stock, thy reverse, thy
distance, thy montant. Is he dead, my Ethiopian?   25
Is he dead, my Francisco? Ha, bully? What says my
Æsculapius? My Galen? My heart of elder? Ha, is
he dead, bully stale? Is he dead?

15. Villainy] *F;* Villan-a *Johnson;* Villain *Dyce*². 16. S.D.] *Q; not in F.* 24.
punto] *Q;* puncto *F.* 26. Francisco] *F;* francoyes *Q.* 27. Galen] *Rowe;*
Galien *F;* gallon *Q1; Gallen Q3.* 28. bully stale] *F* (bully-Stale); bullies taile *Q.*

15. *villainy*] Caius' form of 'villain',
as at I. iv. 62.

22. *foin*] lunge—often used of the
tactical pass that keeps the opponent
at a distance (as probably in *Lr.*, IV. vi.
251) rather than of a home thrust (as
Quickly probably misuses it in *2H4*,
II. i. 17). Doll no doubt gives it a
second meaning in *2H4*, II. iv. 252.

23. *traverse*] Another fencing and
also military term, of movement from
side to side.

24. *punto*] direct thrust. F's 'puncto'
is not necessarily wrong, but 'punto'
seems to be the normal form and is
used e.g. in the 'good Quarto', Q2, of
Rom., II. iv. 27. The Host is ridiculing
Caius' knowledge of the technical
jargon of fencing much as Mercutio
ridicules Tybalt's. Similarly it is the
pretentious Bobadill who knows all the
terms in Jonson's *Every Man in His
Humour*: 'your *Punto*, your *Reuerso*,

your *Stoccata*, your *Imbroccata*, your
Passada, your *Montanto*' (IV. vii. 77–9).

stock] Anglicized form and abbreviation of *astoccata* or *stoccado*. Cf.
II. i. 214–15 and note.

reverse] The 'punto reverso' of *Rom.*,
II. iv. 27—a back-handed stroke.

25. *distance*] (knowledge of) the
correct distance from one's opponent.
montant] upward thrust ('montanto').

Ethiopian] blackamoor, as in Jeremiah, 13:23. Caius is apparently dark,
or black-bearded, as Frenchmen are
sometimes alleged to be today.

26. *Francisco*] That the reporter of
Q took this to mean 'Frenchman', as
it probably does, is shown by Q's
'francoyes'.

27. *Æsculapius*] The god of medicine,
under his Roman name.

Galen] The famous Greek physician
of the second century A.D.

heart of elder] 'Heart of oak' would

Caius. By gar, he is de coward Jack priest of de vorld; he
  is not show his face.   30

Host. Thou art a Castalian-king-Urinal: Hector of
  Greece, my boy!

Caius. I pray you bear witness that me have stay six or
  seven, two, tree hours for him, and he is no come.

Shal. He is the wiser man, Master Doctor: he is a curer   35
  of souls, and you a curer of bodies; if you should
  fight, you go against the hair of your professions. Is
  it not true, Master Page?

Page. Master Shallow, you have yourself been a great
  fighter, though now a man of peace.   40

---

31. Castalian-king-Urinal:] *F* (Castalion-king-Vrinall:) *;* castallian king vrinall.
Q; Cardalion, king Urinal, Hanmer; Castillian, king urinal; *Capell;* Castilian king,
Urinal! *Steevens*[2], *conj. Farmer;* Castilian king-Urinal *Hudson;* Castilian King
Urinal *Sisson.*   34. two, tree] *F* (two tree).

---

be a compliment to a man's bravery;
'heart of elder' is just the opposite, for
the elder is a low tree, the wood of
which is often spongy, and it had other
derogatory implications as 'Judas'
tree', the one on which he hanged himself. The Host takes the justifiable risk
of assuming that Caius will not follow
this inflated and allusive language.

28. *bully stale*] In effect, this is the
Host's equivalent of 'Master Doctor'.
For 'bully' see note on I. iii. 2; 'stale' is
probably used in the sense of 'urine'
(*O.E.D. sb.*[5]) and is a reference to the
practice of diagnosing by analysing it
(cf. *2H4,* I. ii. 1–6). Conceivably,
however, there is a quibble on other
meanings of 'stale'—e.g. stuffed bird
used as a decoy or a dupe (*O.E.D. sb.*[3]
1, 5) or laughing stock (cf. Nashe's jibe
at those who become 'the scoffe of a
Scholler and the stale of a Courtier',
I. 35). Q's amusing reading 'bullies
taile' is significant as showing that the
reporter or his scribe wrote down what
he *heard.*

29. *Jack priest*] Used before at I. iv.
112; see note on I. iv. 102 and cf. l. 59
below.

31–2.] The Host becomes ever more

grandiloquent, and impossible to paraphrase. The image of 'stale' (l. 28) is
carried on in 'urinal', but it is by no
means certain which words have the
function of nouns and which of adjectives, as the collations show. If the
Host says 'king-urinal' (i.e. king of
urinals), then his 'Castalian' (for
'Castilian') is a pejorative adjective
natural in the days of the feared
Spanish invasion; if he says 'Castalian-
king urinal', then it would mean the
urinal used by the hated Philip II of
Castile. And it is quite possible that the
three words form a compound adjective qualifying 'Hector of Greece' in,
of course, the most ironic way. Hart's
argument for reading 'Castalian' (F
'Castalion') rather than 'Castilian' is
sound: there may well be, as he suggests, a further atrocious quibble on
the water from the Castalian spring.
(Hanmer's explanation that the Host
meant to say 'Cœur de lion' is unconvincing.)

37. *against the hair*] i.e. against the
proper function—a proverbial image
(Tilley H18) from rubbing an animal's
fur the wrong way. Cf. also 'against the
grain'.

Shal. Bodykins, Master Page, though I now be old, and
of the Peace, if I see a sword out, my finger itches to
make one. Though we are justices, and doctors, and
churchmen, Master Page, we have some salt of our
youth in us; we are the sons of women, Master Page.   45
Page. 'Tis true, Master Shallow.
Shal. It will be found so, Master Page. Master Doctor
Caius, I am come to fetch you home. I am sworn of
the Peace; you have showed yourself a wise physi-
cian, and Sir Hugh hath shown himself a wise and   50
patient churchman; you must go with me, Master
Doctor.
Host. Pardon, guest Justice.—A word, Mounseur Mock-
water.
Caius. Mock-vater? Vat is dat?   55
Host. Mock-water, in our English tongue, is valour,
bully.
Caius. By gar, then, I have as much mock-vater as de
Englishman. Scurvy Jack-dog priest! By gar, me
vill cut his ears.   60
Host. He will clapper-claw thee tightly, bully.
Caius. Clapper-de-claw? Vat is dat?

---

53. A word] *Q;* a *Ff;* ah! *Hanmer.*   53–4. Mock-water] *F, Q;* Muck-water
Steevens[3], *conj. Farmer;* Make-water *Sisson, conj. Cartwright.*

41. *Bodykins*] by God's dear body
('bodykin' is the familiar or affectionate diminutive). Cf. 'Od's heartlings'
in III. iv. 56. Shallow's over-frequent
use of the term of address 'Master
Page' is also to be noted as giving an
undignified and even puerile tone to
his speech.
42–3. *to make one*] The modern colloquial equivalent would be 'to be in it'.
44. *salt*] strength or 'drive' (*O.E.D.
sb.*[1] 3. b).
53. *guest Justice*] The Host must
mean that Shallow, like Falstaff, is a
paying guest in his inn, the Garter; he
similarly calls Shallow 'Master guest'
in l. 69.
Mounseur] 'Mounseer' was perhaps
the common anglicized form, often

used mockingly, but the Host may be
allowed his own variation as F gives
it.
53–4. *Mock-water*] The listed emendations will show that the phrase has
caused trouble. What is clear is that
the 'stale-urinal' image is being continued, with a quibble on 'make
water'—one sign of the opposite of
valour. Whether there is some further
reference to the analysis of urine is
uncertain.
59. *Jack-dog*] a mongrel, *or* a male
dog, not castrated; see I. iv. 102 and
note.
61. *clapper-claw*] drub, thrash, as in
Troil., v. iv. 1, where it is used deri-
sively by Thersites.
tightly] soundly. Cf. I. iii. 75 and note.

Host. That is, he will make thee amends.

Caius. By gar, me do look he shall clapper-de-claw me,
    for, by gar, me vill have it.   65

Host. And I will provoke him to 't, or let him wag.

Caius. Me tank you for dat.

Host. And, moreover, bully—[*To the others, aside*] But
    first, Master guest, and Master Page, and eke
    Cavaliero Slender, go you through the town to   70
    Frogmore.

Page. Sir Hugh is there, is he?

Host. He is there. See what humour he is in; and I will
    bring the doctor about by the fields. Will it do well?

Shal. We will do it.   75

Page, Shal., and Slen. Adieu, good Master Doctor.

                        [*Exeunt Page, Shallow, and Slender.*]

Caius. By gar, me vill kill de priest, for he speak for a
    jack-an-ape to Anne Page.

Host. Let him die; sheathe thy impatience; throw cold
    water on thy choler; go about the fields with me   80
    through Frogmore, I will bring thee where Mistress
    Anne Page is, at a farm-house a-feasting; and thou
    shalt woo her. Cried game; said I well?

Caius. By gar, me dank you vor dat; by gar, I love you;
    and I shall procure-a you de good guest: de earl, de   85
    knight, de lords, de gentlemen, my patients.

---

68. S.D.] *As Capell; not in* F.   76. *Page, Shal., and Slen.*] *Malone; All.* F; *Page.
Slen. Capell.*   S.D.] *Rowe; not in* F; *Exit all but the Host and Doctor.* Q.   80–1.
go . . . Frogmore] F; com go with me / Through the fields to *Frogmore*, and Q.
83. her. Cried game;] F (her: Cride-game,) ; *hir cried game:* Q; her Cride-game;
Rowe; her. Cry'd game, *Pope;* her. Try'd Game; *Theobald;* her. Cry aim, *Warburton;* her. Cried I aim? *Halliwell, conj. Douce;* her. Cried, Game? *Keightley;*
her. Cried game? *Sisson.*

66. *wag*] Normally means 'depart',
as in I. iii. 6 and II. i. 219 and l. 90
below, but the Host probably means
here something more like 'run for his
life'.

71. *Frogmore*] Then a small village—
on the opposite side of Windsor from
where Caius has been sent for the duel.

80. *go*] i.e. if you go. Alternatively
the F comma after 'Frogmore' may be
replaced by a semi-colon.

83. *Cried game*] Q confirms the F
reading; 'cry aim'—as in III. ii. 40—is
therefore irrelevant. 'Cried game'
must be a hunting cry, equivalent to
'the hunt is up': the game has been
located and the chase is on. And Caius
assumes that Evans is the 'game', not
realizing that he himself is too. (By
1702 the phrase was apparently no
longer current: Dennis omits it from
his version of the play.)

Host. For the which I will be thy adversary toward Anne
    Page. Said I well?
Caius. By gar, 'tis good; vell said.
Host. Let us wag, then.   90
Caius. Come at my heels, Jack Rugby.   *Exeunt.*

87. *adversary*] Caius, again misled, thinks that the word means something like 'advocate', instead of the opposite. (Q confirms the reading.)

ACT III

SCENE I

Enter EVANS *and* SIMPLE.

Evans. I pray you now, good Master Slender's servingman, and friend Simple by your name, which way
have you looked for Master Caius, that calls himself
Doctor of Physic?

Sim. Marry, sir, the Pitty-ward, the Park-ward, every   5
way; Old Windsor way, and every way but the town
way.

Evans. I most fehemently desire you you will also look
that way.

Sim. I will, sir.   [*Going aside.*]   10

Evans. Pless my soul, how full of chollors I am, and
trempling of mind: I shall be glad if he have de-

ACT III

Scene 1

ACT III SCENE 1] *F;* Act III. Scene 1. Frogmore *near* Windsor. *Pope; Act III.*
Scene I. Fields near Frogmore. *Capell.*   S.D.] *Q; Enter Euans, Simple, Page,*
Shallow, Slender, Host, Caius, Rugby. F.   5. Pitty-ward] *Dyce;* pittie-ward *F1;*
pitty-wary *F2;* pitty-way *conj. Mason;* city-ward *Capell;* petty-ward *Collier1;*
pit-way *Collier2;* Petty-ward *Halliwell.*   Park-ward] *F;* park-way *Collier2.*
10. S.D.] *This ed.; not in F;* Retiring / *Collier;* Exit / *Camb.*

---

5. *the Pitty-ward*] Emendations vary
from 'Petty-ward' (meaning towards
Windsor Little or 'Petty' Park) to
'Pity-ward' (meaning towards the
pietà and so the church of the Blessed
Virgin in Windsor) to 'pit-ward'
(meaning towards the saw-pit mentioned in v. iii. 13). The first is the most
plausible, but emendation may be
unnecessary: F's 'pittie' may be an
alternative spelling of 'petty' (from
French *petit*) and may indicate the
common pronunciation.

the Park-ward] in the direction of
Windsor Great Park.

6. *Old Windsor way*] in the direction
of Old Windsor, two or three miles
from the Windsor of Shakespeare's
day and ours.

11. *chollors*] i.e. choler or bile, which
was supposed to cause quick temper (so
Fluellen is 'valiant, / And, touch'd with
choler, hot as gunpowder', *H5*, iv. vii.
187–8)—but Evans, as usual, seems to
be confused and to mean 'sadness' or
'agitation'.

69

ceived me. How melancholies I am! I will knog his
urinals about his knave's costard when I have good
opportunities for the 'ork. Pless my soul!   15
[*Singing*]   To shallow rivers, to whose falls
              Melodious birds sings madrigals;
              There will we make our peds of roses,
              And a thousand fragrant posies.
              To shallow—   20
Mercy on me! I have a great dispositions to cry.—
[*Singing*]   Melodious birds sing madrigals—
              Whenas I sat in Pabylon—
              And a thousand vagram posies.
              To shallow, etc.   25
Sim. Yonder he is coming, this way, Sir Hugh.

16, 22, 28. *Singing*] As Pope (*Sings, being afraid—in l. 16*); *not in* F.   16–25, 28.]
Verse as Pope; italicized but continuous in F.   26. *Sim.*] F; *Sim.* [*Coming forward*]
Collier; Enter Simple. Sim. Camb.

13. *knog*] knock, rather than knot,
but perhaps both.
14. *urinals*] Evans may have confused with the name of the glass vessel
used in the medical examination of
urine the associated word 'testicles'.
His phrase is repeated at l. 81 (where
Q has 'knock').
costard] The name of a large apple,
applied in derision to the head (cf. the
modern colloquial 'nut').
16–25.] To keep up his spirits, Evans
sings snatches of Marlowe's famous
lyric, 'Come live with me and be my
love', which was probably sung to an
old tune (perhaps the one later printed
in William Corkine's *Second Book of
Airs*, 1612). Although the words were
not published until 1599, they presumably became popular, with the
music, during Marlowe's lifetime;
Chapman seems to take knowledge of
them for granted when he has a variation on them in *The Blind Beggar of
Alexandria* (1596), ix. 24ff. There are
variant texts, but a standard version of
the relevant lines (from stanzas 2 and
3) is: 'And we will sit upon the rocks, /
Seeing the shepherds feed their flocks /
By shallow rivers to whose falls /

Melodious birds sing madrigals. // And
I will make thee beds of roses, / And a
thousand fragrant posies'. Mixed with
Marlowe, however, is the first line of a
metrical version of Psalm 137 (better
known in the form 'By the rivers of
Babylon, there we sat down, yea, we
wept, when we remembered Zion').
The link in Evans's mind may be sadness (many madrigals were sad), the
rivers, and even trees, for the next
verse of the Psalm is 'We hanged our
harps upon the willows in the midst
thereof'. Peter J. Seng (*The Vocal Songs
in the Plays of Shakespeare*, Cambridge,
Mass., 1967, p. 164) asks whether
Evans may not have sung Marlowe's
words to the tune of the psalm, but in
Q the words mixed up with Marlowe's
lines are 'There dwelt a man in
Babylon'—words from an old ballad
that is similarly begun by Sir Toby in
Tw.N., II. iii. 84. The Q reporter remembered both that the parson was
giving himself away by singing an
'indelicate' love lyric and that the lyric
was confused with another song, but
he apparently had no recollection of
any psalm tune.
26. *he*] i.e., presumably, Caius

Evans. He's welcome.—

    [*Singing*]   To shallow rivers, to whose falls—

    Heaven prosper the right!—What weapons is he?

Sim. No weapons, sir. There comes my master, Master   30
    Shallow, and another gentleman; from Frogmore,
    over the stile, this way.

Evans. Pray you, give me my gown, or else keep it in your
    arms.

        Enter PAGE, SHALLOW, *and* SLENDER.

Shal. How now, Master Parson? Good morrow, good   35
    Sir Hugh. Keep a gamester from the dice, and a good
    student from his book, and it is wonderful.

Slen. Ah, sweet Anne Page!

Page. Save you, good Sir Hugh.

Evans. Pless you from His mercy sake, all of you.   40

Shal. What, the sword and the word? Do you study them
    both, Master Parson?

Page. And youthful still, in your doublet and hose this
    raw rheumatic day?

Evans. There is reasons and causes for it.   45

Page. We are come to you to do a good office, Master
    Parson.

Evans. Fery well: what is it?

Page. Yonder is a most reverend gentleman, who, belike

---

34. S.D.] *Q; not in F1; Enter All.* F2.   38, 66, 105.] *Marked 'Aside' Camb.*   41–
2.] *Prose as Pope;* What? . . . Word? / Doe . . . *F.*   49. who, belike] *F* (who (belike)).

coming with Rugby and the Host from 'the fields' on the roundabout way to Frogmore, as planned in II. iii. 73–4 and 80–1, although the first to enter are Page, Shallow, and Slender, coming from 'the town' and Frogmore (II. iii. 70–1).

37. *book*] Apparently Evans is reading a book as he waits, and Shallow (see l. 41 and note) assumes that it is the Bible; but conceivably, as *New Cambridge* suggests, it is the book from which Evans was quoting or singing the Marlowe. Shallow is adapting some such proverb as

Tilley's F351, 'Keep flax from fire and youth from gaming'.

40. *from His mercy sake*] Evans is probably thinking of Psalms 6:4 ('Oh save me for thy mercies' sake') but again has his constructions mixed. (Q reads 'God plesse you all from his mercies sake' and perhaps Shakespeare did write 'God . . .', but the phrase is clear enough without the additional word.)

41. *the word*] Shallow means 'the word of God' (see note on l. 37) but specific allusion to Ephesians 6:17 seems improbable.

having received wrong by some person, is at most   50
odds with his own gravity and patience that ever you
saw.

Shal. I have lived fourscore years and upward; I never
heard a man of his place, gravity, and learning so
wide of his own respect.   55

Evans. What is he?

Page. I think you know him: Master Doctor Caius, the
renowned French physician.

Evans. Got's will and His passion of my heart, I had as
lief you would tell me of a mess of porridge.   60

Page. Why?

Evans. He has no more knowledge in Hibocrates and
Galen, and he is a knave besides: a cowardly knave
as you would desires to be acquainted withal.

Page. I warrant you, he's the man should fight with him.   65

Slen. O sweet Anne Page!

Shal. It appears so by his weapons. Keep them asunder;
here comes Doctor Caius.

Enter HOST, CAIUS [*and* RUGBY].

Page. Nay, good Master Parson, keep in your weapon.

Shal. So do you, good Master Doctor.   70

Host. Disarm them, and let them question; let them keep
their limbs whole, and hack our English.

59. His passion] *F; his—*Passion *Staunton.*   68. S.D.] *Rowe (after l. 66); not in F1;
Enter Doctor and the Host, they offer to fight.* Q *(after l. 66); Enter Caius.* F2 *(after l. 66).*
71–2.] *F; Host.* Disarme, let them question. / *Shal.* Let them keep their limbs
hole, and hack our English. *Q.*

53. *fourscore*] Some commentators
gravely point out that this would make
Shallow some twenty years older than
he 'was' in *2H4*—if the figure is meant
to be exact.

55. *wide of his own respect*] Generally
explained as 'far from' or even 'in-
different to' his own 'reputation'—
but may rather mean 'different
from his normal, true, quality or nature'.

60. *mess of porridge*] Evans may have
meant to refer to the 'mess (dish) of
pottage' for which, as the story is told

in the Geneva Bible, Esau sold his
birthright (in any case the word
'porridge' is an altered form of 'pottage'). Sisson, *N.R.*, p. 11, saw in F's
'porredge' a dialectal form—but
Ralph Crane uses the spelling elsewhere and it probably comes from his
transcript here.

62. *Hibocrates*] Hippocrates, the
most famous physician of ancient
Greece.

65. *he's ... him*] i.e. Evans is the man
whom Caius expects to fight.

71. *question*] argue.

Caius. I pray you let-a me speak a word with your ear.
    Verefore vill you not meet-a me?

Evans. [*Aside to Caius*] Pray you use your patience. 75
    [*Aloud*] In good time.

Caius. By gar, you are de coward; de Jack dog; John ape.

Evans. [*Aside to Caius*] Pray you let us not be laughing-
    stocks to other men's humours; I desire you in friend-
    ship, and I will one way or other make you amends. 80
    [*Aloud*] I will knog your urinal about your knave's
    cogscomb.

Caius. Diable! Jack Rugby, mine host de Jarteer, have I
    not stay for him to kill him? Have I not, at de place
    I did appoint? 85

Evans. As I am a Christians soul, now, look you, this is
    the place appointed. I'll be judgement by mine host
    of the Garter.

Host. Peace, I say, Gallia and Gaul, French and Welsh,
    soul-curer and body-curer. 90

Caius. Ay, dat is very good, excellant.

Host. Peace, I say; hear mine host of the Garter. Am I
    politic? Am I subtle? Am I a Machiavel? Shall
    I lose my doctor? No, he gives me the potions and
    the motions. Shall I lose my parson? My priest? 95
    My Sir Hugh? No, he gives me the proverbs and

---

75. *Aside to Caius*] *Camb.; not in F.*　　75–6. patience. In] *Johnson; patience in F.*
76. *Aloud*] *Bowers; not in F.*　　78, 81. S.D.] *Staunton; not in F.*　　81. urinal] *F;*
vrinalls *Q.*　　82. cogscomb] *F;* cockcomes, for missing your meetings and appointments *Q;* cogs-comb, for missing your meetings and appointments *Pope.*
89. Gallia and Gaul] *F;* gawle and gawlia *Q; Gallia* and *Wallia Hanmer;* Gwallia
and Gaul *Rann, conj. Farmer;* Gallia and Guallia *Collier.*　　92–3. Peace . . . Shall]
Prose as Pope; Peace, . . . Garter, / Am . . . Machiauell? / Shall *F.*　　93. a
Machiavel] *F* (a Machiuell), *Rowe³;* Matchauil *Q.*

77. *Jack dog; John ape*] See notes on
I. iv. 102 and II. iii. 29, 59.

81–2.] See ll. 13–14 and notes.
'Cogscomb' is Evans's form of 'cockscomb', another colloquial term for the
head. As the collations indicate, some
editors add here Q's 'for missing your
meetings and appointments'—which
only spells out the obvious.

89. *Gallia and Gaul*] Wales (French
Galles) and France.

91. *excellant*] The F spelling, used

only here, probably means that Caius
uses the French pronunciation.

93. *Machiavel*] i.e. perfect intriguer.
Machiavelli, as author of *The Prince*,
was understood, or misunderstood, by
the Elizabethans to be advocating the
doctrine of the end justifying the
means (the so-called 'policy': hence
the Host's 'Am I politic?'). The
Machiavel, or Machiavillian (the pun
was conscious), became a stock character in Elizabethan drama.

L

the no-verbs. Give me thy hand, terrestrial, so;
give me thy hand, celestial, so. Boys of art, I have
deceived you both: I have directed you to wrong
places; your hearts are mighty, your skins are   100
whole, and let burnt sack be the issue. Come, lay
their swords to pawn. Follow me, lads of peace;
follow, follow, follow.   *Exit.*

Shal. Trust me, a mad host. Follow, gentlemen, follow.

Slen. O sweet Anne Page! [*Exeunt Shallow, Slender, and Page.*]

Caius. Ha, do I perceive dat? Have you make-a de sot   106
of us, ha, ha?

Evans. This is well; he has made us his vlouting-stog.
I desire you that we may be friends; and let us
knog our prains together to be revenge on this same   110
scall, scurvy, cogging companion, the host of the
Garter.   *

Caius. By gar, with all my heart. He promise to bring
me where is Anne Page; by gar, he deceive me
too.   115

97–8. Give . . . Boys] *As Theobald;* Giue me thy hand (Celestiall) so: Boyes *F;*
Giue me thy hand terestiall, / So giue me thy hand celestiall: / So boyes *Q.*
102. lads] *Q;* Lad *F.*   103. *Exit*] *Q; not in F.*   105. S.D.] *This ed.; not in F;*
Ex. Shal. Slen. Page and Host. *Rowe; Exeunt* Host, Page, *&c. Capell.*

97. *no-verbs*] i.e. tells me, in his capacity as parson, what I must not do.

Give . . . terrestrial] The Q phrase must be included here; the bad text retains what the scribe or compositor of F dropped by accident. The Q reporter could hardly have invented so neat a phrase, and the F 'Celestiall' (addressed to Parson Evans) has no point without the balance of 'terrestrial' (addressed to Caius in the parallel phrase). The antithesis of 'body-curer' and 'soul-curer' of l. 90 is continued.

98. *art*] learning.

101. *burnt sack*] See II. i. 203–4 and note.

issue] outcome, the *only* result.

102. *to pawn*] i.e. because they will not be needed for fighting.

102–3. *Follow . . . follow*] Hart conjectures that 'follow, follow, follow' was the cry used by constables raising the 'hue and cry'.

106. *sot*] fool, idiot.

108. *vlouting-stog*] i.e. flouting-stock, something or somebody to be mocked (cf. 'laughing-stock'). Evans uses the word again to the Host at IV. v. 75—where he is taking the vengeance he 'adumbrates' here.

110. *knog*] knock (in the sense of 'join').

111. *scall*] Another form of 'scald': affected with the scall, a scabby disease of the scalp, and so used, as is 'scurvy' (and 'lousy') to mean 'contemptible'.

cogging] cheating, deceitful (cf. III. iii. 42 and *Oth.,* IV. ii. 132).

companion] Used contemptuously, as often in Shakespeare: rogue, villain.

Evans. Well, I will smite his noddles. Pray you follow.

[*Exeunt.*]

SCENE II

[*Enter*] MISTRESS PAGE [*following*] ROBIN.

Mrs. Page. Nay, keep your way, little gallant; you were
wont to be a follower, but now you are a leader.
Whether had you rather lead mine eyes, or eye your
master's heels?

Rob. I had rather, forsooth, go before you like a man than   5
follow him like a dwarf.

Mrs. Page. O, you are a flattering boy: now I see you'll
be a courtier.

[*Enter* FORD.]

Ford. Well met, Mistress Page. Whither go you?

Mrs. Page. Truly, sir, to see your wife. Is she at home?   10

Ford. Ay, and as idle as she may hang together, for want
of company. I think, if your husbands were dead,
you two would marry.

Mrs. Page. Be sure of that—two other husbands.

Ford. Where had you this pretty weathercock?   15

---

116. S.D.] *Pope; not in F; Exit omnes Q.*

Scene II

SCENE II] *F;* Scene IV. *The Street. Pope;* Scene, *The Street, in* Windsor. *Theobald.*
S.D.] *This ed.; Mist. Page, Robin, Ford, Page, Shallow, Slender, Host, Euans, Caius. F;
Enter Mistress* Page *and* Robin. *Rowe.*   8. S.D.] *Rowe; not in F.*   12. company]
F; your company *Collier*².

116. *noddles*] 'Noddle' is another
colloquialism for 'head', but the plural
is Evans's own.

Scene II

1. *keep your way*] keep going, go on
(as in *Ado*, I. i. 144).

11. *may hang together*] can manage to
be while still surviving (a common
saying). Schmidt compares *Wint.*,
II. ii. 21–3, where, to Paulina's question 'How fares our gracious lady?',
Emilia replies 'As well as one so
great and so forlorn / May hold together'.

15. *weathercock*] The allusion is
probably to the feathers Robin wears
in his cap: weathercocks often had a
pennon (cf. *LLL.*, IV. i. 96–7). Hart
and some other editors see an allusion
to gaudy dress and compare 'Jack-a-
lent' in III. iii. 23.

Mrs. Page. I cannot tell what the dickens his name is
my husband had him of.—What do you call your
knight's name, sirrah?

Rob. Sir John Falstaff.

Ford. Sir John Falstaff?   20

Mrs. Page. He, he; I can never hit on's name. There is
such a league between my goodman and he! Is your
wife at home indeed?

Ford. Indeed she is.

Mrs. Page. By your leave, sir; I am sick till I see her.   25
                                    [*Exeunt Mistress Page and Robin.*]

Ford. Has Page any brains? Hath he any eyes? Hath he
any thinking? Sure, they sleep: he hath no use of
them. Why, this boy will carry a letter twenty mile
as easy as a cannon will shoot point-blank twelve
score. He pieces out his wife's inclination; he gives   30
her folly motion and advantage: and now she's
going to my wife, and Falstaff's boy with her. A man
may hear this shower sing in the wind. And Falstaff's
boy with her! Good plots! They are laid; and our
revolted wives share damnation together. Well, I   35
will take him, then torture my wife, pluck the

22. goodman] *F1;* good man *F4.*   25. S.D.] *Rowe; not in F.*

16. *what the dickens*] An interesting
example of a phrase that has not altered
its colloquial status in nearly four
hundred years. The derivation is uncertain.

18. *sirrah*] The common form of
address to a boy not old enough to be
called 'Master'.

22. *league*] i.e. of friendship. In-
triguing is not implied.

goodman] husband.

29–30. *point-blank twelve score*] with
direct aim in a horizontal line at a distance of twelve score (240) yards or,
perhaps, paces—as contrasted with
shooting an *arrow* accurately at this
distance, the usual phrase for an
exceptional feat (as in *2H4*, III. ii.
51–2).

30. *pieces out*] actually increases the
scope of ('piece' in Shakespeare often

means 'enlarge' or 'add to'; cf.,
particularly, *Ant.*, I. v. 44–6).

31. *folly*] wantonness—as in II. ii.
234 and, e.g., *Lucr.*, 556.

motion] instigation, or provocation
(*O.E.D. sb.* 9).

advantage] favourable opportunity
(*O.E.D. sb.* 4, 5).

32–3. *A man . . . wind*] i.e. trouble
may be anticipated, as a storm may
sometimes be heard coming before it
is felt.

35. *revolted*] i.e. revolted from virtue,
faithless, as in *Troil.*, v. ii. 186. The
exact meaning is perhaps clearest from
the Friar's philosophizing, *Rom.*, II. iii.
19–20: 'Nor aught so good but strain'd
from that fair use / Revolts from true
birth, stumbling on abuse'.

36. *torture*] Perhaps only in the more
general sense of 'torment' (*O.E.D. v.* 2).

borrowed veil of modesty from the so-seeming
Mistress Page, divulge Page himself for a secure and
wilful Actæon; and to these violent proceedings all
my neighbours shall cry aim. [*Clock strikes.*] The   40
clock gives me my cue, and my assurance bids me
search: there I shall find Falstaff. I shall be rather
praised for this than mocked, for it is as positive as
the earth is firm that Falstaff is there. I will go.

Enter PAGE, SHALLOW, SLENDER, HOST, EVANS, CAIUS
[*and* RUGBY].

Shal., *Page, etc.* Well met, Master Ford.   45
Ford. [*Aside*] Trust me, a good knot.—[*Aloud*] I have
    good cheer at home, and I pray you all go with me.
Shal. I must excuse myself, Master Ford.
Slen. And so must I, sir: we have appointed to dine with
    Mistress Anne, and I would not break with her for   50
    more money than I'll speak of.
Shal. We have lingered about a match between Anne
    Page and my cousin Slender, and this day we shall
    have our answer.
Slen. I hope I have your good will, father Page.   55
Page. You have, Master Slender, I stand wholly for you.

40. S.D.] *As Capell* (*Clock heard*)*; not in* F.   41. *cue*] F (Qu), *Rowe*[3].   44.
Enter . . . Caius] *As* Q*; not in* F.   *and Rugby*] *Malone; not in* F *or* Q.   46. *Aside*]
This ed.; not in F.   *Aloud*] *This ed.; not in* F.   49–51.] *Prose as Pope;* And . . .
Sir, | We . . . Anne, | And . . . mony | Then . . . of. F.

<table>
<tr><td>

38. *divulge*] reveal, proclaim openly
(*O.E.D. v.* I. b, 2).

secure] foolishly confident (as in
II. ii. 233).

39. *Actæon*] For Actæon as prototype
of the cuckold, see note on II. i. 115.

40. *cry aim*] applaud the accuracy of
my aim (the phrase, originally used by
the spectator applauding the archer's
skill, had much the same force as the
modern 'well played!' or even 'hear,
hear!').

46. *knot*] IV. ii. 108 and several other
Shakespearian uses (particularly *Tim.*,
III. vi. 99, 'You knot of mouth-friends!')
suggest that the word was often used

</td><td>

pejoratively or ironically, like the
modern 'gang'. If it is so used here,
Page's first words must be an 'aside'.

50. *break with her*] break my word to
her, or even break faith with her: cf.
Cor., IV. vi. 47–8.

52. *lingered about*] Unless it means
'hankered after' (*O.E.D.* 'linger' *v.* 8),
probably means, in effect, 'considered
as possible, without reaching any con-
clusion', 'left open the possibility of';
the closest parallel would be *1H6*,
IV. iv. 19, where it is said that Talbot,
'in advantage lingering, looks for
rescue'.

56. *stand . . . for*] support.

</td></tr>
</table>

But my wife, Master Doctor, is for you altogether.

Caius. Ay, be-gar, and de maid is love-a me: my nursh-a
Quickly tell me so mush.

Host. What say you to young Master Fenton? He capers,   60
he dances, he has eyes of youth; he writes verses, he
speaks holiday, he smells April and May. He will
carry 't, he will carry 't; 'tis in his buttons he will
carry 't.

Page. Not by my consent, I promise you. The gentleman   65
is of no having: he kept company with the wild
Prince and Poins. He is of too high a region; he
knows too much. No, he shall not knit a knot in his
fortunes with the finger of my substance; if he take
her, let him take her simply: the wealth I have waits   70
on my consent, and my consent goes not that way.

63. buttons he] *This ed.;* buttons, he *F;* betmes he *Q;* buttons; he *Steevens;* talons
—he *conj. New Camb.;* fortunes, he *Sisson.*

58. *nursh-a*] Presumably, house-
keeper; cf. I. ii. 3–4 and note.

60. *capers*] is able to make extravagant leaps when dancing—a sign, in
the eyes of the Host, of masculinity and
joy in living.

62. *speaks holiday*] speaks with the
gaiety appropriate to a holiday; cf.
from *AYL.* 'holiday foolery', I. iii. 14,
and Rosalind's 'Come, woo me, woo
me, for now I am in a holiday humour
and like enough to consent', IV. i.
68–70.

smells April and May] has all the
freshness of spring.

63. *carry 't*] succeed, prevail (a
common expression, sometimes in the
fuller form 'carry it away'); not unlike
the modern 'carry it off'); cf. I. i. 217.

'tis in his buttons he] It is perhaps
defence of a kind for the F text that the
May-buttons image sequence is found
also in *The Two Noble Kinsmen*, III. i,
'O Queene Emilia, / Fresher then
May, sweeter / Then hir gold Buttons
on the bowes . . .' (noted in another
context by Kenneth Muir, in *Shakespeare Survey* 11, 52–3)—where 'buttons' means buds or blossoms. Q's 'he
wil cary it, he will carit, / Tis in his

betmes he will carite' is no help, except for the evidence that the phrase
was spoken on the stage without a
pause after 'buttons' or 'betmes' and
understood to mean 'it is obvious (in
some way) that he will win'. Perhaps
'buttons' does mean 'buds' and the
image is of the flower that is yet to open
but whose colour and character are
already determined; more probably
the phrase is parallel to 'it is written in
his face that . . .'.

66. *having*] substance, means.

66–7. *he kept . . . Poins*] For this
obvious attempt to make a link with
the Henry IV plays, see Introduction,
p. lii, and cf. III. iv. 8, and note on
v. v. 103 S.D.

67. *region*] i.e. social sphere.

68–9. *shall . . . substance*] shall not
use my wealth to save his own fortunes,
as one ties a knot in a rope or a piece of
string to prevent its fraying further. It
is just possible that the phrase was
suggested by the parallelism of the
proverb 'he has tied a knot with his
tongue that he can't untie with all his
teeth' (Tilley K167), as Hart thought.

70. *simply*] as she is, without a dowry.

Ford. I beseech you heartily, some of you go home with
    me to dinner; besides your cheer, you shall have
    sport: I will show you a monster. Master Doctor,
    you shall go; so shall you, Master Page, and you,   75
    Sir Hugh.
Shal. Well, fare you well: we shall have the freer wooing
    at Master Page's.   *Exeunt Shallow and Slender.*
Caius. Go home, John Rugby; I come anon.   [*Exit Rugby.*]
Host. Farewell, my hearts; I will to my honest knight   80
    Falstaff, and drink canary with him.   *Exit.*
Ford. [*Aside*] I think I shall drink in pipe-wine first with
    him; I'll make him dance.—Will you go, gentles?
All. Have with you to see this monster.   *Exeunt.*

SCENE III

Enter MISTRESS FORD *and* MISTRESS PAGE.

Mrs. Ford. What, John! What, Robert!
Mrs. Page. Quickly, quickly, is the buck-basket—

77–8.] *Prose as Pope;* Well, . . . well: / We . . . F.   78. S.D.] *Q; not in F.*   79.
Exit Rugby] *Capell; not in F.*   81. *Exit*] *Q; not in F.*   82. *Aside*] *Johnson; not in F.*

Scene III

SCENE III] *F; Scene* VII. *Ford's House. Pope.*   S.D.] *Capell; Enter M. Ford, M.
Page, Seruants, Robin, Falstaffe, Ford, Page, Caius, Euans. F; Enter Mistresse Ford,
with two of her men, and a great buck basket. Q; Enter Mistress* Ford, *Mistress* Page,
and Servants with a Basket. Rowe.

74. *show you a monster*] Hart has a
good note on the popularity of mon-
sters at fairs etc., and well compares
Trinculo's wish that he could display
Caliban in England: 'Not a holiday
fool there but would give a piece of
silver: there would this monster make
a man; any strange beast there makes
a man' (*Tp.*, II. ii. 30–3).

81. *canary*] wine from the Canaries
(which was very popular)—but
'canary' was also the name of a dance;
hence Ford's pun in ll. 82–3.

82. *drink in*] drink, or drink up (with
relish).

pipe-wine] wine from the 'pipe' or
cask—but there is a pun on 'pipe' in
the sense of the musical instrument,
played for the 'dance' (l. 83).

84. *Have with you*] we are coming.

Scene III

2. *buck-basket*] clothes-basket, basket
for dirty clothes. 'Bucking' was the
process of washing in lye (as a bleach)
but also (as early as the fourteenth
century) had the wider meaning of
washing or soaking clothes (*O.E.D.*
'buck' *v.*[1] 1); 'buck', perhaps originally
the tub in which the clothes soaked in

Mrs. Ford. I warrant. What, Robin, I say!

[*Enter* JOHN *and* ROBERT *with a basket.*]

Mrs. Page. Come, come, come.

Mrs. Ford. Here, set it down.   5

Mrs. Page. Give your men the charge; we must be brief.

Mrs. Ford. Marry, as I told you before, John and Robert,
   be ready here hard by in the brew-house, and
   when I suddenly call you, come forth, and, without
   any pause or staggering, take this basket on your   10
   shoulders. That done, trudge with it in all haste, and
   carry it among the whitsters in Datchet Mead, and
   there empty it in the muddy ditch close by the
   Thames side.

Mrs. Page. You will do it?   15

Mrs. Ford. I ha' told them over and over; they lack no
   direction.—Be gone, and come when you are called.
                                              [*Exeunt John and Robert.*]

Mrs. Page. Here comes little Robin.

[*Enter* ROBIN.]

Mrs. Ford. How now, my eyas-musket, what news with
   you?   20

---

3. Robin] *F*; Robert *Bowers.*   S.D.] *This ed.; not in F; Enter Servants with a basket*
Capell.   12. Datchet Mead] *As Rowe; Dotchet* Mead *F1; Dutchet-*Mead *F4.*
17. Exeunt John and Robert] *As Johnson; not in F; Exit Seruant Q.*   18. Enter Robin]
Rowe; not in F.

---

the lye, was later used of the clothes
waiting to be so treated or washed
('buck' *sb.*³ 3). Washing clothes in
rivers is still, of course, common, particularly in the East.

   3. *I warrant*] I'm sure of it.

   Robin] Probably not the boy given
to Page and his wife by Falstaff (although he enters at l. 18) but the
servant of the Fords who is called
'Robert' in l. 1.

   8. *brew-house*] outhouse used for
brewing liquor, privately.

   10. *staggering*] wavering, hesitating
(*O.E.D.* 'stagger' *v.* 1. 2—and cf. *Meas.*,
1. ii. 169).

   12. *whitsters*] professional bleachers.
In Q, in a badly reported version of
this scene, Mistress Ford tells the
servants to explain, if they are asked,
that they are carrying the basket 'to
the Launderers'.

   Datchet Mead] the 'mead' or meadow
between Windsor Little Park and the
Thames.

   19. *eyas-musket*] fledgling sparrow-
hawk. The 'musket' was the male of
the sparrow-hawk; 'eyas' (originally
'nyas') a young hawk taken from the
nest or one incompletely trained. Cf.
the famous reference to the children's
acting companies as 'little eyases' in

Rob. My master, Sir John, is come in at your back door,
Mistress Ford, and requests your company.

Mrs. Page. You little Jack-a-Lent, have you been true
to us?

Rob. Ay, I'll be sworn. My master knows not of your   25
being here, and hath threatened to put me into
everlasting liberty if I tell you of it; for he swears
he'll turn me away.

Mrs. Page. Thou'rt a good boy: this secrecy of thine shall
be a tailor to thee, and shall make thee a new   30
doublet and hose.—I'll go hide me.

Mrs. Ford. Do so.—Go tell thy master I am alone. [*Exit
Robin.*] Mistress Page, remember you your cue.

Mrs. Page. I warrant thee; if I do not act it, hiss me.

Mrs. Ford. Go to, then: we'll use this unwholesome   35
humidity, this gross watery pumpion; we'll teach
him to know turtles from jays.   [*Exit Mistress Page.*]

Enter FALSTAFF.

Fal. Have I caught thee, my heavenly jewel? Why, now
let me die, for I have lived long enough: this is the
period of my ambition. O this blessed hour!   40

32–3. *Exit Robin*] *Rowe (after l. 33); not in F.*   33. cue] *F (Qu), Rowe³.*   37.
Exit Mistress Page] *Rowe (after l. 34); not in F.*   *Enter Falstaff*] *Q; not in F.*   38.
thee] *F; not in Q.*

---

competition with adults, *Ham.*, II. ii. 355.

23. *Jack-a-lent*] brightly dressed puppet, like the later 'Guy', set up by children in Lent as a butt at which to throw stones. Here the emphasis is probably on the bright colours of the dress (though *O.E.D.* takes it to be on the insignificance); at v. v. 128 it is on the function of the puppet as the equivalent of a coconut shy.

36. *pumpion*] Or 'pompion', the earlier form of the now commoner word 'pumpkin'.

37. *turtles from jays*] turtle-doves (proverbial for their faithfulness—cf. II. i. 78) from jays (notorious for their bright plumage—and the term was thus applied to 'made-up' women and

even, as here, to immoral women or prostitutes).

38. *Have . . . jewel?*] The words are a quotation, incongruous in Falstaff's mouth, from a song in Sir Philip Sidney's romantic sonnet-sequence *Astrophel and Stella*. 'Thee' is not in the original (and Q omits it, as do some editors) but, as Hart well says, 'when a quotation is made in conversation, it is commonly altered to suit circumstances'. It is hardly likely that Falstaff burst into song with this line, although a musical setting of the Sidney poem has been found and printed by John P. Cutts (*Shakespeare Quarterly*, XI, 1960, 89–92).

40. *period*] conclusion; aim and end.

Mrs. Ford. O sweet Sir John!

Fal. Mistress Ford, I cannot cog, I cannot prate,
Mistress Ford. Now shall I sin in my wish: I would
thy husband were dead; I'll speak it before the best
lord: I would make thee my lady.   45

Mrs. Ford. I your lady, Sir John? Alas, I should be a
pitiful lady.

Fal. Let the court of France show me such another. I see
how thine eye would emulate the diamond: thou
hast the right arched beauty of the brow that be-   50
comes the ship-tire, the tire-valiant, or any tire of
Venetian admittance.

Mrs. Ford. A plain kerchief, Sir John: my brows become
nothing else, nor that well neither.

Fal. Thou art a tyrant to say so; thou wouldst make an   55
absolute courtier, and the firm fixture of thy foot
would give an excellent motion to thy gait in a semicircled farthingale. I see what thou wert if Fortune

---

51. tire-valiant] *F* (Tyre-valiant); tire vellet *Q*; tire-volant *conj. Steevens*; tire-velvet *conj. Tollet.*   53-4.] *Prose as Pope*; A . . . *Iohn*: | My . . . neither. *F.*
55. Thou . . . tyrant] *F*; By the Lord thou art a traitor *Q*.   58-9. I . . . friend]
This ed.; I see what thou wert if Fortune thy foe, were not Nature thy friend *F1*;
I see what thou wert if Fortune thy foe were not, Nature thy friend *F2*; I see what
thou wert, if fortune thy foe were not, nature is thy friend *Pope*; I see what thou
wert, if fortune thy foe, were but nature thy friend *conj. Staunton*; I see what thou
wert, if Fortune thy foe were, not, Nature, thy friend *Alexander.*

---

42. *cog*] Either 'lie' (cf. III. i. 111) or
'fawn', 'wheedle' (*O.E.D.* v.³ 5).

51. *ship-tire*] elaborate head-dress in
the form of a ship (or, perhaps, the
sails of one). Falstaff is not making this
up: such head-dresses were worn.

tire-valiant] No other use of this word
has been recorded; the meaning is
generally assumed to be 'fanciful' or
'extreme' head-dress, taking 'valiant'
as an intensive adjective. In view of
the possible reference to sails in 'ship-
tire', is there perhaps a kind of concealed pun on 'valiant'–'gallant'–'top-
gallant'?

51-2. *of Venetian admittance*] acceptable, or in fashion, in Venice. Italian
fashions were eagerly imitated and
were often elaborate.

53. *become*] suit.

55. *tyrant*] *New Cambridge* is surely
right in rejecting Q's 'traitor' on the
ground that there is a pun on 'tire'.

56. *absolute*] consummate, perfect.

fixture] placing (an apparently rare
use, for which no parallel has been
found; Falstaff is speaking in would-be
formal language).

57-8. *semicircled farthingale*] The
farthingale, or petticoat stretched over
whalebone hoops, could take many
different shapes; the semicircular one
Falstaff is thinking of projected in a
semicircle at the back but was flat at
the front.

58-9. *I see . . . friend*] Staunton was
perhaps the first editor to understand
these words but, paradoxically, he

(thy foe) were—not Nature—thy friend. Come,
thou canst not hide it.   60

Mrs. Ford. Believe me, there's no such thing in me.

Fal. What made me love thee? Let that persuade thee
there's something extraordinary in thee. Come, I
cannot cog and say thou art this and that, like a
many of these lisping hawthorn-buds that come like   65
women in men's apparel, and smell like Bucklersbury in simple time; I cannot; but I love thee, none
but thee; and thou deserv'st it.

Mrs. Ford. Do not betray me, sir. I fear you love Mistress
Page.   70

Fal. Thou mightst as well say I love to walk by the
Counter-gate, which is as hateful to me as the reek
of a lime-kill.

62–3. thee there's] *As Q1* (thee / Ther's); thee. Ther's *F;* thee: ther's *Q3;* thee,
there's *Theobald²*.   73. lime-kill] *F, Q;* lime-kiln *Rowe*.

wished to emend them; Peter Alexander showed how they could be retained and be punctuated satisfactorily. (See *Shakespeare Survey,* 5, 3.) Falstaff is flattering Mistress Ford: Nature, he insists, *is* her friend (she is beautiful) but Fortune is as yet her foe (she is a citizen's wife, not Falstaff's 'Lady'), and he can imagine how distinguished she would be if she had Fortune as well as Nature on her side. (Staunton's paraphrase is: 'I see what you would be if Fortune were as bountiful to you as Nature has been'.) 'Fortune (thy foe)' would be recognized immediately by an Elizabethan audience as a variation on 'Fortune my foe', the name of a popular tune to which many different sets of words were written. There is a similar allusion in *H5*, III. vi. 41.

62–3. *thee there's*] F's punctuation is possible but Q's makes rather better sense and is adopted, from a fairly well reported speech, as giving what was presumably spoken on the stage.

65. *hawthorn-buds*] The budding of the hawthorn is associated with the coming of spring and fine weather for

the shepherd in *MND.,* I. i. 185; and in *3H6,* II. v. 42–3, the king thinks of the hawthorn bush as giving 'sweeter shade / To shepherds looking on their silly sheep' than canopies give to worried kings. Perhaps, then, Falstaff chooses the term as a contemptuous description of perfumed wooers not only because of the spring associations (cf. the Host's description of Fenton in III. ii. 60–2) but also because of a latent connection with the 'complaining' amorous shepherds of pastoral literature.

66–7. *Bucklersbury*] The street in the City of London where, *inter alia,* herbs were sold.

67. *simple time*] summer, when the simples or herbs used for medicinal purposes (cf. I. iv. 58 and note) were collected and sold.

71–2. *the Counter-gate*] the gate of the Counter, or prison for debtors, in the City, of which a Falstaff may be thought to have had special fear. Elizabethan prisons were notorious also for the foul stench that came from them; the Counter is therefore in Falstaff's mind the very opposite of the

Mrs. Ford. Well, heaven knows how I love you, and you
    shall one day find it.   75
Fal. Keep in that mind: I'll deserve it.
Mrs. Ford. Nay, I must tell you, so you do; or else I
    could not be in that mind.

[*Enter* ROBIN.]

Rob. Mistress Ford, Mistress Ford! Here's Mistress Page
    at the door, sweating and blowing, and looking   80
    wildly, and would needs speak with you presently.
Fal. She shall not see me: I will ensconce me behind the
    arras.
Mrs. Ford. Pray you do so; she's a very tattling woman.
                        Falstaff hides behind the arras.

[*Enter* MISTRESS PAGE.]

What's the matter? How now?   85
Mrs. Page. O Mistress Ford, what have you done?
    You're shamed, you're overthrown, you're undone
    for ever!
Mrs. Ford. What's the matter, good Mistress Page?
Mrs. Page. O well-a-day, Mistress Ford, having an   90
    honest man to your husband, to give him such
    cause of suspicion!
Mrs. Ford. What cause of suspicion?
Mrs. Page. What cause of suspicion? Out upon you:
    how am I mistook in you!   95

74–5. *Prose as F3;* Well . . . you, / And . . . *F1.*   77–8.] *Prose as F3;* Nay . . . doe; /
Or . . . *F1.*   78. *Enter Robin] As Capell; not in F.*   79. *Rob.] F1; Within. | Rob.*
F2.   84. *Falstaff . . . arras] As Q; not in F;* Falstaff *hides himself Theobald.   Enter*
Mistress Page] F2; not in F1; Enter Mistress Page, *and* Robin Malone.   86–8.]
Prose as F3; O . . . done? / You'r sham'd, y'are ouerthrowne, y'are vndone for
euer. *F.*

nearby Bucklersbury, fragrant with
sweet-smelling herbs.
    73. *lime-kill*] The now obsolete
dialectal form 'kill' (for 'kiln') is confirmed by Q.
    81. *presently*] immediately.
    82. *ensconce*] hide (as in II. ii. 24).
    83. *arras*] curtain of woven tapestry,

hung in front of walls. It does not
necessarily follow from the action here
that there was an arras on the Elizabethan stage, in front of the (hypothetical) inner stage or against the
rear wall; if there were no arras, a
pillar or any other available hiding-
place would have served.

Mrs. Ford. Why, alas, what's the matter?

Mrs. Page. Your husband's coming hither, woman, with all the officers in Windsor, to search for a gentleman that he says is here now in the house, by your consent, to take an ill advantage of his   100 absence. You are undone.

Mrs. Ford. 'Tis not so, I hope.

Mrs. Page. Pray heaven it be not so, that you have such a man here—but 'tis most certain your husband's coming, with half Windsor at his heels, to search   105 for such a one, I come before to tell you. If you know yourself clear, why, I am glad of it; but if you have a friend here, convey, convey him out. Be not amazed, call all your senses to you, defend your reputation, or bid farewell to your good life for ever.   110

Mrs. Ford. What shall I do? There is a gentleman, my dear friend; and I fear not mine own shame so much as his peril. I had rather than a thousand pound he were out of the house.

Mrs. Page. For shame, never stand 'you had rather'   115 and 'you had rather': your husband's here at hand! Bethink you of some conveyance; in the house you cannot hide him. O, how have you deceived me! Look, here is a basket; if he be of any reasonable stature, he may creep in here; and throw foul   120 linen upon him, as if it were going to bucking; or— it is whiting-time—send him by your two men to Datchet Mead.

Mrs. Ford. He's too big to go in there. What shall I do?

Fal. [*Coming forward*] Let me see 't, let me see 't, O, let   125 me see 't! I'll in, I'll in. Follow your friend's counsel; I'll in.

Mrs. Page. What, Sir John Falstaff?—Are these your letters, knight?

125. *Coming forward*] Camb.; not in F; *Enter* Falstaff *Rowe; starting from his Conceal-ment Capell.*   128–9. —Are . . . knight?] F (Are . . . Knight?); (*Aside.*) Fie sir *Iohn* is this your loue? Go too. Q; [*in his ear*] Are . . . knight? *New Camb.*

107. *clear*] innocent.
109. *amazed*] bewildered.
115. *stand*] Perhaps 'rely on' (cf.

II. i. 214); perhaps 'waste time over'.
122. *whiting-time*] time for bleaching clothes; cf. 'whitsters' in l. 12.

Fal. I love thee; help me away. Let me creep in here.   130
  I'll never—

> *Gets into the basket; they cover him with 'foul linen'.*

Mrs. Page. Help to cover your master, boy.—Call your
  men, Mistress Ford.—You dissembling knight!
Mrs. Ford. What, John! Robert! John!

> [*Enter* JOHN *and* ROBERT.]

Go take up these clothes here quickly. Where's the   135
cowl-staff? Look, how you drumble! Carry them to
the laundress in Datchet Mead; quickly, come.

> [*Enter* FORD, PAGE, CAIUS, *and* EVANS.]

Ford. Pray you come near: if I suspect without cause,
  why then make sport at me; then let me be your
  jest, I deserve it.—How now? Whither bear you   140
  this?
John. To the laundress, forsooth.
Mrs. Ford. Why, what have you to do whither they bear
  it? You were best meddle with buck-washing!
Ford. Buck? I would I could wash myself of the buck!   145
  Buck, buck, buck! Ay, buck; I warrant you, buck;
  and of the season too, it shall appear. [*Exeunt John,
  Robert, and Robin with the basket.*] Gentlemen, I have

130. I love thee] *F;* I loue thee, and none but thee *Q.*   131. S.D.] *As Rowe; not
in F; Sir Iohn goes into the basket, they put cloathes ouer him, the two men carries it away:
Foord meetes it, and all the rest, Page, Doctor, Priest, Slender, Shallow. Q.*   134. S.D.]
As Capell; not in F; Exit Robin. Re-enter Servants. Malone.   137. S.D.] *Rowe; not
in F.*   142. John] *This ed.; Ser. F.*   147–8. S.D.] *This ed.; not in F; Exeunt
Servants with the Basket. Rowe.*

130. *love thee*] The additional words
in Q, included by some editors, are
probably the result of confusion with
ll. 67–8.

136. *cowl-staff*] a wooden rod used to
carry a 'cowl' (tub) or similar object;
the staff was put through the two
handles.

  drumble] move sluggishly, lag
(*O.E.D. v.*[1] 1). Wright found the
word in Warwickshire, among other
counties, but Nashe's uses of it,
recorded by Hart, perhaps confirm

that it was not necessarily dialectal.

143. *what have you to do*] what concern
is it of yours.

145–7.] Ford is, of course, concerned
with the other implications of 'buck'
—the stag whose horns symbolize
cuckoldry.

147. *of the season*] in season—perhaps
with a further quibble: the buck is in
season in the sense that it (Falstaff) is
in such good (fat) condition; and
perhaps, worse, the female he seeks is
in season, ready for a mate.

dreamed to-night; I'll tell you my dream. Here,
here, here be my keys; ascend my chambers;   150
search, seek, find out. I'll warrant we'll unkennel
the fox. Let me stop this way first. [*Locking the door*]
So, now uncape.

Page. Good Master Ford, be contented; you wrong
yourself too much.   155

Ford. True, Master Page.—Up, gentlemen, you shall
see sport anon; follow me, gentlemen.   [*Exit.*]

Evans. This is fery fantastical humours and jealousies.

Caius. By gar, 'tis no the fashion of France; it is not
jealous in France.   160

Page. Nay, follow him, gentlemen; see the issue of his
search.   [*Exeunt Page, Caius, and Evans.*]

Mrs. Page. Is there not a double excellency in this?

Mrs. Ford. I know not which pleases me better, that my
husband is deceived, or Sir John.   165

Mrs. Page. What a taking was he in when your husband
asked who was in the basket!

---

152. S.D.] *Capell; not in* F.   153. uncape] F; uncouple *Hanmer;* uncope *New
Camb.;* uncase *Sisson.*   157. *Exit*] *Capell; not in* F.   162. S.D.] *Capell; not in* F;
Exit omnes (after l. 158) Q; *Exeunt (after l. 160)* F2; *Exeunt (after l. 160). Manent
Mistress* Page *and Mistress* Ford *(after l. 162)* Rowe.   167. who] F; what *Harness.*

---

149. *to-night*] last night.

151. *unkennel*] unearth, uncover. Cf.
Ham., III. ii. 86.

153. *uncape*] If the F text is correct,
'uncape' presumably means 'uncover',
but as a clothing, not a hunting,
image. (Warburton said it meant 'dig
out the fox'.) *New Cambridge's* emendation 'uncope' is based on the meaning
of 'cope' as to tie or sew up the lips of a
ferret to prevent its biting the rabbits
it dislodges (as a greyhound is muzzled
today); it also, however, would be odd
used intransitively. Q's 'Ile . . . ferit
him' in Ford's soliloquy at the end of
III. v may be an attempt to recall either
'uncape' or 'unkennel the fox', neither
of which is reproduced in the correct
place.

156. *True*] Probably Ford agrees in
the sense that too much wrong is done

him; or perhaps he seems to agree
with Page to placate him for the
minute.

166. *taking*] state of overwhelming
fear (as in *Lucr.,* 453)—though sometimes used of emotion in general.

166–7. *when . . . basket!*] In fact, Ford
asked no such question, nor did he ask
what was in the basket, as Falstaff
alleges at III. v. 93–4. But it does not
help at all to introduce from Q, as *New
Cambridge* does, after 'How now?' in
l. 140, Q's 'Who goes heare?' which
obviously refers to the bearers of the
basket. Hart's statement (in a note on
III. v. 93–4) that 'in the Folio text the
question is not asked. This is an over-
sight which the Quarto has right' is
misleading; Q has only: 'How now
who goes heare? whither goes this? /
Whither goes it? set it downe.'

Mrs. Ford. I am half afraid he will have need of washing—so throwing him into the water will do him a
benefit.   170
Mrs. Page. Hang him, dishonest rascal! I would all of
the same strain were in the same distress.
Mrs. Ford. I think my husband hath some special suspicion of Falstaff's being here, for I never saw him
so gross in his jealousy till now.   175
Mrs. Page. I will lay a plot to try that, and we will yet
have more tricks with Falstaff: his dissolute disease
will scarce obey this medicine.
Mrs. Ford. Shall we send that foolish carrion, Mistress
Quickly, to him, and excuse his throwing into the   180
water, and give him another hope, to betray him to
another punishment?
Mrs. Page. We will do it: let him be sent for to-morrow
eight o'clock to have amends.

[*Enter* FORD, PAGE, CAIUS, *and* EVANS.]

Ford. I cannot find him; maybe the knave bragged of   185
that he could not compass.
Mrs. Page. [*Aside to Mrs. Ford*] Heard you that?
Mrs. Ford. You use me well, Master Ford, do you?
Ford. Ay, I do so.
Mrs. Ford. Heaven make you better than your thoughts! 190
Ford. Amen!
Mrs. Page. You do yourself mighty wrong, Master Ford.
Ford. Ay, ay; I must bear it.

179. foolish] *F2;* foolishion *F1.*   183–4. to-morrow eight] *F1;* to morrow by
eight *F2.*   184. S.D.] *Capell; not in F; Enter all. Q; Re-enter* Ford, Page, *&c.
Rowe; Re-enter* Ford, Page, *and the rest at a distance. Johnson.*   187. S.D.] *As
Capell; not in F.*   189. Ay, I] *F* (I, I); Ay, ay, I *Rowe.*   190. you] *F; me conj.
Capell* (*1783*).   193. Ay, ay; I] *F* (I, I: I).

168–9. *need of washing*] Not only
because of the dirtiness of the clothes
but also because of the physical results
of his own fear.
176. *try*] test.
178. *obey*] i.e. respond to, be totally
cured by.

179. *carrion*] From being applied to
corrupted flesh, 'carrion' came to be a
general term of contempt, particularly
for a woman; so Capulet uses it,
unforgivably, to Juliet, *Rom.*, III.
v. 157.
186. *compass*] achieve.

Evans. If there be anypody in the house, and in the
    chambers, and in the coffers, and in the presses,   195
    heaven forgive my sins at the day of judgement!
Caius. By gar, nor I too: there is nobodies.
Page. Fie, fie, Master Ford, are you not ashamed? What
    spirit, what devil suggests this imagination? I
    would not ha' your distemper in this kind for the   200
    wealth of Windsor Castle.
Ford. 'Tis my fault, Master Page, I suffer for it.
Evans. You suffer for a pad conscience Your wife is as
    honest a 'omans as I will desires among five
    thousand, and five hundred too.   205
Caius. By gar, I see 'tis an honest woman.
Ford. Well, I promised you a dinner. Come, come, walk
    in the Park. I pray you pardon me; I will hereafter
    make known to you why I have done this. Come,
    wife, come, Mistress Page, I pray you pardon me;   210
    pray heartly pardon me.
Page. Let's go in, gentlemen—[*aside*] but, trust me, we'll
    mock him.—I do invite you to-morrow morning
    to my house to breakfast; after, we'll a-birding
    together—I have a fine hawk for the bush. Shall it 215
    be so?
Ford. Anything.
Evans. If there is one, I shall make two in the company.
Caius. If there be one or two, I shall make-a the turd.
Ford. Pray you go, Master Page.   [*Exit, with Page.*]   220

---

200. the] *F* (*corrected*).   211. heartly] *F* (hartly).   212. *aside*] *This ed.; not in F.*
214. breakfast;] *F* (breakfast:) *; Breakfast, Rowe.*   220. S.D.] *This ed., as New*
Camb.; not in F.

195. *presses*] cupboards (a surviving
meaning).
201. *Windsor Castle*] The reference is
'natural' from a citizen of Windsor but
serves also to remind the audience of
the supposed setting.
202. *fault*] misfortune (as in *Per.*,
IV. ii. 79).
207–8. *walk in the Park*] i.e. until the
promised dinner is ready.
211. *heartly*] heartily, sincerely.

212. *go in*] The direction is quite
logical on the unlocalized Elizabethan
stage, and they do go 'in' (away from
the audience), not 'in' to the house.
214. *a-birding*] hunting small birds
with sparrow-hawks. The hawk chased
the smaller birds even from the bush in
which they had taken shelter (hence
l. 215) and then they could be shot. (In
true falconry the falcon itself did the
killing.)

M

Evans. I pray you now, remembrance to-morrow on the
    lousy knave mine host.
Caius. Dat is good, by gar; with all my heart!
Evans. A lousy knave, to have his gibes and his
    mockeries!   *Exeunt.*   225

SCENE IV

Enter FENTON *and* ANNE PAGE.

Fent. I see I cannot get thy father's love;
    Therefore no more turn me to him, sweet Nan.
Anne. Alas, how then?
Fent.   Why, thou must be thyself.
    He doth object I am too great of birth,
    And that my state being gall'd with my expense,   5
    I seek to heal it only by his wealth;
    Besides these, other bars he lays before me—
    My riots past, my wild societies—
    And tells me 'tis a thing impossible
    I should love thee but as a property.   10
Anne. Maybe he tells you true.
Fent. No, heaven so speed me in my time to come!
    Albeit I will confess thy father's wealth
    Was the first motive that I woo'd thee, Anne,
    Yet, wooing thee, I found thee of more value   15

Scene IV

SCENE IV] *F; Scene* XII. *Changes to* Page's house. *Pope; . . . Before Page's house*
Chambers.   S.D.] *As Rowe; Enter Fenton, Anne, Page, Shallow, Slender, Quickly,*
Page, Mist. Page. F.   12. *Fent.*] *Q3; not in F.*

221–5.] Obviously Caius and Evans
have 'knogged' their 'prains together'
and have planned their revenge on the
Host for the trick played on them over
the duel, but the audience still does
not know what form the vengeance is
to take.

Scene IV

5. *state*] estate.
   gall'd] Literally, chafed in such a
way as to produce a sore, and so,
metaphorically, seriously depleted.
   8.] See Introduction, p. lii, and
cf. III. ii. 66–7.
   10. *property*] There may be one or
two secondary meanings: stage property, and means to an end. Cf. IV. iv.
77 and *Cæs.* IV. i. 39–40.
   12.] i.e. may heaven not favour
me in future if his accusations are justified.

Than stamps in gold or sums in sealed bags;
And 'tis the very riches of thyself
That now I aim at.

Anne.   Gentle Master Fenton,
Yet seek my father's love; still seek it, sir.
If opportunity and humblest suit   20
Cannot attain it, why then—hark you hither!

[*They converse apart.*]

[*Enter* SHALLOW, SLENDER, *and* MISTRESS QUICKLY.]

Shal. Break their talk, Mistress Quickly. My kinsman
shall speak for himself.

Slen. I'll make a shaft or a bolt on 't. 'Slid, 'tis but
venturing.   25

Shal. Be not dismayed.

Slen. No, she shall not dismay me: I care not for that, but
that I am afeard.

Quick. [*To Anne*] Hark ye, Master Slender would speak a
word with you.   30

Anne. I come to him. [*Aside*] This is my father's choice.
O, what a world of vile ill-favour'd faults
Looks handsome in three hundred pounds a year!

Quick. And how does good Master Fenton? Pray you, a
word with you.   35

Shal. [*To Slender*] She's coming; to her, coz. O boy, thou
hadst a father!

21. then—hark] *Theobald;* then harke *F.*   *They converse apart*] *Capell, as Theobald;*
not in *F.*   Enter . . . *Quickly*] *Rowe; not in F.*   22-3.] *Prose as Pope;* Breake . . .
Quickly. | My . . . *F.*   27-8.] *Prose as Pope;* No . . . me: / I . . . *F.*   29. *To Anne*]
This ed.; not in F.   31. *Aside*] *As Capell; not in F; to Fenton New Camb.*   34-7.]
Prose as Pope; And . . . *Fenton?* / Pray . . . with you. / *Shal.* Shee's . . . Coz: / O . . . *F.*
35.] *Capell adds 'drawing him aside'.*   36. S.D.] *This ed.; not in F.*

16. *stamps*] coins (on which a device
has been stamped or impressed—
O.E.D. 'stamp' *sb.* III. 15).

21.] *New Cambridge,* which rejects
Capell's S.D. and prints the line
without the dash, takes Anne to
mean 'if all else fails come back to
me'.

24. *I'll make . . . on 't*] The proverb
(Tilley S264) derives from the contrast between the slim shaft of the true

arrow (or even of the bow with which
it was fired) and the shorter and thicker
arrow known as the 'bolt' or 'quarrel'
(used with the crossbow): 'do it one
way or another'.

'*Slid*] by God's (eye)lid.

36. *to her, coz*] 'Coz' and 'cousin'
(l. 42) meant 'kinsman' and not only
'cousin' in the modern sense; for 'to
her', giving encouragement, cf. I. iii. 51
and note.

Slen. I had a father, Mistress Anne; my uncle can tell you
  good jests of him. Pray you, uncle, tell Mistress Anne
  the jest how my father stole two geese out of a pen, 40
  good uncle.

Shal. Mistress Anne, my cousin loves you.

Slen. Ay, that I do, as well as I love any woman in
  Gloucestershire.

Shal. He will maintain you like a gentlewoman. 45

Slen. Ay, that I will, come cut and long-tail, under the
  degree of a squire.

Shal. He will make you a hundred and fifty pounds
  jointure.

Anne. Good Master Shallow, let him woo for himself. 50

Shal. Marry, I thank you for it; I thank you for that good
  comfort. She calls you, coz; I'll leave you.

Anne. Now, Master Slender.

Slen. Now, good Mistress Anne.

Anne. What is your will? 55

Slen. My will? Od's heartlings, that's a pretty jest
  indeed! I ne'er made my will yet, I thank heaven:
  I am not such a sickly creature, I give heaven praise.

Anne. I mean, Master Slender, what would you with me?

Slen. Truly, for mine own part, I would little or nothing 60
  with you. Your father and my uncle hath made
  motions. If it be my luck, so; if not, happy man be
  his dole! They can tell you how things go, better than
  I can. You may ask your father; here he comes.

52.] *Collier*[2] *adds 'Stands back'.*

38. *uncle*] Slender probably does use
the word in our sense; but see note on
Dramatis Personæ, l. 4.

46. *come cut and long-tail*] Proverbial
(Tilley C938) for 'no matter who or
what is concerned' (since horses and
dogs must fall into one of two classes,
those with uncut and those with docked
tails). A typical use is in *George-a-
Greene* (attributed to Robert Greene),
v. i, where George, having beaten
all the shoemakers of Bradford, asks
'What, have you any more? / Call
all your town forth, cut and long tail'.

under] Not 'beneath' but 'in accordance with' (*O.E.D. prep.* III).

56. *Od's heartlings*] by God's little
heart—another mild oath.

62. *motions*] proposals.

62–3. *happy man be his dole*] Slender's
speech is larded with clichés: this is
another proverb (Tilley M158) meaning, roughly, 'good luck to any man
who is successful' ('dole' in the sense of
destiny, or lot—*O.E.D. sb.*[1] 4). Cf.
Shr., I. i. 144.

[*Enter* PAGE *and* MISTRESS PAGE.]

Page. Now, Master Slender; love him, daughter Anne.— 65
    Why, how now, what does Master Fenton here?
    You wrong me, sir, thus still to haunt my house.
    I told you, sir, my daughter is disposed of.
Fent. Nay, Master Page, be not impatient.
Mrs. Page. Good Master Fenton, come not to my child.   70
Page. She is no match for you.
Fent. Sir, will you hear me?
Page.   No, good Master Fenton.
    Come, Master Shallow; come, son Slender; in.
    Knowing my mind, you wrong me, Master Fenton.
            [*Exeunt Page, Shallow, and Slender.*]
Quick. Speak to Mistress Page.   75
Fent. Good Mistress Page, for that I love your daughter
    In such a righteous fashion as I do,
    Perforce, against all checks, rebukes and manners,
    I must advance the colours of my love,
    And not retire. Let me have your good will.   80
Anne. Good mother, do not marry me to yond fool.
Mrs. Page. I mean it not; I seek you a better husband.
Quick. [*Aside*] That's my master, Master Doctor.
Anne. Alas, I had rather be set quick i' th' earth,
    And bowl'd to death with turnips!   85
Mrs. Page. Come, trouble not yourself. Good Master Fenton,
    I will not be your friend nor enemy.

64. S.D.] *Rowe; not in F.*   66. Fenton] *Q3; Fenter F.*   74. S.D.] *Rowe; not in F.*
83. *Aside*] *Bowers; not in F.*   86. yourself. Good] *Warburton* (your self; good);
your selfe good *F.*   86–7.] *Arranged as Rowe³;* Come, . . . good M. | *Fenton,* . . .
enemy: *F.*

66. *Fenton*] F's 'Fenter' is only a compositor's error, more probably from temporary conflation with 'Slender' than from misreading (although 'on' could easily be mistaken for 'er' in secretary hand).

78. *checks*] reproofs, censure.

79. *advance the colours*] A military metaphor: raising the flag as an indication of giving battle.

84–5. *set quick . . . turnips*] be fixed, alive, in the earth (up to the neck) and be killed by having turnips bowled at me. Anne's—and Shakespeare's—vivid imagining may have begun from a real, or mythical, treatment of madmen by burying them up to the neck in earth or worse (Hart cites some evidence for this), although Aaron's punishment in *Tit.* is to be 'set . . . breast-deep in earth' and starved to death.

My daughter will I question how she loves you,
And as I find her, so am I affected.
Till then, farewell, sir; she must needs go in;   90
Her father will be angry.

Fent. Farewell, gentle mistress; farewell, Nan.

                [Exeunt Mistress Page and Anne.]

Quick. This is my doing now. 'Nay', said I, 'will you cast
away your child on a fool, and a physician? Look
on Master Fenton.' This is my doing.   95

Fent. I thank thee; and I pray thee, once to-night
Give my sweet Nan this ring. There's for thy pains.

Quick. Now heaven send thee good fortune! *[Exit
Fenton.]* A kind heart he hath: a woman would run
through fire and water for such a kind heart. But   100
yet I would my master had Mistress Anne; or I
would Master Slender had her; or, in sooth, I
would Master Fenton had her. I will do what I can
for them all three, for so I have promised, and I'll
be as good as my word, but speciously for Master   105
Fenton. Well, I must of another errand to Sir John
Falstaff from my two mistresses; what a beast am I
to slack it!   *Exit.*

---

92. S.D.] *Rowe (after l. 91); not in F.*
98–9. S.D.] *F2 (after l. 97); not in F1.*

94. and] *F;* or *Hanmer, conj. Johnson.*

89. *affected*] inclined (from 'affect' meaning to 'like' or 'respond to').

94. *a fool, and a physician*] 'A fool or a physician' was a common phrase (Tilley M125); in adapting it, Quickly, as usual, is wiser than she knows, in that the phrase both describes Caius and states the choice between Slender and Caius.

96. *once*] (Probably) some time; cf. *1H4*, v. ii. 73, and *Cæs.*, iv. iii. 191—although occasionally the word is used merely as an intensive with an imperative.

105. *speciously*] Quickly's error, repeated at iv. v. 106, for 'specially'.

106–8. *I must . . . slack it*] No allowance whatever for theatrical illusion is made by those who complain either that Quickly has had no time to be given this errand (which, after all, Mistress Page and Mistress Ford planned in iii. iii. 176–84) or that she does in fact 'slack it' since she apparently leaves it until nearly eight o'clock 'the following morning'. 'Double time' is frequent in *Wiv.*

SCENE V

Enter FALSTAFF.

Fal. Bardolph, I say!

[*Enter* BARDOLPH.]

Bard. Here, sir.
Fal. Go fetch me a quart of sack; put a toast in 't. [*Exit
     Bard.*] Have I lived to be carried in a basket, like a
     barrow of butcher's offal, and to be thrown in the   5
     Thames? Well, if I be served such another trick, I'll
     have my brains ta'en out and buttered, and give
     them to a dog for a New Year's gift. The rogues
     slighted me into the river with as little remorse as
     they would have drowned a blind bitch's puppies,   10
     fifteen i' th' litter; and you may know by my size that
     I have a kind of alacrity in sinking: if the bottom

Scene v

SCENE v] *F;* Scene xv. *The Garter-Inn. Pope.*   S.D.] *Q; Enter Falstaffe, Bardolfe,
Quickly, Ford. F; Enter* Falstaff *and* Bardolph. *Rowe.*   1. S.D.] *As New Camb.;
not in F.*   3–4. S.D.] *Theobald; not in F.*   4–6. Have . . . Thames?] *F;* Haue
I liued to be carried in a basket and throwne into the Thames like a barow of
Butchers offoll. *Q.*   9. slighted] *F;* slided *Q;* sleighted *conj. New Camb.*   10.
blind bitch's] *As F;* bitch's blind *Theobald.*

---

3. *toast*] Toast was commonly put in
both beer (to put a 'head' on it) and
wine.

5. *barrow*] barrowful. Wheatley
follows Daniel in preferring the Q
reading, not seeing that 'barrow'
could mean the contents of a barrow
rather than the barrow itself.

7. *buttered*] Hart quotes lines from
The Pilgrim (1621)—'The thing is
mad, / Abominably mad, her brains
are buttered'—that suggest that
'buttered brains was a synonym for
foolishness'.

8. *New Year's gift*] Gifts were custo-
marily given on 1 January (which was
New Year's Day even when it was the
practice not to change the year number, in reckoning dates, until Lady
Day, 25 March).

9. *slighted*] Elsewhere in Shakespeare
(e.g. *2H4*, v. ii. 94) 'slight' means
'treat with contempt' or 'treat as insignificant' and perhaps that is what
it means here, though in a different
construction. Q has 'the rogues slided
me in' which—if it is not a mishearing
or a misunderstanding—may indicate
that F 'slighted' is an error, or that
Shakespeare did intend a kind of pun.

11–12. *you may know . . . sinking*] The
literal-minded duly point out that,
according to the laws of physics, size
and speed in sinking are not necessarily
related. Dorset was later to make a
delightful use of Shakespeare's phrase
in his satire 'To Mr Edward Howard'
—'So in this way of writing, without
thinking, / Thou hast a strange alacrity
in sinking'.

were as deep as hell, I should down. I had been
drowned but that the shore was shelvy and shallow—
a death that I abhor: for the water swells a man; and   15
what a thing should I have been when I had been
swelled! I should have been a mountain of mummy.

[Enter BARDOLPH *with sack.]*

Bard. Here's Mistress Quickly, sir, to speak with you.
Fal. Come, let me pour in some sack to the Thames
water: for my belly's as cold as if I had swallowed   20
snowballs for pills to cool the reins. Call her in.
Bard. Come in, woman!

Enter MISTRESS QUICKLY.

Quick. By your leave; I cry you mercy. Give your worship
good morrow.
Fal. Take away these chalices. Go brew me a pottle of   25
sack finely.
Bard. With eggs, sir?
Fal. Simple of itself; I'll no pullet-sperm in my brewage.
[Exit Bardolph.] How now?
Quick. Marry, sir, I come to your worship from Mistress   30
Ford.
Fal. Mistress Ford! I have had ford enough; I was
thrown into the ford; I have my belly full of ford.

---

17. S.D.] *As Capell; not in F; Enter* Bardolph. *Theobald.*   22. S.D.] *Q; not in F.*
28. pullet-sperm] *F* (Pullet-Spersme).   29. S.D.] *Capell; not in F.*

---

14. *shelvy*] 'Shelves' in *3H6*, v. iv. 23,
Lucr., 335, and at least twice in
Marlowe's (and Nashe's) *Dido* means
sandbanks (once it is perhaps used of
reefs or rocks): *O.E.D.* 'shelf' *sb.²*
Falstaff may thus mean that the bed of
the river had sandbanks so that the
water was not deep; alternatively he
could mean that the bed 'shelved' or
sloped gradually (*O.E.D.* 'shelve' *v.³*
1).
    17. *mummy*] Perhaps just 'dead
flesh', as *O.E.D.* takes it (obviously
Falstaff is not thinking of a desiccated
body) but the word was also applied

to 'a pulpy substance or mass' (*O.E.D.*
sb.¹ 1. c).
    21. *reins*] kidneys.
    24. *morrow*] morning—and as the
subsequent exchange with Ford shows,
it *is* morning, about 8 a.m. See III.
iv. 106–8 and note.
    25. *chalices*] drinking cups or goblets
(as in *Ham.*, IV. vii. 161)—but Falstaff,
complaining that from such goblets he
cannot get more than a sip, may also
be thinking of the sacramental vessels.
    pottle] half a gallon, or a vessel of that
size (as in II. i. 203).
    28. *Simple*] pure, 'straight'.

Quick. Alas the day, good heart, that was not her fault!
　She does so take on with her men; they mistook their　35
　erection.
Fal. So did I mine, to build upon a foolish woman's
　promise.
Quick. Well, she laments, sir, for it, that it would yearn
　your heart to see it. Her husband goes this morning　40
　a-birding; she desires you once more to come to her,
　between eight and nine. I must carry her word
　quickly; she'll make you amends, I warrant you.
Fal. Well, I will visit her; tell her so. And bid her think
　what a man is; let her consider his frailty, and then　45
　judge of my merit.
Quick. I will tell her.
Fal. Do so. Between nine and ten, sayst thou?
Quick. Eight and nine, sir.
Fal. Well, be gone; I will not miss her.　　　　　　　50
Quick. Peace be with you, sir.　　　　　　　　*Exit.*
Fal. I marvel I hear not of Master Brook; he sent me
　word to stay within. I like his money well.—O, here
　he comes.

Enter FORD *as* BROOK.

Ford. Bless you, sir!　　　　　　　　　　　　55
Fal. Now, Master Brook, you come to know what hath
　passed between me and Ford's wife?
Ford. That, indeed, Sir John, is my business.
Fal. Master Brook, I will not lie to you: I was at her
　house the hour she appointed me.　　　　　　60
Ford. And sped you, sir?

51. S.D.] *Q; not in F.*　　54. S.D.] *As Q; not in F.*

35. *does so take on with*] The phrase is
used again in IV. ii. 18: shows how
angry she is with.
36. *erection*] Quickly's version of
direction (instruction).
39. *yearn*] move to compassion
(*O.E.D.* v.¹ 7). Hilda Hulme (p. 125)
suspects a further indecency, on the
meaning 'to become erect'.
45. *consider his frailty*] Falstaff, like

the devil, can quote—or adapt—
Scripture: 'the flesh is frail', then as
now, was a popular variation on the
Biblical 'the flesh is weak' (Tilley
F363).
50. *miss*] fail.
61. *sped you*] did you succeed (past
tense of the verb 'to speed')—no doubt
with special emphasis on sexual
success.

Fal. Very ill-favouredly, Master Brook.

Ford. How so, sir? Did she change her determination?

Fal. No, Master Brook, but the peaking cornuto her
husband, Master Brook, dwelling in a continual   65
larum of jealousy, comes me in the instant of our
encounter, after we had embraced, kissed, protested,
and, as it were, spoke the prologue of our comedy;
and at his heels a rabble of his companions, thither
provoked and instigated by his distemper, and, for-   70
sooth, to search his house for his wife's love.

Ford. What, while you were there?

Fal. While I was there.

Ford. And did he search for you, and could not find you?

Fal. You shall hear. As good luck would have it, comes   75
in one Mistress Page; gives intelligence of Ford's
approach; and, in her invention and Ford's wife's
distraction, they conveyed me into a buck-basket—

Ford. A buck-basket?

Fal. Yes, a buck-basket!—rammed me in with foul   80
shirts and smocks, socks, foul stockings, greasy
napkins, that, Master Brook, there was the rankest
compound of villainous smell that ever offended
nostril.

77. in] *F*; by *Q*.   78. distraction] *F*; direction *Hanmer, conj. Warburton.*   80.
Yes] *F1*; By the Lord *Q*; Yea *F2*.   81. greasy] *F*; and greasie *Rowe.*

62. *ill-favouredly*] i.e. unpleasantly or
disagreeably (the corresponding adjective, used before in I. i. 275, usually
means 'ugly').

64. *peaking*] sneaking, skulking, or
mean-spirited (*O.E.D.* 1). The quibble
seen by some editors on the 'peak' of
the (cuckold's) horn may be imaginary.

cornuto] horned beast, cuckold.
('Cornute', an anglicized form of the
Italian word, is also found.)

66. *larum*] A common aphetic form
of 'alarum': alarm.

me] Another instance of the 'ethic
dative' in Falstaff's speech. Cf. I. iii. 52
and note.

67. *encounter*] Often, but by no means
always, in Shakespeare means 'ama-

tory meeting'. The tone of the word is
best suggested in *Troil.*, IV. v. 58–9, by
the derivative 'encounterer': 'these
encounterers, so glib of tongue, / That
give accosting welcome ere it comes'—
part of Ulysses' scornful description of
Cressida.

protested] made protestations (of
affection).

70. *distemper*] lack of 'temper' (in the
sense of balance).

78. *distraction*] Q confirms the F
reading and so rules out the emendation 'direction'.

80. *rammed*] There is probably a
quibble on 'ram' and 'buck', each
meaning the male of certain horned
species.

82. *that*] with the result that.

Ford. And how long lay you there?   85
Fal. Nay, you shall hear, Master Brook, what I have
    suffered to bring this woman to evil, for your good.
    Being thus crammed in the basket, a couple of
    Ford's knaves, his hinds, were called forth by their
    mistress to carry me in the name of foul clothes to   90
    Datchet Lane; they took me on their shoulders;
    met the jealous knave their master in the door,
    who asked them once or twice what they had in
    their basket. I quaked for fear lest the lunatic
    knave would have searched it; but fate, ordaining   95
    he should be a cuckold, held his hand. Well, on
    went he for a search, and away went I for foul
    clothes. But mark the sequel, Master Brook: I
    suffered the pangs of three several deaths. First, an
    intolerable fright, to be detected with a jealous   100
    rotten bell-wether; next, to be compassed like a
    good bilbo in the circumference of a peck, hilt to
    point, heel to head; and then to be stopped in like
    a strong distillation with stinking clothes that
    fretted in their own grease—think of that—a man   105

100. with] F; by Rowe³.

89. *knaves, his hinds*] Originally
'hind', like 'knave', meant only
'servant', particularly a farm-servant,
but it was commonly used in a derisory
way to mean 'boor'.

93–4. *who . . . basket*] See III. iii. 166–7
and note.

95–6. *fate . . . cuckold*] Falstaff is alluding to the maxim that 'cuckolds come
by destiny' (Tilley C889).

100. *with*] by.

101. *rotten*] rotting (with disease).

bell-wether] the castrated male sheep
that wore a bell round its neck and
was used to lead the flock: hence,
often, leader of the 'mob'—and
Falstaff sees Ford as that too (cf. l.
69).

compassed] Not 'encompassed' but
'curved' (*O.E.D.* 'compass' *v*.¹ v.14)—
'head to foot', as Falstaff goes on to

explain, since he had to curl up to fit
into the basket.

102. *good bilbo*] Part of the test of
quality in the bilbo or 'Bilboa' sword
(cf. I. i. 146 and note) would be to bend
it 'hilt to point' to make sure that it
would not snap.

peck] a vessel that would hold a
'peck', a quarter of a bushel, of dry
goods.

103. *stopped*] stuffed (*O.E.D.* 'stop'
v. 1).

104. *distillation*] Here, that which
has been, or is being, distilled—i.e.
condensed after being converted into
vapour by heat.

105. *fretted*] fermented (*O.E.D.*
'fret' *v*.¹ 7, 10)—and did so in their own
'grease', not needing the addition of
Falstaff's. Cf. the image in II. i. 65–6,
which Falstaff unwittingly is repeating.

of my kidney—think of that—that am as subject to
heat as butter; a man of continual dissolution and
thaw: it was a miracle to 'scape suffocation. And
in the height of this bath, when I was more than
half stewed in grease, like a Dutch dish, to be   110
thrown into the Thames and cooled, glowing hot,
in that surge, like a horse-shoe—think of that—
hissing hot—think of that, Master Brook!

Ford. In good sadness, sir, I am sorry that for my sake
you have suffered all this. My suit, then, is des-   115
perate: you'll undertake her no more?

Fal. Master Brook, I will be thrown into Etna, as I have
been into Thames, ere I will leave her thus. Her
husband is this morning gone a-birding; I have
received from her another embassy of meeting.   120
'Twixt eight and nine is the hour, Master Brook.

Ford. 'Tis past eight already, sir.

Fal. Is it? I will then address me to my appointment.
Come to me at your convenient leisure and you
shall know how I speed; and the conclusion shall   125
be crowned with your enjoying her. Adieu. You
shall have her, Master Brook; Master Brook, you
shall cuckold Ford.   *Exit.*

Ford. Hum! Ha! Is this a vision? Is this a dream? Do I
sleep? Master Ford, awake; awake, Master Ford: 130

---

112. surge] *F* (serge); forge *conj. Capell* (*1783*).   128. *Exit*] *Q*; *not in F.*

---

106. *of my kidney*] The phrase survives in colloquial use to mean 'make-
up' or, sometimes, 'type', but in
Falstaff's use it is, of course, particularly vivid as carrying on the physical
images of fat, blubber, and grease.

107. *dissolution*] dissolving, turning
into liquid.

110. *Dutch dish*] Presumably the
cooking of the Low Countries was
proverbially oily or 'greasy'.

112. *surge*] The word had once
meant simply 'stream' (*O.E.D. sb.* 1. a)
but had come to have its modern
meaning of violently moving water
and so adds to the comic exaggeration

when applied to the Thames, so placid
until Falstaff is tipped in.

114. *sadness*] seriousness (the normal
Elizabethan meaning).

117–18. *Etna . . . Thames*] A
brilliant adaptation of 'go through
fire and water'.

120. *embassy*] ambassador, or party
of ambassadors; and even though used
elsewhere by Shakespeare of messages
of love, has a deliberately comic effect
of incongruity here since it refers to
Mistress Quickly.

127–8. *Brook . . . Ford*] Again a neat
verbal jest is ruined if 'Broome' replaces 'Brook'.

there's a hole made in your best coat, Master Ford.
This 'tis to be married; this 'tis to have linen and
buck-baskets! Well, I will proclaim myself what I
am. I will now take the lecher; he is at my house;
he cannot 'scape me; 'tis impossible he should; he   135
cannot creep into a halfpenny purse, nor into a
pepper-box; but, lest the devil that guides him
should aid him, I will search impossible places.
Though what I am I cannot avoid, yet to be what I
would not shall not make me tame: if I have horns   140
to make one mad, let the proverb go with me—I'll
be horn-mad.   *Exit.*

141. one] *F;* me *Halliwell, conj. Dyce (Remarks).*

131. *a hole made . . . coat*] 'To pick a
hole in a man's coat' was a proverbial
phrase (Tilley H522) meaning to find
a fault in somebody who was thought
of, or who thought of himself, as im-
peccable. Cf. *H5,* III. vi. 88–9.

136. *halfpenny purse*] A small purse
for carrying halfpennies and other such
coins. Cf. *LLL.,* v. i. 77, 'thou half-
penny purse of wit'.

142. *horn-mad*] See note on I. iv. 45.

ACT IV

SCENE I

Enter Mistress Page, [Mistress] Quickly, *and* William.

Mrs. Page. Is he at Master Ford's already, think'st thou?

Quick. Sure he is by this, or will be presently; but truly he is very courageous mad about his throwing into the water. Mistress Ford desires you to come suddenly.

Mrs. Page. I'll be with her by and by: I'll but bring my   5
young man here to school. Look, where his master comes; 'tis a playing-day, I see.

[Enter Evans.]

How now, Sir Hugh, no school to-day?

Evans. No; Master Slender is let the boys leave to play.

Quick. Blessing of his heart!   10

Mrs. Page. Sir Hugh, my husband says my son profits nothing in the world at his book. I pray you, ask him some questions in his accidence.

ACT IV

Scene i

Act IV Scene i] *F;* Act IV. Scene i. Page'*s house. Pope; Act IV. Scene I. A Street.*
Capell.   S.D.] *Rowe; Enter Mistris Page, Quickly, William, Euans. F.*   7. S.D.]
Rowe (after l. 8); not in F.   9. let] *F;* get *Collier².*

iv. i] For comment on this scene, as probably intended for an educated audience, see Introduction, p. xxix. It avoids two successive Falstaff scenes. Q, which has nothing corresponding to iv. i, gets over the difficulty by transposing iii. iv and iii. v, and (necessarily) by omitting the mention in the original iii. iv of Quickly's errand to Falstaff.

2. *presently*] immediately (as in iii. iii. 81). 'By and by' (l. 5) has weakened in meaning in exactly the same way.

3. *courageous*] Perhaps Quickly intended another word (but it is hardly likely to have been 'outrageous' as Hart and others say). As usual, her malapropism is, ironically, appropriate.

9.] Apparently, distinguished visitors to schools had the same privilege as they have today, of 'asking' for a holiday for the pupils.

13. *accidence*] the part of grammar that deals with the inflexions of

Evans. Come hither, William. Hold up your head; come.

Mrs. Page. Come on, sirrah, hold up your head. Answer 15
your master, be not afraid.

Evans. William, how many numbers is in nouns?

Will. Two.

Quick. Truly I thought there had been one number more,
because they say 'Od's nouns'.   20

Evans. Peace your tattlings! What is 'fair', William?

Will. Pulcher.

Quick. Polecats? There are fairer things than polecats,
sure.

Evans. You are a very simplicity 'oman: I pray you,   25
peace.—What is *lapis*, William?

Will. A stone.

Evans. And what is 'a stone', William?

Will. A pebble.

Evans. No, it is *lapis*: I pray you remember in your prain. 30

Will. Lapis.

Evans. That is a good William. What is he, William, that
does lend articles?

words. Here, of course, in the practice of Elizabethan schools, the language in question is Latin; and William is almost certainly being tested on the opening pages of the text-book that Edward VI commanded to be used in all schools, *A Shorte Introduction of Grammar* ('for the bryngynge vp of all those that entende to atteyne the knowlege of the Latine tongue'), by William Lilly and John Colet, first published in 1549 and often reprinted. Such 'rehersing of the wordes' is recommended to the schoolmaster, in the preface.

15. *sirrah*] Cf. I. iii. 75 and III. ii. 18 and notes.

18. *Two*] William is correct: as Lilly told him, 'In Nounes be two Numbers, the Singular and the Plurall'.

20. *Od's nouns*] Quickly has misunderstood the common expletive, which is a corruption of '(By) God's (i.e. Christ's) wounds' ('nouns' being

pronounced with the vowel [u:]).

22. pulcher] One of Lilly's examples of an adjective or 'Noune Adiective'.

23. *Polecats*] Quickly's confusion is more easily understood if, as is probable, the Elizabethan pronunciation of the first syllable rhymed with 'pull', but again she is giving herself away: polecats were notorious for their odour—and the word was slang for 'prostitutes'.

26. lapis] This is the noun that Lilly uses to exemplify a singular form and also the third declension; and the schoolmaster is advised in the preface to have the pupil both turn the Latin into English and turn the English back into Latin.

29. *pebble*] The F spelling 'peeble' probably indicates William's pronunciation (a common one), and makes clearer the joke ('stone', of course, also meant 'testicle').

Will. Articles are borrowed of the pronoun, and be thus
    declined: *Singulariter nominativo hic, hæc, hoc.*   35
Evans. *Nominativo hig, hag, hog.* Pray you mark: *genitivo
    huius.* Well, what is your accusative case?
Will. *Accusativo hinc.*
Evans. I pray you have your remembrance, child: *accusa-
    tivo hing, hang, hog.*   40
Quick. 'Hang-hog' is Latin for bacon, I warrant you.
Evans. Leave your prabbles, 'oman.—What is the
    focative case, William?
Will. O—*vocativo,* O.
Evans. Remember, William: focative is *caret.*   45
Quick. And that's a good root.

38. *hinc*] *F;* hunc *Halliwell.*   40. *hing*] *F;* hung *Pope.*   41. Latin] *F3* (Latine);
latten *F1.*

34–5.] More text-book material—
and William has learnt it off, word for
word from his edition of Lilly (probably 1577), without understanding
any of it. Evans continues the quotation from Lilly with his *'genitivo huius'*
in ll. 36–7.

35. nominativo] This, the form used
in Lilly's text-book, is the ablative
case of the Latin word for 'nominative'
and means '*in* the nominative' (case),
as *genitivo* and *accusativo* in ll. 36 and
38–9 mean 'in the genitive' and 'in
the accusative'.

40. hing, hang, hog] i.e. *hinc, hanc,
hoc.* William has given only the
masculine accusative, and has given
it incorrectly (it should be *hunc*). Evans
adds the feminine and neuter forms but
repeats William's error (unless Pope's
emendation is to be accepted—and it
surely spoils the joke).

41. *Hang-hog*] Quickly's miraculous
inference is not necessarily more
amusing if, with Zachary Grey (I. 110–
11) and Halliwell, one sees a reference
to Sir Nicholas Bacon's rejoinder to
one Hog, a prisoner who claimed kin-
ship and asked that the sentence of
death passed on him should therefore
be commuted: 'you and I cannot be
of kindred unless you be hang'd; for

Hog is not Bacon, till it be well hang'd'.

42. *prabbles*] Elsewhere (see I. i. 51–2
and note) Evans speaks of 'pribbles
and prabbles' and means 'quarrels'.
Here 'silly objections', even 'prattling'.

43. *focative*] Evans's mispronunciation of 'vocative'—which, unfortunately, in conjunction with William's
reply, suggests a 'four-letter word'.

44.] F prints all three words in italic,
its way of drawing attention to
William's learnt-off replies; but it also
has l. 50 in italic, and l. 44 is funnier if
William's 'O' is intended to show his
distress at not being able to give an
answer, and thereby giving an intel-
ligible one, that the vocative is the form
used in address—'O woman' (or whatever the noun may be). Alternatively, Baldwin (I. 561–5) thinks that
William's mind goes back to Lilly's
section on the vocative of nouns, where
the example cited is 'O *magister*, *O
mayster*'.

45. caret] Latin for 'is missing'
(regularly used by Lilly in such con-
texts—e.g. 'vocatiuo caret') and,
perhaps, 'is *caret*' shows how little
Latin even Evans has learnt. Quickly
thinks he has said 'carrot'—but that
was also a slang term for the penis
(Partridge, p. 84).

Evans. 'Oman, forbear.

Mrs. Page. Peace.

Evans. What is your genitive case plural, William?

Will. Genitive case?   50

Evans. Ay.

Will. Genitive *horum, harum, horum*.

Quick. Vengeance of Ginny's case; fie on her! Never
    name her, child, if she be a whore.

Evans. For shame, 'oman.   55

Quick. You do ill to teach the child such words.—He
    teaches him to hick and to hack, which they'll do
    fast enough of themselves, and to call 'horum'—fie
    upon you!

Evans. 'Oman, art thou lunatics? Hast thou no under- 60
    standings for thy cases, and the numbers of the
    genders? Thou art as foolish Christian creatures as
    I would desires.

Mrs. Page. [*To Quickly*] Prithee hold thy peace.

Evans. Show me now, William, some declensions of your 65
    pronouns.

Will. Forsooth, I have forgot.

Evans. It is *qui, quæ, quod*: if you forget your *quies*, your
    quæs, and your *quods*, you must be preeches. Go your
    ways, and play; go.   70

Mrs. Page. He is a better scholar than I thought he was.

Evans. He is a good sprag memory. Farewell, Mistress
    Page.

52. Genitive] *F;* Genitivo *Singer.*   53. Ginny's] *This ed.;* Ginyes *F;* Giney's
Theobald; Jenny's *Capell;* Jinny's *Ridley.*   60. lunatics] *Capell;* Lunaties *F;*
Lunacies *Rowe.*   61. of] *F;* and *Collier².*   the] *F;* thy *conj. Grant White.*
64. *To Quickly*] *Munro; not in F.*   68. quæ] *Pope;* que *F.*   69. quæs] *Pope;*
Ques *F.*   preeches] *F;* preeched *conj. Grant White.*

53. *Vengeance of*] A mild asseveration: 'a plague on'.

case] Another slang term—this time,
for the female pudend.

57. *to hick and to hack*] (Apparently)
to hiccup from excessive drinking and
to take sexual pleasure where it can be
found: cf. II. i. 50 and note.

67. *I have forgot*] Or, possibly,
William has not reached pp. 16 and 17
of his Lilly.

68–9. quies . . . quæs . . . quods] If
pronounced by Evans as 'keys . . .
case . . . cods', the words would suggest
to an Elizabethan audience still
further indecencies: 'case' as in l. 53,
'cods' for 'testicles', and 'keys' for the
part that 'unlocks' the 'case'.

69. *preeches*] breeches—i.e. breeched,
meaning whipped.

72. *sprag*] Perhaps Evans's pronunciation of 'sprack', but Wright records

Mrs. Page. Adieu, good Sir Hugh. [*Exit Evans.*] Get you
   home, boy. Come, we stay too long.   *Exeunt.*   75

SCENE II

Enter FALSTAFF *and* MISTRESS FORD.

Fal. Mistress Ford, your sorrow hath eaten up my
   sufferance. I see you are obsequious in your love,
   and I profess requital to a hair's breadth, not only,
   Mistress Ford, in the simple office of love, but in all
   the accoutrement, complement, and ceremony of it.   5
   But are you sure of your husband now?
Mrs. Ford. He's a-birding, sweet Sir John.
Mrs. Page. [*Within*] What ho, gossip Ford! What ho!
Mrs. Ford. Step into th' chamber, Sir John.   [*Exit Falstaff.*]

[*Enter* MISTRESS PAGE.]

74. S.D.] *Steevens³; not in F.*

Scene II

SCENE II] *F;* Scene II. Ford's *House. Pope;* [4.2] *The hall in Master Ford's house; the
buck-basket in a corner New Camb.*   S.D.] *Rowe; Enter Falstoffe, Mist. Ford, Mist.
Page, Seruants, Ford, Page, Caius, Euans, Shallow. F.*   5. accoutrement] *Capell;*
accustrement *F1;* accoustrement *F2.*   8. *Within*] *Rowe; not in F.*   9. *Exit
Falstaff*] *Rowe; not in F.*   Enter . . . Page] *As F2; not in F1.*

later uses of 'sprag' in the same sense of
'lively' or 'smart'.

Scene II

1–2. *your sorrow . . . sufferance*] i.e. my
suffering is completely insignificant in
comparison with your sorrow, and I
have forgotten it.

2. *obsequious*] compliant, anxious to
please (*O.E.D.* 1).

3. *to a hair's breadth*] Already a stock
phrase (Tilley H29).

4. *office*] function or (perhaps) deed,
act.

5. *accoutrement*] There would be a
strong case for preserving F's 'accustrement' as an older form of the word
rather than an old spelling. It normally

means 'apparel' (or 'equipment'), as
in *AYL.*, III. ii. 402, and is rather odd
here—but of course Falstaff is using his
precious, wooing, manner as in III. iii.

complement] This also is hard to paraphrase, for the word did mean con-
summation (*O.E.D. sb.* 3) as well as
accompaniment; and in view of
'ceremony' in the same word-group, it
may be meant in the wider sense of
elaborate forms of polite address
('complement' and 'compliment' were
not always distinguished).

8. *gossip*] A term of affectionate
greeting used by one woman to
another (*O.E.D. sb.* 2). From the OE
godsibb, the word once also meant a
godfather or godmother.

Mrs. Page. How now, sweetheart, who's at home besides   10
yourself?

Mrs. Ford. Why, none but mine own people.

Mrs. Page. Indeed?

Mrs. Ford. No, certainly.—[*Aside to her*] Speak louder.

Mrs. Page. Truly, I am so glad you have nobody here.   15

Mrs. Ford. Why?

Mrs. Page. Why, woman, your husband is in his old lines
again: he so takes on yonder with my husband; so
rails against all married mankind; so curses all Eve's
daughters, of what complexion soever; and so   20
buffets himself on the forehead, crying, 'Peer out,
peer out!', that any madness I ever yet beheld
seemed but tameness, civility, and patience to this
his distemper he is in now. I am glad the fat knight
is not here.   25

Mrs. Ford. Why, does he talk of him?

Mrs. Page. Of none but him, and swears he was carried
out, the last time he searched for him, in a basket;
protests to my husband he is now here, and hath
drawn him and the rest of their company from their   30
sport, to make another experiment of his suspicion.
But I am glad the knight is not here; now he shall
see his own foolery.

Mrs. Ford. How near is he, Mistress Page?

Mrs. Page. Hard by, at street end; he will be here anon.   35

Mrs. Ford. I am undone: the knight is here.

Mrs. Page. Why, then, you are utterly shamed, and he's
but a dead man. What a woman are you? Away

14. S.D.] *As Theobald; not in F.*   17. lines] *F;* vaine *Q;* lunes *Theobald.*

17. *lines*] The Q reading 'in his old
vaine againe' confirms F 'lines' and
almost rules out the emendation
'lunes' (fits of lunacy).

18. *takes on*] is angry. Cf. III. v. 35.

21. *crying, 'Peer out . . . '*] i.e. calling
on the horns of the cuckold to appear
(perhaps quoting an old children's
rhyme, in which the words are addressed to the snail).

23. *to*] compared to.

35. *street end*] This is either an alter-

native form of the possessive or the
construction (Abbott 430) where a
kind of compound noun replaces the
expected possessive. It is frequent with
a proper noun, as in 'Carthage Queen'
(*MND.*, I. i. 173) or 'These should be
Carthage walls' (Marlowe and Nashe's
Dido, II. i. 1).

anon] at once. Like 'presently' and
'by and by', the word has lost force
(and is consequently often misunderstood: cf. *1H4*, II. iv. 31–112).

with him, away with him; better shame than
murder.   40

Mrs. Ford. Which way should he go? How should I
bestow him? Shall I put him into the basket again?

[*Enter* FALSTAFF.]

Fal. No, I'll come no more i' th' basket. May I not go out
ere he come?

Mrs. Page. Alas, three of Master Ford's brothers watch   45
the door with pistols, that none shall issue out;
otherwise you might slip away ere he came. But
what make you here?

Fal. What shall I do? I'll creep up into the chimney.

Mrs. Ford. There they always use to discharge their   50
birding-pieces. Creep into the kill-hole.

Fal. Where is it?

Mrs. Ford. He will seek there, on my word. Neither press,
coffer, chest, trunk, well, vault, but he hath an
abstract for the remembrance of such places and   55
goes to them by his note. There is no hiding you in
the house.

Fal. I'll go out, then.

42. S.D.] *As F2; not in F1.*   51.] *F;* birding-pieces. | *Mrs. Page.* Creep into the
kill-hole. *Dyce, conj. Malone.*   kill-hole] *F;* kiln-hole *Capell.*

42. *the basket*] *New Camb.* is undoubtedly right in having the buck-basket
on the stage from the beginning of the
scene (unless it is 'discovered', by the
drawing of a curtain, at this point).
Ll. 103–4 prove that the servants do
not carry it on at l. 98. The Quarto
version, which begins the scene with
lines corresponding to 99–101, probably implies a recollection that the
basket had to be brought on the stage
before Falstaff enters.

48. *what make you*] what are you
doing.

50–1. *discharge their birding-pieces*]
Because it was a safe way to discharge
the fire-arms or to dislodge the soot (or
both). For the method of hunting
birds, cf. note on III. iii. 214. The

frequent references to 'birding pieces'
confirm that a recognizable type of gun
was used specifically for this 'sport'.

51. *Creep into the kill-hole*] Malone
conjectured that these words should be
given to Mistress Page. He referred to
Mistress Ford's vetoing of the proposal,
in l. 53; but saw also that Mistress
Ford could be tantalizing Falstaff by
pretending to change her mind.
(Ralph Crane's speech prefixes, not
always clearly distinguished and
sometimes not in line with the relevant
speech, may well have caused confusion. Cf. l. 59, note.) The 'kill-hole'
is the door or opening of the kiln or
oven.

53. *press*] cupboard, as in III. iii. 195.

55. *abstract*] list or catalogue.

Mrs. Page. If you go out in your own semblance, you die,
  Sir John—unless you go out disguised.   60
Mrs. Ford. How might we disguise him?
Mrs. Page. Alas the day, I know not: there is no woman's
  gown big enough for him; otherwise he might put on
  a hat, a muffler, and a kerchief, and so escape.
Fal. Good hearts, devise something: any extremity rather   65
  than a mischief.
Mrs. Ford. My maid's aunt, the fat woman of Brainford,
  has a gown above.
Mrs. Page. On my word, it will serve him. She's as big as
  he is; and there's her thrummed hat, and her muffler 70
  too. Run up, Sir John.
Mrs. Ford. Go, go, sweet Sir John; Mistress Page and I
  will look some linen for your head.
Mrs. Page. Quick, quick! We'll come dress you straight;
  put on the gown the while.   [*Exit Falstaff.*]   75
Mrs. Ford. I would my husband would meet him in this
  shape. He cannot abide the old woman of Brainford;
  he swears she's a witch, forbade her my house, and
  hath threatened to beat her.

59–60. *Mrs. Page.* If . . . disguised.] *Malone; Mist. Ford.* If . . . disguis'd. *F;
Mistress Ford.* If . . . Sir John. / *Mistress Page.* Unless you go disguised. *conj. Greg.*
61. *Mrs. Ford.* How . . . him?] *F1;* How . . . him? *F2.*   67. Brainford] *F;*
Brentford *Capell.*   75. S.D.] *As F2; not in F1.*

59. Mrs. Page] Redistribution of
some words from F is necessary, since
F gives Mistress Ford two successive
speeches. Sir Walter Greg, in a private
letter recorded in the 1954 *New
Cambridge*, p. 134, suggested that only
'unless you go out disguised' should be
given to Mistress Page; and Wilson
accepted this.

64. *muffler*] a scarf 'to cover part
of the face and the neck' (*O.E.D.*
1. a).

kerchief] a form of cover for the head
(*O.E.D.* 1) rather than neckerchief
(*O.E.D.* 2), for Falstaff is dressed in a
muffler *and* 'some linen for your head'
(l. 73) which is, presumably, the
kerchief.

65. *Good hearts*] A term of affection,

probably more commonly used by
women to other women.

67. *fat woman of Brainford*] For possible reference to a recorded resident of
Brainford, see Introduction, p. lxii.
Brainford is Brentford, then a village
(on the Thames, about half-way between Windsor and London), now a
suburb of London.

70. *thrummed hat*] 'Thrums' are 'the
ends of the warp-threads left unwoven
and remaining attached to the loom
when the web is cut off' or waste yarn
(*O.E.D.* 'thrum' *sb.*² 1, 2)—but the
verb was used not only of the adapting
of such material but also of fringing
generally (*v.*² b). A fringed hat would
be more appropriate here as offering
more cover for the face.

Mrs. Page. Heaven guide him to thy husband's cudgel;   80
and the devil guide his cudgel afterwards!

Mrs. Ford. But is my husband coming?

Mrs. Page. Ay, in good sadness, is he, and talks of the
basket too, howsoever he hath had intelligence.

Mrs. Ford. We'll try that: for I'll appoint my men to   85
carry the basket again, to meet him at the door with
it, as they did last time.

Mrs. Page. Nay, but he'll be here presently; let's go
dress him like the witch of Brainford.

Mrs. Ford. I'll first direct my men what they shall do   90
with the basket. Go up; I'll bring linen for him
straight.

Mrs. Page. Hang him, dishonest varlet, we cannot
misuse him enough.

We'll leave a proof, by that which we will do,   95
Wives may be merry and yet honest too.
We do not act that often jest and laugh;
'Tis old, but true: 'Still swine eats all the draff'.

[*Exit.*]

[*Enter* JOHN *and* ROBERT.]

Mrs. Ford. Go, sirs, take the basket again on your
shoulders. Your master is hard at door; if he bid   100
you set it down, obey him. Quickly, dispatch.   [*Exit.*]

John. Come, come, take it up.

92.] *Capell adds 'Exit'.*   93–4.] *Prose as Pope;* Hang . . . Varlet, / We . . . misuse
enough: *F.*   94. him] *F2; not in F1.*   98. draff] *F* (draugh).   *Exit] Capell;
not in F.*   *Enter John and Robert.*] *This ed.; not in F1;* Enter M. Ford, Page, Priest,
Shallow, the two men carries the basket, and Ford meets it. *Q;* Enter Ser. *F2 (after l. 101);*
Enter Servants with the Basket. *Rowe (after l. 101);* Re-enter Mistress Ford *with her
two Men. Capell.*   101. *Exit] Capell; not in F; Exeunt* Mrs. Page *and* Mrs. Ford.
Theobald.   102, 104. *John] This ed.; 1 Ser. F.*

83. *in good sadness*] in all seriousness.

84. *intelligence*] information—as in
l. 136.

85. *try*] test.

93. *dishonest*] Probably in a stronger
sense, the opposite of 'honest' (l. 96)
meaning 'chaste'.

97.] i.e. women who jest and laugh
are not the immoral ones; and our mirth
is not assumed for ulterior purposes.

98. *Still swine . . . draff*] A proverb

(Tilley S681). 'Still' means 'quiet', and
'draff' 'dregs' or 'hog's-wash'. The
saying is used in a comparable way by
Heywood in *If You Know Not Me You
Know Nobody,* Part 2: 'The still sowe
eats all the draffe; and no question the
most smoother tongued fellow, the
more arrant knave'.

100. *hard at door*] right at the door,
close to it. (*O.E.D.* 'hard' *adv.* 6). Cf.
'hard by', in l. 35 above.

Robert. Pray heaven it be not full of knight again.
John. I hope not; I had as lief bear so much lead.

[*Enter* FORD, PAGE, SHALLOW, CAIUS, *and* EVANS.]

Ford. Ay, but if it prove true, Master Page, have you   105
any way then to unfool me again?—Set down the
basket, villain! Somebody call my wife. Youth in a
basket! O you pandarly rascals, there's a knot, a
ging, a pack, a conspiracy against me. Now shall the
devil be shamed.—What, wife, I say! Come, come   110
forth: behold what honest clothes you send forth
to bleaching!
Page. Why, this passes, Master Ford; you are not to go
loose any longer, you must be pinioned.
Evans. Why, this is lunatics; this is mad as a mad dog.   115
Shal. Indeed, Master Ford, this is not well, indeed.
Ford. So say I too, sir.

[*Enter* MISTRESS FORD.]

Come hither, Mistress Ford—Mistress Ford, the
honest woman, the modest wife, the virtuous
creature, that hath the jealous fool to her husband!   120
I suspect without cause, mistress, do I?
Mrs. Ford. Heaven be my witness you do, if you
suspect me in any dishonesty.

103. Robert] *This ed.; 2 Ser.* F.   104. as lief] *F2;* liefe as *F1.*   S.D.] *Rowe;
not in* F.   107. villain] *F;* villains *Collier².*   109. ging] *F2;* gin *F1;* gang *Rowe.*
117. S.D.] *Hanmer; not in* F; *after l. 115 Theobald.*

104. S.D. Caius] Actually the main 'justification' for bringing Caius on here is that he appears in the corresponding III.iii; he does not speak. Q does not mention him in its version of the scene; but cf. III. iii. 219 and IV. ii. 29–31.

105ff.] Ford is obviously replying to a query by Page whether he is not making a fool of himself: the stress is on the 'un' of 'unfool' (which is apparently of Shakespeare's coining).

107–8. *Youth in a basket*] Proverbial (Tilley Y51) for a triumphant lover—but Tilley is able to cite only the two examples given by Hart.

108. *knot*] gang. Cf. III. ii. 46 and note.

109. *ging*] gang or pack. This F2 reading makes good sense—but F1's 'gin' is not completely impossible, meaning snare or trap.

109–10. *Now . . . shamed*] i.e. the truth will be known—an allusion to the proverb (Tilley T566) 'Speak the truth and shame the devil'.

113. *passes*] surpasses, is beyond belief. ('Passing' was used in the same way for 'surpassingly', as in 'passing strange'.) The phrase is repeated in l. 126.

Ford. Well said, brazen-face, hold it out.—Come forth,
      sirrah!   [*Pulling clothes out of the basket.*]   125
Page. This passes!
Mrs. Ford. Are you not ashamed? Let the clothes alone.
Ford. I shall find you anon.
Evans. 'Tis unreasonable; will you take up your wife's
      clothes? Come, away.   130
Ford. Empty the basket, I say!
Mrs. Ford. Why, man, why?
Ford. Master Page, as I am a man, there was one con-
      veyed out of my house yesterday in this basket:
      why may not he be there again? In my house I am   135
      sure he is; my intelligence is true, my jealousy is
      reasonable. Pluck me out all the linen.
Mrs. Ford. If you find a man there, he shall die a flea's
      death.
Page. Here's no man.   140
Shal. By my fidelity, this is not well, Master Ford; this
      wrongs you.
Evans. Master Ford, you must pray, and not follow the
      imaginations of your own heart: this is jealousies.
Ford. Well, he's not here I seek for.   145
Page. No, nor nowhere else but in your brain.
Ford. Help to search my house this one time. If I find not
      what I seek, show no colour for my extremity; let

125. S.D.] *As Rowe; not in F.*   130. Come, away] *F;* Come away *Rowe.*   132.
Mrs. Ford] *F;* Page *conj. Lambrechts.*

124. *hold it out*] Cf. *LLL.*, v. ii. 395,
'Can any face of brass hold longer
out?', i.e. remain unchanged for a
longer time. The different but corresponding modern idiom is 'keep it
up'.

136. *intelligence*] information (a
surviving meaning).

137. *me*] The ethic dative again.

141. *By my fidelity*] upon my word, by
my faith. (Even the oaths uttered by
Shallow can sound precious.)

142. *wrongs you*] i.e. is unworthy of
you. Cf. III. iii. 192.

143. *you must pray*] Because Evans
thinks that Ford is possessed by the
devil. Page had made the same assumption in III. iii. 199 (and it is note-
worthy that many of the phrases in
IV. ii echo, probably deliberately,
those of Ford's earlier search).

143–4. *the imaginations of your own
heart*] Evans is alluding to Jeremiah
13:10.

148. *show no colour*] May mean either
'offer no excuse or explanation'
(*O.E.D.* 'colour' *sb.* III) or 'do not
defend, take the part of' (comparing
'show the colours'). Cf. *Cæs.*, II. i.
28–30.

extremity] going to extremes or,
perhaps, extravagance (*O.E.D.* 5).

me for ever be your table-sport; let them say of me,
'As jealous as Ford, that searched a hollow walnut   150
for his wife's leman'. Satisfy me once more; once
more search with me.

[*Exeunt John and Robert with the basket.*]

Mrs. Ford. What, ho, Mistress Page, come you and the
old woman down; my husband will come into the
chamber.   155

Ford. Old woman? What old woman's that?

Mrs. Ford. Why, it is my maid's aunt of Brainford.

Ford. A witch, a quean, an old cozening quean! Have I
not forbid her my house? She comes of errands,
does she? We are simple men; we do not know   160
what's brought to pass under the profession of
fortune-telling. She works by charms, by spells, by
th' figure, and such daubery as this is, beyond our
element; we know nothing. Come down, you witch,
you hag, you; come down, I say!   165

152. S.D.] *This ed.; not in F, Q.*   157.] *F; Why my maidens Ant, Gilliā of
Brainford. Q.*   163. daubery] *F (dawbry).   is,] F; is Wheatley.*

149. *table-sport*] the subject of your
dinner-table jokes.

150. *a hollow walnut*] the proverbial
unlikely small hiding-place.

151. *leman*] lover (often, unlawful
lover). Shakespeare may be using the
word here—and in *Tw.N.*, II. iii. 26,
and *2H4*, v. iii. 49—as a conscious
archaism (Byron, of course, revived it
in *Childe Harold*).

157.] By naming the old woman
'Gillian', Q makes more probable
some reference to a real (or proverbial)
person. See Introduction, p. lxii, and
cf. l. 168 and note.

158. *cozening*] cheating—both because of her fortune-telling and because he suspects her 'errands' of
being immoral.

quean] disreputable female (of any
kind, though often used of har-
lots).

162–3. *by th' figure*] by drawing the
appropriate diagrams—no doubt including the 'lines, circles, letters, and

characters' that Marlowe's Faustus
names as the 'heavenly' 'metaphysics
of magicians / And necromantic books'
(Scene 1, 48–50). In astrology, 'figure'
was also used for diagrams of the
'aspects' of the planets, or a horoscope.
These interpretations seem more probable than an allusion to the witch's
frequent use of a wax figure of her
victim on which to cast spells etc. But
see next note.

163. *daubery*] Although 'daub' could
mean to cover with clay (and perhaps
therefore to model in clay) and also to
paint inartistically (as the model
would no doubt have been painted),
'daubery' here probably derives rather
from 'daub' as meaning 'put on a
false show' (*O.E.D. v.* 7. b) and so
means 'trickery' generally.

163–4. *beyond our element*] *Either*
'beyond our legitimate sphere of
activity or knowledge' *or*, spoken
ironically, 'beyond our feeble understanding' (cf. 'out of one's element').

Mrs. Ford. Nay, good, sweet husband!—Good gentlemen, let him not strike the old woman.

Enter FALSTAFF *in woman's clothes, and* MISTRESS PAGE.

Mrs. Page. Come, Mother Prat, come, give me your
hand.

Ford. I'll prat her. [*Beating him*] Out of my door, you   170
witch, you rag, you baggage, you polecat, you
runnion, out, out! I'll conjure you, I'll fortune-tell
you.   [*Exit Falstaff.*]

Mrs. Page. Are you not ashamed? I think you have
killed the poor woman.   175

Mrs. Ford. Nay, he will do it. 'Tis a goodly credit for
you!

Ford. Hang her, witch!

Evans. By yea and no, I think the 'oman is a witch
indeed. I like not when a 'oman has a great peard;   180
I spy a great peard under his muffler.

Ford. Will you follow, gentlemen? I beseech you,
follow; see but the issue of my jealousy; if I cry out

167. not] *Q3; not in F.*   S.D.] *Q (Enter Falstaffe disguised like an old woman, and
misteris Page with him, Ford beates him, and hee runnes away.); not in F1; Enter Fal. F2.*
170. S.D.] *As Rowe (after 'witch'); not in F.*   171. rag] *F1* (Ragge); *Hagge Q3;
Rag F2; Hag F3.*   172. runnion] *F;* ronyon *Capell.*   173. S.D.] *F2; not in F1.*
181. his] *F;* her *Q.*

168. *Mother Prat*] The name is not
found in Q or in any other recorded
allusion to Gillian of Brainford.

170. *prat*] Hart thought that this
was an instance of the more or less
meaningless repetition, in a threat, of
a word previously used (like 'fortune-
tell' in l. 172); *New Cambridge* compares 'prat(s)' defined by *O.E.D.* (*sb.²*)
as 'buttocks'. But cf. *O.E.D.* 'prat' *v.*
meaning 'to practise tricks'—which
would be exactly parallel to 'I'll
conjure you' in l. 172.

171. *rag*] Emendation is unnecessary: 'rag' is similarly applied in
Tim., IV. iii. 271, to somebody worthless.

polecat] See note on IV. i. 23.

172. *runnion*] The word—also used
contemptuously of a woman, by the
First Witch, in *Mac.,* I. iii. 6, in the
form 'ronyon'—is probably from MF
rongne, F *rogne,* the mange or scurf,
whence *rongneux,* scurvy (cf. 'the
roynish clown' in *AYL.,* II. ii. 8),
although *O.E.D.* is uncertain and is
content to say 'an abusive term applied
to a woman'.

181. *his*] Emendation of F is again
superfluous: Evans in his excitement
gets his pronouns mixed—and so is
wiser than he knows. Certainly Evans
does not suspect the truth: as Hart
shows, citing e.g. *Mac.,* I. iii. 46, beards
were thought to be common among
witches.

thus upon no trail, never trust me when I open
again.   185

Page. Let's obey his humour a little further: come
gentlemen.   *Exeunt Ford, Page, Shallow, Caius, and Evans.*

Mrs. Page. Trust me, he beat him most pitifully.

Mrs. Ford. Nay, by th' mass, that he did not: he beat
him most unpitifully, methought.   190

Mrs. Page. I'll have the cudgel hallowed and hung o'er
the altar; it hath done meritorious service.

Mrs. Ford. What think you: may we, with the warrant
of womanhood and the witness of a good conscience,
pursue him with any further revenge?   195

Mrs Page. The spirit of wantonness is sure scared out of
him; if the devil have him not in fee-simple, with
fine and recovery, he will never, I think, in the way
of waste attempt us again.

Mrs. Ford. Shall we tell our husbands how we have   200
served him?

Mrs. Page. Yes, by all means—if it be but to scrape the
figures out of your husband's brains. If they can
find in their hearts the poor unvirtuous fat knight
shall be any further afflicted, we two will still be   205
the ministers.

---

187. S.D.] *Q* (*Exit omnes*); *not in F1; Exeunt F2.*

184. *upon no trail*] when there is not
in fact a scent for the hounds to follow
(and 'cry out' is the technical hunting
term for the barking of the dogs).

open] give tongue when following a
scent (*O.E.D. v.* II. 21)—a regular
hunting term, thus carrying on the
image of 'upon no trail'.

186. *obey his humour*] accede to his
'distempered', unbalanced requests.

196. *wantonness*] lust (i.e. a stronger
sense than the current one).

197. *in fee-simple*] The legal term for
absolute possession, for ever, with no
flaw in the title and no 'limitation'.

197-8. *with fine and recovery*] Both
'fine' and 'recovery' have more than
one meaning in law, but almost certainly the reference here is to the pro-

cesses, based on legal fiction, by which
an entailed estate is transferred. Mistress Page would thus mean, in short,
that unless the devil's title to Falstaff
is now final, beyond any possibility of
change, Falstaff will not err in this
way again. (Elizabethans were particularly interested in legal procedure,
and Shakespeare's knowledge of law
is not exceptional.)

199. *waste*] Yet another legal term:
roughly, any unauthorized act of da-
mage or destruction by a tenant, one
who does not have full legal owner-
ship—and so correctly applied to Falstaff's relations with the merry wives.

203. *figures*] imaginings (distinct
from the use of 'figure' in l. 163).

206. *ministers*] Perhaps again in a

Mrs. Ford. I'll warrant they'll have him publicly
shamed; and methinks there would be no period
to the jest should he not be publicly shamed.

Mrs. Page. Come, to the forge with it, then; shape it: I   210
would not have things cool.   *Exeunt.*

SCENE III

Enter HOST *and* BARDOLPH.

Bard. Sir, the German desires to have three of your
horses: the Duke himself will be to-morrow at court,
and they are going to meet him.

Host. What duke should that be comes so secretly? I hear
not of him in the court. Let me speak with the   5
gentlemen. They speak English?

210. it, then; shape] *as Hudson;* it, then shape *F;* it then, shape *Hanmer.*

Scene III

SCENE III] *F;* Scene VI. *Changes to the* Garter-Inn. *Pope.*   1. German desires] *F;*
Germans desire *Capell.*

legal sense: the officers whose duty it
is to ad*minister* the law.

    208. *period*] full-stop, end.

Scene III

IV. iii] For the problems of inter-
preting this scene, see Introduction,
pp. xlvi ff. Briefly, one must deduce that
Caius and Evans, carrying out their
threat to take vengeance on the Host,
have hired somebody (some commentators would say Pistol, Nym, and
John Rugby) to impersonate the
retainers of a German duke and hire
the Host's horses—perhaps without
paying the hire and certainly pro-
posing not to return them. The
German duke may be Count Mömpelgard. It is even more debatable
whether the holding of Falstaff's
horses as security (V. v. 115–16) is
linked with this; indeed it is not clear
whether Ford–Brook (V. v. 238–40)
does finally release Falstaff from the

obligation to pay the money for which
the horses have been held.

    1. *German desires*] Most editors ac-
cept the emendation 'Germans desire'
but where all is so cryptic, alteration is
most unwise. Obviously there is more
than one retainer (Q says 'heere be
three Gentlemen come from the Duke
the Stanger sir, would haue your
horse') but perhaps there is one spokes-
man.

    4. *What duke . . . secretly?*] The line
has more meaning if Hotson's theory
is accepted—that the play was written
for a ceremony to which Count
Mömpelgard, Duke of Würtemberg,
was carefully not invited: he 'comes so
secretly' that he does not come at all.
See Introduction, p. xlvii. *Pace New
Cambridge,* there is no contradiction
with ll. 9–10: the Host has reservations for the retainers, not for the Duke
who would no doubt have more aristocratic lodgings.

Bard. Ay, sir; I'll call him to you.

Host. They shall have my horses, but I'll make them pay;
    I'll sauce them. They have had my house a week at
    command; I have turned away my other guests.   10
    They must come off; I'll sauce them. Come.   *Exeunt.*

SCENE IV

Enter PAGE, FORD, MISTRESS PAGE, MISTRESS FORD, *and*
EVANS.

Evans. 'Tis one of the best discretions of a 'oman as ever
    I did look upon.

Page. And did he send you both these letters at an
    instant?

Mrs. Page. Within a quarter of an hour.   5

Ford. Pardon me, wife. Henceforth do what thou wilt:
    I rather will suspect the sun with cold

---

7. him] *F; them Q.*   9. house] *Q; houses F.*   11. come off] *F; compt off*
Theobald, conj. Warburton; count off *Hanmer, conj. Warburton;* not come off *Capell.*

Scene IV

SCENE IV] *F;* Scene VII. *Changes to* Ford's house. *Pope.*   S.D.] *F; Enter Ford,*
Page, their wiues, Shallow, and Slender. Syr Hu. Q.   7. cold] *Rowe;* gold *F.*

---

7. *him*] The F pronoun is retained, consistently with 'German' in l. 1. Q, equally consistently, has Bardolph say 'Ile call them to you sir'.

9. *sauce*] The metaphor is more probably from seasoning food (cf. *AYL.,* III. v. 69, 'I'll sauce her with bitter words') than, as Hilda Hulme suggests, pp. 45–6, from paying more for the sauce than for the food. *New Cambridge* is surely right in preserving the image by paraphrasing 'make it hot for them'. *O.E.D.* cites only this passage for the meaning 'charge extortionate prices', comparing the much later phrase 'to pay sauce'.

9–10. *at command*] Generally explained as 'reserved for their use upon arrival' but Schmidt's paraphrase 'at pleasure' is supported by many paral-

lels from other plays, and makes sense in that the Host would be less likely to 'turn away' his other guests before the 'Germans' arrived. Perhaps, however, he would have known more about them if they had already been in residence.

11. *come off*] 'pay up' (*O.E.D.*).

Scene IV

6–16. The verse form here, and in most of the scene, may be intended to elevate the tone. Some, however, see signs of revision or of the 'source' play.

7. *suspect . . . with*] suspect . . . of. (Hart glosses 'suspect' as 'accuse', comparing *Oth.,* IV. ii. 145–7—where also the word may surely *mean* 'suspect'. *O.E.D.* gives him no support.)

cold] *New Cambridge* suggests that F's

Than thee with wantonness; now doth thy honour
   stand,
In him that was of late an heretic,
As firm as faith.
Page.   'Tis well, 'tis well; no more.   10
Be not as extreme in submission
As in offence.
But let our plot go forward: let our wives
Yet once again, to make us public sport,
Appoint a meeting with this old fat fellow,   15
Where we may take him, and disgrace him for it.
Ford. There is no better way than that they spoke of.
Page. How? To send him word they'll meet him in the
   Park at midnight? Fie, fie, he'll never come.
Evans. You say he has been thrown in the rivers, and has   20
   been grievously peaten, as an old 'oman: methinks
   there should be terrors in him that he should not
   come; methinks his flesh is punished, he shall have
   no desires.
Page. So think I too.   25
Mrs. Ford. Devise but how you'll use him when he comes,
   And let us two devise to bring him thither.
Mrs. Page. There is an old tale goes that Herne the hunter,
   Sometime a keeper here in Windsor Forest,

11–12.] *As Capell; one line F.*   28–9.] *As Q3;* There . . . the / Hunter (sometime . . . Forrest) / *F.*

'gold' must be 'an error of dictation'—
but compositors' minds do sometimes
wander and there is always the possibility of 'foul case'.

   9. *heretic*] unbeliever, or one who
held false beliefs.

   28–45.] Two problems present
themselves here: that Q calls the
hunter 'Horne' and that it specifies
that Falstaff is to be disguised like him,
whereas Page in F refers to 'this shape'
(l. 44), leaving the audience to infer
what the 'shape' is, at least until
Mistress Page in l. 63 speaks of dis-
horning the 'spirit'. (v. i. 5–6 later
mentions horns and chain.) As the
collation on l. 42 shows, Theobald

incorporated two lines from Q in his
text, and most editors import at least
the second. See Introduction, p. xxxvi.
The relevant lines in Q (which gives
no other account of 'Horne') are: 'Oft
haue you heard since *Horne* the hunter
dyed, / That women to affright their
litle children, / Ses that he walkes in
shape of a great stagge. / Now for that
Falstaffe hath bene so deceiued, / As
that he dares not venture to the house, /
Weele send him word to meet vs in the
field, / Disguised like *Horne*, with huge
horns on his head, / The houre shalbe
iust betweene twelue and one, / And at
that time we will meet him both'.

   29. *Sometime*] once, formerly.

Doth all the winter-time, at still midnight,   30
Walk round about an oak, with great ragg'd horns,
And there he blasts the tree, and takes the cattle,
And makes milch-kine yield blood, and shakes a
    chain
In a most hideous and dreadful manner.
You have heard of such a spirit, and well you know   35
The superstitious idle-headed eld
Receiv'd, and did deliver to our age,
This tale of Herne the hunter for a truth.
Page. Why, yet there want not many that do fear
    In deep of night to walk by this Herne's oak.   40
    But what of this?
Mrs. Ford.   Marry, this is our device,
    That Falstaff at that oak shall meet with us.
Page. Well, let it not be doubted but he'll come;
    And in this shape when you have brought him
        thither,
    What shall be done with him? What is your plot?   45
Mrs. Page. That likewise have we thought upon, and thus:
    Nan Page (my daughter) and my little son
    And three or four more of their growth we'll dress
    Like urchins, ouphs, and fairies, green and white,

---

31. ragg'd] *F1* (rag'd-), *F2;* ragged *Rowe;* jag'd *Capell.*   32. tree] *F;* trees *Hanmer.*   33. makes] *F2;* make *F1.*   42. us.] *F;* us. / We'll send him word to meet us in the Field, / Disguis'd like *Herne,* with huge Horns on his Head. *Theobald (from Q, which has 'Horne', not 'Herne')* ; us, / Disguis'd like *Herne,* with huge horns on his head. *Capell.*   43. come;] *As F* (come,) ; come, *Capell.*   44. shape when] *F2;* shape, when *F1;* shape; when *Capell.*

---

31. *ragg'd*] shaggy, rough or jagged (*O.E.D. a.*[1] 1, 2)—used by Shakespeare several times of rocks.

32. *blasts*] Either 'blights' (*O.E.D. v.* 5) or 'kills as if with lightning'. The word was especially associated with evil supernatural influence; cf. *Ham.,* I. iv. 41, 'airs from heaven or blasts from hell'.

takes] 'possesses', bewitches ('taking' is similarly used of a malign influence, as in *Lr.,* III. iv. 61).

33. *shakes a chain*] Then, as now, a presumed habit of ghosts. Cf. v. i. 5.

36. *eld*] ancients (in the sense of

people of earlier ages, as suggested by *O.E.D. sb.*[2] 5. b).

39. *want not*] fail not, are.

43. *let it not be doubted*] Some commentators have felt that Page is too easily persuaded and that the text must have been cut. Dramatic illusion, however, allows for a playwright to omit part of a sequence of evidence, and especially in the comedies Shakespeare relies on this.

48. *growth*] size, age.

49. *urchins*] goblins or elves (*O.E.D.* I. c).

ouphs] The same word as oaph, auph,

With rounds of waxen tapers on their heads,   50
And rattles in their hands; upon a sudden,
As Falstaff, she, and I are newly met,
Let them from forth a sawpit rush at once
With some diffused song; upon their sight,
We two in great amazedness will fly;   55
Then let them all encircle him about,
And fairy-like to pinch the unclean knight,
And ask him why, that hour of fairy revel,
In their so sacred paths he dares to tread
In shape profane.

Mrs. Ford.   And till he tell the truth,   60
Let the supposed fairies pinch him sound,
And burn him with their tapers.

Mrs. Page.   The truth being known,
We'll all present ourselves, dis-horn the spirit,
And mock him home to Windsor.

Ford.   The children must
Be practis'd well to this, or they'll ne'er do 't.   65

Evans. I will teach the children their behaviours; and I
will be like a jack-an-apes also, to burn the knight
with my taber.

---

57. *to pinch*] F; *too, pinch Warburton; to—pinch Steevens², conj. Tyrwhitt.*
60. *Mrs. Ford*] *Rowe; Ford F.*

or auf: children of elves (magical dwarfs) and particularly changelings, substituted by fairies for human children.

54. *diffused*] divided among them, as a kind of part-song. *New Cambridge* compares the S.D. 'Burthen (dispersedly)' in *Tp.*, I. ii. 382. (The other 'explanation' is 'wild' or 'irregular'.)

57. *to pinch*] 'To' may seem unusual after 'let', but the construction is not unlike others described in Abbott 349. Cf. also 'thou . . . / didst let . . . / thy rude hand to act / The deed', *John*, IV. ii. 237–41. Cf. also 'to marry' in l. 84 and 'to pinch' in IV. vi. 43. For 'pinch', cf. V. v. 46 and 103 S.D., and notes.

61. *sound*] soundly.

63. *dis-horn*] Greg, in the letter to

Wilson quoted in *New Cambridge* p. 134 (see note on IV. ii. 59), argued that 'There would be little point in saying "take off his horns"—it must mean "strip him of his Horne disguise"' (and so maintained that the name must be 'Horne'). To take off the dressed-up Falstaff's horns, however, is symbolic enough of exposing him in his true character.

67. *jack-an-apes*] monkey (see I. iv. 102 and note). Q has it that in the last scene Evans is dressed 'like a Satyre' and some editors insert a S.D. accordingly—and *New Cambridge* actually says that 'a satyr . . . was a kind of "ape"'. Falstaff's 'Heavens defend me from that Welsh *fairy*' (V. v. 82) hardly suggests that the satyr-disguise was intended in the F version, even if it

Ford. That will be excellent. I'll go buy them vizards.

Mrs. Page. My Nan shall be the queen of all the fairies,   70
    Finely attired in a robe of white.

Page. That silk will I go buy.—[*Aside*] And in that time
    Shall Master Slender steal my Nan away,
    And marry her at Eton.—Go, send to Falstaff
      straight.

Ford. Nay, I'll to him again in name of Brook;   75
    He'll tell me all his purpose. Sure, he'll come.

Mrs. Page. Fear not you that. Go get us properties
    And tricking for our fairies.

Evans. Let us about it: it is admirable pleasures and fery
    honest knaveries.   [*Exeunt Page, Ford, and Evans.*]   80

Mrs. Page. Go, Mistress Ford,
    Send quickly to Sir John to know his mind.
                   [*Exit Mistress Ford.*]
    I'll to the Doctor, he hath my good will,
    And none but he to marry with Nan Page.
    That Slender, though well landed, is an idiot;   85
    And he my husband best of all affects.
    The Doctor is well money'd, and his friends
    Potent at court: he, none but he, shall have her,
    Though twenty thousand worthier come to crave
      her.   [*Exit.*]

69.] *As one line, Pope;* That . . . excellent, / Ile . . . vizards. *F.*   70–1.] *As Rowe³;*
as prose F.   72. *Aside*] *Pope (after l. 73); not in F.*   time] *F;* tire *Theobald.*
79–80.] *Prose as Pope;* Let . . . it, / It . . . knaueries. *F.*   80. S.D.] *Rowe; not in F.*
82. quickly] *F; Quickly Theobald.*   S.D.] *Rowe; not in F.*   84. he to] *F;*
he, to *Pope.*   89. S.D.] *F2; not in F1.*

does not rule out the possibility. ('Welsh goat' in v. v. 138 probably has no reference to costume at all.) Hart may be right in deducing, with the support of a passage in Nashe, that 'jack-an-apes' also meant an evil spirit (or evil fairy).

69. *vizards*] visors or masks (cf. IV. vi. 39).

74. *Eton*] Eton is within sight of Windsor, across the river.

77. *properties*] In the sense in which it is still used in the theatre, of any portable article necessary in the production.

78. *tricking*] adornments (the verb 'trick' commonly means 'dress up').

85. *well landed*] possessed of much land (as compared with the 'well moneyed' Caius, who has no landed inheritance).

86. *affects*] likes, approves.

O

SCENE V

Enter HOST *and* SIMPLE.

Host. What wouldst thou have, boor? What, thick-skin?
Speak, breathe, discuss; brief, short, quick, snap.

Sim. Marry, sir, I come to speak with Sir John Falstaff
from Master Slender.

Host. There's his chamber, his house, his castle, his   5
standing-bed, and truckle-bed; 'tis painted about
with the story of the Prodigal, fresh and new. Go,
knock and call; he'll speak like an Anthropophaginian unto thee; knock, I say.

Sim. There's an old woman, a fat woman, gone up into   10
his chamber. I'll be so bold as stay, sir, till she come
down; I come to speak with her, indeed.

Host. Ha? A fat woman? The knight may be robbed;
I'll call.—Bully knight, bully Sir John! Speak from
thy lungs military. Art thou there? It is thine host,   15
thine Ephesian, calls.

Scene v

SCENE v] *F;* Scene VIII. *The* Garter-Inn. *Pope.*   S.D.] *Q; Enter Host, Simple,*
Falstaffe, Bardolfe, Euans, Caius, Quickly. F.

1. *thick-skin*] blockhead or bumpkin. Cf. *MND.*, III. ii. 13.

2. *discuss*] disclose, speak up. Cf. I. iii. 89 and note.

snap] Apparently an adjective or adverb, connected with the verb 'snip' or 'snap', and meaning 'sudden(ly)' or 'rapid(ly)'. The closest parallel is *LLL.*, v. i. 62–3, 'a quick venue of wit! snip, snap, quick and home!'

5. *castle*] There is no need to suspect an allusion to Falstaff's original name, Oldcastle, in *1H4*. A man's home is still his castle.

6. *truckle-bed*] a small low bed on 'truckles', i.e. castors, that could be run under a normal bed when not in use.

'tis painted . . .] It is not quite clear whether the Host is referring to the painted hangings round the bed or round the room; both were known. In wealthier homes, woven tapestry was used.

7. *the Prodigal*] the Prodigal Son of Christ's parable, as told in Luke 15.

8–9. *Anthropophaginian*] Strictly, a cannibal, an eater of human flesh. The noun is familiar from Othello's traveller's tales to Desdemona of 'the Cannibals that each other eat, / The Anthropophagi and men whose heads / Do grow beneath their shoulders' (I. iii. 143–5). Nashe (in *Christ's Tears*) and Dekker (in *The Wonderful Year*) also use forms of the word, the latter contributing the added information that the 'Anthropophagi are Scithians'. *If* the Host knows what the word means, he must be ironically cheering Simple up with the expectation that Falstaff will really 'bite his head off'.

16. *Ephesian*] The word is generally explained as 'boon companion', on a

Fal. [*Above*] How now, mine host?

Host. Here's a Bohemian-Tartar tarries the coming
down of thy fat woman. Let her descend, bully, let
her descend; my chambers are honourable. Fie! 20
Privacy? Fie!

Enter FALSTAFF.

Fal. There was, mine host, an old fat woman even now
with me, but she's gone.

Sim. Pray you, sir, was 't not the wise woman of Brain-
ford?   25

Fal. Ay, marry, was it, mussel-shell: what would you
with her?

Sim. My master, sir, my master Slender, sent to her, seeing her go thorough the streets, to know, sir, whether
one Nym, sir, that beguiled him of a chain, had the 30
chain or no.

Fal. I spake with the old woman about it.

Sim. And what says she, I pray, sir?

17. *Above*] *As Theobald; not in F; Enter* Falstaff. *Rowe.*   21. S.D.] *Q (after l. 23);
not in F.*   28. My . . . Slender] F (My Master (Sir) my master *Slender,*)*; My
master, sir, master Slender *Steevens²*.

supposed analogy with 'Corinthian'
(Corinth being noted for loose living);
and the same explanation is given of
2H4, II. ii. 164, where Prince Hal asks
the Page what company Falstaff is
keeping and is told 'Ephesians, my
lord, of the old church'. In *Sewanee
Review*, LXVII, 1959, 204–19, however,
J. A. Bryant has suggested that much
more is involved in *H4*: Hal's famous
self-commitment, in his early soliloquy,
to 'redeeming time when men think
least I will' is seen to be a quotation
from Ephesians 5:16; the theme is
identified with Paul's plea to the
Ephesians 4:22, 'that ye put off concerning the former conversation the
old man which is corrupt according to
the deceitful lusts'. 'Ephesians' in *2H4*
therefore presumably means, specifically, Ephesians in need of salvation.
Whether any of this deeper meaning
carries over, ironically, to the Host's

description of himself (as such an un-
regenerate sinner) is an open question.

18. *Bohemian-Tartar*] The Tartars,
proverbially savages, are not normally
associated with Bohemia. The Host
enjoys making up epithets, as perhaps
does Pistol: 'Phrygian Turk' in I. iii. 84
is a close parallel.

tarries] awaits.

26. *mussel-shell*] Johnson explained,
reasonably enough, that Simple is so
christened because he is standing with
his mouth open; Hart, objecting—in
a rather literal way—that this image
would apply only to the whole mussel,
with *two* shells, preferred to think that
the reference was to 'an empty worthless object'. *New Cambridge*'s suggestion
of a further possible pun on 'muzzle'
(it accepts the emendation 'tyke', i.e.
mongrel, in l. 51) piles one hypothesis
on another.

Fal. Marry, she says that the very same man that
   beguiled Master Slender of his chain cozened him   35
   of it.

Sim. I would I could have spoken with the woman herself; I had other things to have spoken with her too,
   from him.

Fal. What are they? Let us know.   40

Host. Ay, come; quick.

Sim. I may not conceal them, sir.

Host. Conceal them, or thou diest.

Sim. Why, sir, they were nothing but about Mistress
   Anne Page, to know if it were my master's fortune   45
   to have her or no.

Fal. 'Tis, 'tis his fortune.

Sim. What, sir?

Fal. To have her, or no. Go; say the woman told me so.

Sim. May I be bold to say so, sir?   50

Fal. Ay, sir; like who more bold.

Sim. I thank your worship; I shall make my master glad
   with these tidings.   [*Exit.*]

Host. Thou art clerkly, thou art clerkly, Sir John. Was
   there a wise woman with thee?   55

Fal. Ay, that there was, mine host; one that hath taught
   me more wit than ever I learned before in my life;
   and I paid nothing for it neither, but was paid for
   my learning.

Enter BARDOLPH.

42. *Sim.*] *Rowe; Fal. F.*   conceal] *F; reveal conj. Farmer.*   43. or] *F; and
Hanmer.*   51. Ay, sir; like] *F* (I Sir: like); *I* tike *Q;* Ay, sir Tike; like *Steevens²,
conj. Farmer;* Ay, sir Tike; *Reed.*   53. *Exit] Rowe; not in F.*   59. S.D.] *Q; not
in F.*

42.] Rowe's emendation, giving the
line to Simple, not Falstaff, seems
inescapable, but there is no need to
emend 'conceal' to 'reveal', which
Simple undoubtedly means: one
character after another in this comedy
falls into malapropism. The Host
echoes Simple's word ironically in the
next line.

51. *like who more bold*] Emendation is
unnecessary (and Q's 'tike' is either,

as Hart argued, a simple misprint, or a
reporter's groping attempt to 'improve'). The F reading is ably defended by Sisson, *N.R.*, p. 72, as idiomatic
and meaning 'as bold as the boldest'.

54. *clerkly*] learned like a clerk
(scholar).

58. *was paid*] was rewarded, by being
thrashed. Falstaff is ringing the
changes on the popular maxim 'Bought
wit is best' (Tilley W545).

Bard. Out, alas sir, cozenage, mere cozenage!   60
Host. Where be my horses? Speak well of them, varletto.
Bard. Run away with the cozeners: for so soon as I came
    beyond Eton, they threw me off, from behind one of
    them, in a slough of mire; and set spurs and away,
    like three German devils, three Doctor Faustuses.   65
Host. They are gone but to meet the Duke, villain; do not
    say they be fled. Germans are honest men.

Enter EVANS.

Evans. Where is mine host?
Host. What is the matter, sir?
Evans. Have a care of your entertainments: there is a   70
    friend of mine come to town tells me there is three
    cozen-Germans that has cozened all the hosts of

---

62. with] *F;* with by *Collier².*   67. S.D.] *Q (after ll. 78–84); not in F.*   71–2.
three cozen-Germans] *F* (three Cozen-Iermans) *;* three sorts of cosen garmombles
Q.

60. *cozenage*] double-dealing.

mere] absolute—as in the often
misunderstood line in the 'Seven ages
of man' speech in *AYL.,* II. vii. 165,
'second childishness and mere obli-
vion'.

61. *varletto*] 'Varlet' is too simple for
the Host.

62. *the cozeners*] There is no doubting
the identification of these with the
'gentlemen' who hired the Host's
horses in IV. iii. (q.v.).

64. *slough*] marsh or bog—and
Wheatley's suggestion of a pun on
Slough, then a mere village, near
Windsor, is not unattractive.

65. *Doctor Faustuses*] Another reference to Marlowe's famous play (see
note on I. i. 120)—this time to the
titular hero, the German scholar who
sold his soul to the devil in return for
magical power. There may be particular reference to (a) the scenes (xiii
and xiv, ed. J. D. Jump) in which
Faustus's vengeance on three men who
try to murder him involves having one
(or perhaps all three) of them dragged
through 'a lake of mud and dirt'; and

(b) the scene (xv) in which he sells a
horse to a 'horse-courser' and changes
it into straw when the courser disobeys
instructions by riding the horse into
water.

67. *Germans . . . men*] The speech, not
in Q, so far from 'softening down' the
Mömpelgard allusion, as *New Cambridge* believes, would presumably have
raised a laugh from a 'knowing' court
audience.

68–84.] It seems clear that Evans
and Caius, who warn the Host to avoid
what has already happened, do so by
malice aforethought, having arranged
the loss themselves. Each, significantly,
uses the hypocritical 'I tell you for
good will'.

70. *entertainments*] Not, probably,
supplies or equipment but, in Evans's
version of English, those whom you
'entertain'—'guests' at the Inn.

72. *cozen-Germans*] A quibble on
'cousins-german(e)' or 'cousin-ger-
man(e)s' (full cousins) and on
cozening-Germans, rogues pretending
to be Germans, and even 'cousin-Ger-
mans', i.e. German 'relations'. (There

Readins, of Maidenhead, of Colebrook, of horses
and money. I tell you for good will, look you; you
are wise, and full of gibes and vlouting-stocks, and   75
'tis not convenient you should be cozened. Fare you
well.   *Exit.*

Enter CAIUS.

Caius. Vere is mine host de Jarteer?
Host. Here, Master Doctor, in perplexity and doubtful
    dilemma.   80
Caius. I cannot tell vat is dat; but it is tell-a me dat you
    make grand preparation for a Duke de Jamanie: by
    my trot, dere is no Duke that the court is know to
    come. I tell you for good will; adieu.   *Exit.*
Host. Hue and cry, villain, go!—Assist me, knight, I am   85
    undone!—Fly, run, hue and cry, villain, I am
    undone!   *Exeunt Host [and Bardolph].*

77. *Exit*] Q; *not in* F.   *Enter Caius*] Q (*before ll. 68–77*); *not in* F.   84. *Exit*] Q;
not in F.   85. Hue] *Rowe;* Huy F.   86. hue] *Rowe;* huy F.   87. S.D.] *Capell;*
not in F; *Exit* Q.

was a proverb 'Call me cousin but
cozen me not'—Tilley C739.) The
notorious Q reading, 'three sorts of
cosen garmombles', may retain a kind
of bad pun on, or anagram of,
Mömpelgard, perhaps a relic of an
authentic text but more probably a
substitution made by a reporter who
remembered only that there had been
a joke involving the Duke. The word
'garmombles', or something like it, did
exist; Nashe uses the similar 'geremumble' at least twice, as a term of
abuse: in *Strange News* he calls Gabriel
Harvey 'the foresaid fanaticall *Phobe-
tor, geremumble, tirleriwhisco,* or what
you will', and in *Nashe's Lenten Stuff*
he employs 'geremumble' as a verb,
meaning apparently to garbage (gut)
fish (I. 321 and III. 207).

73. *Readins*] Reading, a village not
far from Windsor (Maidenhead and
Colebrook or Colnbrook were others);
now of course a large town.

75. *gibes*] Evans may or may not
mean this. If he does mean it he is

referring sarcastically to the Host's
gibes at him in III. i. Certainly
'vlouting-stocks' recalls his words to
Caius on that occasion, 'Pray you let
us not be laughing-stocks to other
men's humours' (ll. 78–9) and 'he has
made us his vlouting-stog' (l. 108).

79. *doubtful*] Either 'doubting'
(*O.E.D.* 2) or 'apprehensive' (*O.E.D.*
5).

82. *Jamanie*] i.e. Germany. Shakespeare may be indicating the pronunciation but there is reason for
thinking that 'Iarman' may have been
his own normal spelling of the word.
Compare F's 'Iermans' in l. 72. The
point was made by R. C. Bald
(*Shakespeare Survey* II. 58).

83–4. *no Duke . . . come*] See IV. iii. 4
and note.

85. *villain . . . knight*] 'Villain' is
addressed to Bardolph, as before
(l. 66); 'knight' to Falstaff—who, as
he proceeds to say, is too sorry for
himself to worry about other people's
troubles.

Fal. I would all the world might be cozened, for I have
been cozened and beaten too. If it should come to
the ear of the court how I have been transformed,   90
and how my transformation hath been washed and
cudgelled, they would melt me out of my fat drop
by drop, and liquor fishermen's boots with me; I
warrant they would whip me with their fine wits
till I were as crest-fallen as a dried pear. I never   95
prospered since I forswore myself at primero.
Well, if my wind were but long enough, I would
repent.

Enter MISTRESS QUICKLY.

Now, whence come you?
Quick. From the two parties, forsooth.   100
Fal. The devil take one party, and his dam the other,
and so they shall be both bestowed. I have suffered
more for their sakes—more than the villainous
inconstancy of man's disposition is able to bear.
Quick. And have not they suffered? Yes, I warrant,   105
speciously one of them: Mistress Ford, good heart,
is beaten black and blue, that you cannot see a
white spot about her.
Fal. What tell'st thou me of black and blue? I was
beaten myself into all the colours of the rainbow;   110
and I was like to be apprehended for the witch of
Brainford. But that my admirable dexterity of wit,

---

97. long enough] *F;* long inough to say my prayers *Q.*   98. S.D.] *Q (after l. 99);
not in F.*

93. *liquor*] oil or grease (as boots are
sometimes oiled today to make them
resistant to water).

95. *as crest-fallen . . . pear*] A daringly
mixed metaphor, of course; 'crest-
fallen' describes the defeated cock, and
'fallen' provides the link to the image
of the pear that has fallen to the ground
and shrivelled up.

96. *forswore myself*] (Presumably)
cheated, by lying about the cards I
held.

primero] a popular game of cards.

97. *long enough*] The additional
words imported by many editors from
Q no doubt make the joke obvious—
and for that reason are unlikely to have
been written by Shakespeare for
Falstaff.

101.] Cf. I. i. 135 and note.

102. *bestowed*] placed, and looked
after.

106. *speciously*] specially (as before,
in III. iv. 105).

my counterfeiting the action of an old woman,
delivered me, the knave constable had set me i' th'
stocks, i' th' common stocks, for a witch.   115

Quick. Sir, let me speak with you in your chamber: you
shall hear how things go and, I warrant, to your
content. Here is a letter will say somewhat. Good
hearts, what ado here is to bring you together! Sure,
one of you does not serve heaven well, that you are   120
so crossed.

Fal. Come up into my chamber.   *Exeunt.*

SCENE VI

Enter FENTON *and* HOST.

Host. Master Fenton, talk not to me, my mind is heavy.
I will give over all.

Fent. Yet hear me speak. Assist me in my purpose
And, as I am a gentleman, I'll give thee
A hundred pound in gold more than your loss.   5

Host. I will hear you, Master Fenton; and I will, at the
least, keep your counsel.

Fent. From time to time I have acquainted you
With the dear love I bear to fair Anne Page,
Who mutually hath answer'd my affection,   10
So far forth as herself might be her chooser,
Even to my wish. I have a letter from her
Of such contents as you will wonder at,
The mirth whereof so larded with my matter

113. an old] *F; a wood Theobald; a wode Hanmer.*

Scene VI
SCENE VI] *F; Scene VI. Another Room. Capell.*

113. *an old woman*] i.e. an ordinary
old lady, as distinct from 'a witch'.
121.   *crossed*] thwarted (*O.E.D.*
'cross' *v.* 12, 14).
122.] It will be seen that Shakespeare does not attempt the particularly difficult task of showing how
Falstaff could have been persuaded to

risk a third meeting with Mistress
Ford; he is content to indicate the
direction that Quickly's lies might
have taken.

Scene VI

2. *give over*] give up.
14. *larded with my matter*] mixed or

That neither singly can be manifested   15
Without the show of both. Fat Falstaff
Hath a great scene; the image of the jest
I'll show you here at large. Hark, good mine host.
To-night at Herne's oak, just 'twixt twelve and one,
Must my sweet Nan present the Fairy Queen—   20
The purpose why, is here—in which disguise,
While other jests are something rank on foot,
Her father hath commanded her to slip
Away with Slender, and with him at Eton
Immediately to marry; she hath consented.   25
Now, sir, her mother, even strong against that match,
And firm for Doctor Caius, hath appointed
That he shall likewise shuffle her away,
While other sports are tasking of their minds,

16. Fat] *F1;* fat Sir *Iohn F2;* wherein fat *Malone (as Q).*   17. great scene] *F;* mightie scare *Q;* great scene in it *Capell;* great share *Dyce²;* great scare *Craig.* 25–6.] *This ed.;* Immediately . . . Now Sir, / Her . . . match *F;* Immediately . . . consented: / Now, Sir, / Her . . . match, *Malone.*   26. even strong] *F;* ever strong *Pope;* still *Q.*   27. Caius] *F; Cayus,* in a robe of red *Q.*

interpenetrated with the problem I am discussing with you. Fenton's language hereabouts is extremely formal—even stilted.

16–17. *Fat Falstaff . . . scene*] *New Cambridge,* which argues that throughout the play there are signs that Falstaff replaced a character in the 'source play' who must have been a different kind of wooer, maintains that 'verse and sense are improved' if the passage is read without these words— and that the same is true of the corresponding Q line 'Wherein fat *Falstaffe* had [sic] a mightie scare'. What the Q line does prove is that the reporter was trying to recall a text like F.

17–18. *the image . . . at large*] i.e. I'll describe to you in detail the form the jest will take.

20. *present*] act the part of.

21. *here*] Perhaps Fenton points to the letter from Anne.

22. *something rank*] somewhat over-abundantly. 'Rank' is used as an adverb, as in *Troil.,* I. iii. 196.

26.] The rearrangement of the F lines adopted here involves no problems, of 'patchwork' or otherwise; many a line in Elizabethan drama has twelve syllables of which the term of address (such as 'My lord') forms the first two.

even] Pope's emendation 'ever' may well be correct but is not essential; and Q's 'still against that match' could be an attempted recalling of either. Wheatley maintained that 'even' means 'equally'.

27.] Q's mention of a *red* dress here gives the best reason for thinking that red was the third colour involved in the multiple intrigue of Act v, but neither F nor Q is consistent in its account of what actually happens. See Introduction, pp. xxx-xxxii.

28. *shuffle*] smuggle or steal, 're-move . . . in a hurried, secret, or underhand manner' (*O.E.D. v.* 5. b).

29. *tasking of*] employing (the modern idiom is 'taxing').

And at the dean'ry, where a priest attends,   30
Straight marry her; to this her mother's plot
She seemingly obedient likewise hath
Made promise to the Doctor. Now, thus it rests:
Her father means she shall be all in white;
And in that habit, when Slender sees his time   35
To take her by the hand and bid her go,
She shall go with him: her mother hath intended,
The better to denote her to the Doctor—
For they must all be mask'd and vizarded—
That quaint in green she shall be loose enrob'd,   40
With ribands pendant flaring 'bout her head;
And when the Doctor spies his vantage ripe,
To pinch her by the hand, and, on that token,
The maid hath given consent to go with him.

Host. Which means she to deceive, father or mother?   45

Fent. Both, my good host, to go along with me:
And here it rests—that you'll procure the vicar
To stay for me at church, 'twixt twelve and one,
And, in the lawful name of marrying,
To give our hearts united ceremony.   50

Host. Well, husband your device; I'll to the vicar.
Bring you the maid, you shall not lack a priest.

Fent. So shall I evermore be bound to thee;
Besides, I'll make a present recompense.   *Exeunt.*

38. denote] *Capell, conj. Steevens;* deuote *F1* (*probably a turned* 'n'); devote *F2.*
49. in] *F* (*corrected*); id (*uncorrected*).

30. *dean'ry*] Hart takes this to mean the deanery attached to St George's Chapel (in the grounds of Windsor Castle). The alternative is to believe that the word is used very loosely of a parsonage.

40. *quaint*] neat(ly) or pleasant(ly). The word had no pejorative implication at all in Elizabethan usage, as is perhaps adequately shown by *Ado,* III. iv. 22–3, 'for a fine, quaint, graceful, and excellent fashion, yours is worth ten on 't'.

41. *pendant*] hanging down (from her hair or head-dress).

flaring] waving all round.

43. *To pinch*] For the use of the full infinitive, cf. IV. iv. 57 and note.

token] agreed signal.

50. *give . . . ceremony*] Again Fenton's language is so formal as to seem stilted or precious; he can only mean 'unite us with the full sanction of religious rites'.

51. *husband your device*] look after your (own part of the) plan. For 'husband' used in a similar context to mean 'manage' a plan involving trickery, cf. *Shr., Ind.* I. 68. Conceivably the Host also intends a pun—but the Host in this scene is a strangely chastened version of the earlier character.

54. *present*] immediate.

ACT V

SCENE I

Enter FALSTAFF *and* [MISTRESS] QUICKLY.

Fal. Prithee no more prattling; go. I'll hold. This is the
third time; I hope good luck lies in odd numbers.
Away, go! They say there is divinity in odd numbers,
either in nativity, chance, or death. Away!

Quick. I'll provide you a chain, and I'll do what I can to   5
get you a pair of horns.

Fal. Away, I say, time wears; hold up your head, and
mince.   [*Exit Mistress Quickly.*]

[*Enter* FORD *as* BROOK]

How now, Master Brook? Master Brook, the matter
will be known to-night, or never. Be you in the Park   10
about midnight, at Herne's oak, and you shall see
wonders.

ACT V

Scene I

ACT V SCENE I] *F; Act V Scene I. A Room in the garter Inn. Capell.*   S.D.] *Rowe;
Enter Falstoffe, Quickly, and Ford. F.*   2–4. I hope . . . death] *As F;* They say
there is good luck in old numbers *Q.*   8. *Exit Mistress Quickly*] *Rowe (after l. 6);
not in F.*   Enter Ford as Brook] *As Rowe; not in F.*

1. *hold*] meet the commitment, keep
the appointment (cf. *O.E.D.* 'hold' *v.*
1. 9).

1–4. *This is the third time . . . death*]
Falstaff is alluding to the group of
proverbs best known from 'third time
lucky'. Tilley cites 'There is luck in
odd numbers' (L582); 'all things
thrive at thrice' (T175); and 'the
third time pays for all' (T319—quoted
in *Tw.N.*, v. i. 40).

3. *divinity*] Perhaps 'divination'
(*O.E.D.* 5); more probably, 'divine

power' (*O.E.D.* 3), as in *Ham.*, v. ii. 10.

7. *wears*] is running out (*O.E.D. v.*[1]
IV. 19).

8. *mince*] When used of speech or
walking, the verb normally has a
pejorative sense in Shakespeare, implying affectation; cf. also Portia's
smiling boast that when she and
Nerissa are disguised as males, 'I'll
prove the prettier fellow of the two, /
. . . and turn two mincing steps /
Into a manly stride' (*Mer.V.*, III. iv.
64–8).

Ford. Went you not to her yesterday, sir, as you told me
you had appointed?

Fal. I went to her, Master Brook, as you see, like a poor   15
old man, but I came from her, Master Brook, like
a poor old woman. That same knave Ford, her
husband, hath the finest mad devil of jealousy in him,
Master Brook, that ever governed frenzy. I will tell
you he beat me grievously, in the shape of a woman;   20
for in the shape of man, Master Brook, I fear not
Goliath with a weaver's beam, because I know also
life is a shuttle. I am in haste; go along with me: I'll
tell you all, Master Brook. Since I plucked geese,
played truant, and whipped top, I knew not what   25
'twas to be beaten, till lately. Follow me; I'll tell you
strange things of this knave Ford, on whom to-night
I will be revenged, and I will deliver his wife into
your hand. Follow. Strange things in hand, Master
Brook! Follow.   *Exeunt.*   30

SCENE II

Enter PAGE, SHALLOW, *and* SLENDER.

Page. Come, come, we'll couch i' th' castle-ditch till we

22. Goliath] *Steevens*ᵃ*;* Goliah *Ff.*

Scene II
SCENE II] *F;* Act V. Scene I. Windsor-Park. *Pope; Scene II. A Street. Capell.*

22. *Goliath . . . beam*] The comparison
of Goliath's spear to a weaver's beam
is made in 1 Samuel 17:7, and at least
twice thereafter in the Old Testament;
cf. also 1 Chronicles 11:23.

22–3. *also life is a shuttle*] As 'also'
indicates, Falstaff is adding another
half-quotation from the Bible about a
weaver, this time from Job 7:6: 'My
days are swifter than a weaver's shuttle,
and are spent without hope'.

24. *plucked geese*] Apparently pluck-

ing feathers from a living goose, to use
the feathers for some game, was a
schoolboy prank.

25. *whipped top*] made my top spin
and continue spinning by lashing it
with a whip.

Scene II
1. *couch*] lie hidden.

castle-ditch] Some editors identify
this as the Castle-ditch, on one side of
Windsor Castle.

see the light of our fairies. Remember, son Slender,
my daughter.

Slen. Ay, forsooth; I have spoke with her, and we have a
nay-word how to know one another: I come to her   5
in white, and cry 'mum'; she cries 'budget'; and by
that we know one another.

Shal. That's good too; but what needs either your 'mum'
or her 'budget'? The white will decipher her well
enough. It hath struck ten o'clock.   10

Page. The night is dark; light and spirits will become it
well. Heaven prosper our sport! No man means evil
but the devil, and we shall know him by his horns.
Let's away; follow me.   *Exeunt.*

SCENE III

Enter MISTRESS PAGE, MISTRESS FORD, *and* DOCTOR CAIUS.

Mrs. Page. Master Doctor, my daughter is in green:
when you see your time, take her by the hand, away
with her to the deanery, and dispatch it quickly. Go
before into the Park; we two must go together.

3. my daughter] *F2;* my *F1.*

Scene III

SCENE III] *F; Scene III. Another Street, leading to the Park. Capell; Scene III. The
Street in Windsor. Malone.*

3. *daughter*] F1 has a blank space
where this, or some similar word,
should be. Apparently the compositor's attention was distracted, or type
was dropped. There is no corresponding scene in Q, but F2's addition is
acceptable.

5. *nay-word*] pass-word (as in II. ii.
121).

6. *mum . . . budget*] Slender (or Anne,
in irony) has chosen an appropriately
childish greeting. 'Mumbudget' (related to the surviving 'mum's the
word'—Tilley M1310) was used of an
inability or a refusal to speak (Tilley

M1311); *O.E.D.* conjectures, with
convincing citations, that it was 'the
name of some children's game in
which silence was required'. Thomas
Hardy later uses 'to come mum-
budgeting' in the sense of 'to come
secretly'.

8. *what needs*] what is the need for;
cf. Apemantus' indignant 'What needs
these feasts, pomps and vain-glories?'
(*Tim.*, I. ii. 248–9).

11. *become*] suit.

13. *devil . . . horns*] A neat adaptation
of 'the devil is known by his horns'
(Tilley D252).

Caius. I know vat I have to do. Adieu.   [*Exit.*]   5
Mrs. Page. Fare you well, sir.—My husband will not
    rejoice so much at the abuse of Falstaff as he will
    chafe at the Doctor's marrying my daughter; but
    'tis no matter: better a little chiding than a great
    deal of heartbreak.   10
Mrs. Ford. Where is Nan now? And her troop of fairies?
    And the Welsh devil Hugh?
Mrs. Page. They are all couched in a pit hard by Herne's
    oak, with obscured lights, which, at the very instant
    of Falstaff's and our meeting, they will at once dis-   15
    play to the night.
Mrs. Ford. That cannot choose but amaze him.
Mrs. Page. If he be not amazed, he will be mocked; if he
    be amazed, he will every way be mocked.
Mrs. Ford. We'll betray him finely.   20
Mrs. Page. Against such lewdsters and their lechery

---

5. *Exit*] *F2; not in F1.*   12. Welsh devil Hugh] *As Capell;* Welch-deuill
Herne *F;* Welch-deuill *Herne Q3;* Welch devil *Evans Theobald;* Welsh devil
Hart.

9–10. *better . . . heartbreak*] This may
be a proverb, or Mistress Page's variation on one. There are several that
could be relevant, including 'Better
once a mischief than always an in-
convenience' (Tilley M995) and
'Better a snotty child than his nose
wiped off' (C296).

12. *Welsh devil Hugh*] The F reading
'Welch-deuill Herne' is retained by
New Cambridge, as 'Welsh devil-hern',
and defended on the argument that
Evans was dressed as a satyr [which is
far from certain], that 'a satyr was a
kind of devil, for the Elizabethans'
[which is debatable], and that 'thus he
was a "devil-hern" in two senses: (i)
"hern" or "harn"=brain; here used
of the head, v. N.E.D. "harn", (ii) his
function was to "devil" Herne–Falstaff'. This is not easily acceptable.
Nor, *pace* Hart, is there particular
significance in the fact that 'Herne',
unlike most proper names, is not in
italics in F; on the same page, [E5ᵛ],

'Ioue' and 'Iupiter' are in roman, not
italic. Capell's emendation 'Hugh'
may be accepted on the assumption
either that the compositor had read
ahead and had in his mind 'Herne's'
from l. 13, or that the later line had
caught his eye. Some support is lent to
the emendation by Ford's 'Well said,
fairy Hugh' in v. v. 132 and Falstaff's
'Heavens defend me from that Welsh
fairy' in v. v. 82.

17. *amaze*] Probably 'terrify' or
'frighten', but the other frequent
meaning in Elizabethan English is
'bewilder', which can hardly be ruled
out here.

18. *mocked*] *New Cambridge* sees a
quibble here and in l. 19, on the two
senses of 'deceived' and 'ridiculed'.

21. *lewdsters*] The meaning is obvious
but no earlier use of the word has been
recorded.

21–2.] No doubt the couplet is to
give the effect of epigram, and to
sound authoritative.

Those that betray them do no treachery.

Mrs. Ford. The hour draws on. To the oak, to the oak!

Exeunt.

SCENE IV

Enter EVANS [*disguised*] *and* [WILLIAM *and other children as*] *Fairies.*

Evans. Trib, trib, fairies; come; and remember your parts. Be pold, I pray you; follow me into the pit; and when I give the watch-'ords, do as I pid you. Come, come; trib, trib.   *Exeunt.*

SCENE V

Enter FALSTAFF [*disguised as Herne*] *wearing a buck's head.*

Fal. The Windsor bell hath struck twelve; the minute draws on. Now, the hot-blooded gods assist me! Remember, Jove, thou wast a bull for thy Europa;

Scene IV

SCENE IV] *F; Scene IV. The Park. Capell.*   S.D.] *As Camb.; Enter Euans and Fairies. F; Enter Sir* Hugh, Pistol, Quickly, Anne Page, *and Others, vizarded, and disguis'd for Fairies. Capell; The Fairies approach, dancing . . . : Sir Hugh Evans . . .; Pistol . . .; Quickly . . .; Anne Page with William, and many other boys . . . New Camb.*

Scene V

SCENE V] *F; Scene V. Another Part of the Park. Capell.*   S.D.] *As Q (Enter sir Iohn with a Bucks head vpon him) ; Enter Falstaffe, Mistris Page, Mistris Ford, Euans, Anne Page, Fairies, Page, Ford, Quickly, Slender, Fenton, Caius, Pistoll. F.*   1. struck] *F* (stroke).   2. hot-blooded gods] *Rowe³;* hot-bloodied-Gods *F1;* hot-bloodied-god *F4;* hot-blooded God *Rowe¹⁻².*

Scene IV

S.D.] Some editors bring on Pistol, Anne, and Quickly, but the S.D. in F does not name them. For Evans's disguise, see IV. iv. 67 and note.

1. *Trib*] i.e. trip, or as Falstaff might have said, 'mince'.

Scene V

3. *Jove . . . Europa*] Jove–Jupiter– Zeus fell in love with Europa, daughter of the King of Tyre, changed himself into a bull, and when she climbed upon his back, swam across the sea with her to Crete.

love set on thy horns. O powerful love, that in some
respects makes a beast a man; in some other, a man   5
a beast. You were also, Jupiter, a swan for the love
of Leda. O omnipotent love, how near the god drew
to the complexion of a goose! A fault done first in the
form of a beast: O Jove, a beastly fault! And then
another fault in the semblance of a fowl: think on 't,   10
Jove, a foul fault! When gods have hot backs, what
shall poor men do? For me, I am here a Windsor
stag, and the fattest, I think, i' th' forest. Send me a
cool rut-time, Jove, or who can blame me to piss my
tallow?—Who comes here? My doe?   15

Enter MISTRESS FORD *and* MISTRESS PAGE.

Mrs. Ford. Sir John! Art thou there, my deer, my male
deer?
Fal. My doe with the black scut? Let the sky rain
potatoes; let it thunder to the tune of 'Greensleeves',
hail kissing-comfits, and snow eringoes; let there   20

15. S.D.] *Q; not in F.*

6–7. *Jupiter . . . Leda*] To rape
Leda, Jupiter disguised himself as a
swan.
  8. *complexion*] Probably a quibble on
the two senses, appearance and disposition or nature.
  8, 9, 10, 11. *fault*] Hilda Hulme,
p. 112, shows that 'fault' often had the
stronger meaning of 'sin' (particularly
sexual sin).
  11. *hot*] lustful.
  14–15. *cool . . . tallow*] Falstaff wants
cool weather because lust—carrying
on the thought of l. 11—is hot and
likely to cause his 'tallow' or fat to
melt. Ray, citing as proverbial 'He has
piss'd his tallow', comments that 'this
is spoken of bucks who grow lean after
rutting time, and may be applied to
men'. If there is a specific reference to
the belief that the male deer at rutting
time ate red mushrooms or toadstools
to cause it to urinate freely, to relieve
the 'heat' (in both senses), Shakespeare's authority may well have been
Turberville, ch. 17, first cited by
Farmer.
  16, 17. *deer*] There is, of course, a
quibble on 'dear' (frequent in Shakespeare: cf. e.g. *1H4*, v. iv. 107–8); and
cf. l. 23 and note.
  18. *scut*] The normal meaning is the
short tail of the rabbit or deer—itself
no elegant phrase to apply to Mistress
Ford—but it seems also to have come
to mean the pudend.
  19. *potatoes*] For another reference to
the common belief in the aphrodisiac
power of potatoes—odd as that seems
today—cf. *Troil.*, v. ii. 56.
  Greensleeves] Named because it is a
love song; cf. II. i. 61 and note.
  20. *kissing-comfits*] perfumed 'com-
fits' (sweetmeats of preserved fruit,
sugar-plums) to sweeten the breath.
  eringoes] candied roots of the sea-
holly, *Eryngium maritinum*, also considered to be aphrodisiac.

come a tempest of provocation, I will shelter me
here.

Mrs. Ford. Mistress Page is come with me, sweetheart.

Fal. Divide me like a bribed buck, each a haunch; I will
keep my sides to myself, my shoulders for the fellow   25
of this walk—and my horns I bequeath your
husbands. Am I a woodman, ha? Speak I like
Herne the hunter? Why, now is Cupid a child of
conscience: he makes restitution. As I am a true
spirit, welcome!   *Noise of horns within.*   30

Mrs. Page. Alas, what noise?

Mrs. Ford. Heaven forgive our sins!

Fal. What should this be?

Mrs. Ford.⎫
Mrs. Page.⎭ Away, away!   *They run off.*

Fal. I think the devil will not have me damned, lest the   35

22.] *Capell adds 'embracing her'.*   24. bribed] *F* (brib'd-)*; bribe- *Theobald.*
30. S.D.] *As* Q (*There is a noise of hornes, the two women run away.*)*; not in F.*   34.
S.D.] *As Rowe; not in F.*   35–7.] *Prose as Pope;* I . . . damn'd, / Least . . . fire; /
He . . . thus. *F.*

---

21. *provocation*] i.e. sexual temptation
or excitation. The inferiority of Q in
this scene cannot be better shown than
by quoting the lines 'Welcome Ladies'
and 'This makes amends for all' that
virtually replace, from ll. 18–22, 'Let
the sky . . . here'.

23. *sweetheart*] No doubt there is a
quibble on 'hart', as on 'deer' in ll. 16
and 17. The F spelling 'sweet hart'
may be intended to indicate this.

24. *bribed buck*] Following up
O.E.D.'s demonstration that 'bribed'
could mean 'stolen' (*ppl. a.* and 'bribe'
v. 1), *New Cambridge* interprets the F
phrase to mean a stolen buck which
had to be cut up quickly and divided
among the poachers if the theft was
not to be discovered by the keeper; but
ll. 24–6 perhaps imply that it is the
keeper who has been bribed to allow
the deer to be taken. The breaking-up
of the deer was a regular part of the
hunting ritual.

25–6. *fellow of this walk*] the keeper

responsible for this particular 'walk' or
part of Windsor Forest. (He was entitled to the right shoulder of a deer
legitimately killed.) Hart sees a
quibble on the sense of the male deer
who uses this section of the forest as his
domain; *New Cambridge* suggests one
on the meaning that Falstaff 'will keep
his shoulders to fight the keeper, should
he appear'—but neither seems probable. As Falstaff goes on to say, he is
trying to speak like Herne or any good
hunter, in the jargon of the hunt. *The
Book of Saint Albans*, cited by Kinnear,
advises the beginner to learn the
language if he wishes to be 'counted a
perfect woodman'.

27. *woodman*] forester or hunter—
but because of the quibble on the
object of the 'hunt' (the 'deer' or
'dear'), it came to mean also one who
pursued women: cf. *Meas.*, IV. iii. 170.

29. *makes restitution*] i.e. restores that
of which I was previously wrongly
deprived—yourself.

P

oil that's in me should set hell on fire; he would
never else cross me thus.

Enter EVANS *[disguised as before;* PISTOL *as Hobgoblin];*
MISTRESS QUICKLY *as the Fairy Queen;* [ANNE PAGE *and]*
children as Fairies [with tapers].

Quick. Fairies, black, gray, green, and white,
    You moonshine revellers, and shades of night,
    You orphan heirs of fixed destiny,   40
    Attend your office and your quality.
    Crier Hobgoblin, make the fairy oyes.
Pist. Elves, list your names; silence, you airy toys.

37. S.D.] *This ed.; Enter Fairies.* F; *Enter sir Hugh like a Satyre, and boyes drest like*
Fayries, mistresse Quickly, like the Queene of Fayries: they sing a song about him, and
afterward speake. Q; *Enter Sir* Hugh Evans, *like a satyr;* Mrs. Quickly, *and* Pistol;
Anne Page, *as the Fairy Queen, attended by her brother and others, dressed like fairies,*
with waxen tapers on their heads. Malone.   38, 91. *Quick.*] As F (*Qui.*); *Queen* |
Collier, conj. Harness; Anne | *Halliwell, conj. Harness.*   40. orphan heirs] F;
Ouphen-heirs *Theobald, conj. Warburton;* ouphs, and heirs *Keightley.*   43. *Pist.*]
F; *Eva. Theobald;* Puck *conj. Harness.*

37. S.D.] It is worthy of note that
F's '*Enter Fairies*' is the only entry it
gives *within* a scene during the whole
play; the 'copy' may thus have been
different here. F's speech prefixes
('*Qui.*' at ll. 38 and 91 and '*Qu.*' at 56
and 85), together with Q's S.D. and
five speech prefixes '*Quic.*', are the
authority for Quickly's playing the
Fairy Queen. (The full Q S.D. seems
to rule out the theory that the speech
prefixes mean no more than that the
one boy-actor played both parts.) She
has replaced Anne, as part of the coun-
ter-scheming. The rhyming couplets
are used to give the effect of incantation.
    39. *shades*] spirits, spectres.
    40.] The line has given rise to much
comment, involving emendation and
conjecture about wider meanings of
'orphan' as 'friendless'. Fairies, however, did not normally have parents,
and were 'orphan' in that sense; and
perhaps they were 'heirs of fixed
destiny' in that different fairies had
different fixed functions, times, and
places (e.g. the fairies being ad-

dressed can come out only at night).
    41. *Attend*] attend to, perform.
    office] duty.
    quality] profession or calling (*O.E.D.*
5)—as in *Gent.*, IV. i. 58.
    42. *Crier . . . oyes*] 'Crier' as in 'town
crier': one who 'cries' 'oyes' or 'oyez'
('hear ye'). The corresponding line in
Q (which differs too much in this scene
to be collated in the ordinary way) is
'Giue them their charge *Puck* ere they
part away'. 'Hobgoblin' was an alternative name for Puck or Robin
Goodfellow.
    43. *Pist.*] Pistol does not appear at
all in this scene in Q, and the corresponding lines, in two speeches, are
given to Evans. Again it is possible,
but unlikely, that the F speech prefix
meant only that the actor who played
Pistol played Hobgoblin here. The
masque tradition of actors stepping
out of their parts may explain how
Pistol (and Quickly and Evans) now
speak without their previous characteristic idiom.
    airy toys] creatures as insubstantial

  Cricket, to Windsor chimneys shalt thou leap; 44
  Where fires thou find'st unrak'd and hearths unswept,
  There pinch the maids as blue as bilberry:
  Our radiant Queen hates sluts and sluttery.
Fal. They are fairies; he that speaks to them shall die.
  I'll wink and couch: no man their works must eye.
               [*Lies face downwards.*]
Evans. Where's Bead? Go you, and where you find a maid 50
  That ere she sleep has thrice her prayers said
  Raise up the organs of her fantasy,
  Sleep she as sound as careless infancy;
  But those as sleep and think not on their sins,

---

44. shalt thou leap] *F; when thoust leapt Collier*².   49. S.D.] *This ed.; not in F;
Lyes down upon his Face Rowe.*   50. Bead] *F (Bede); Pead Q.*   52. Raise] *F;
Rein Hanmer, conj. Warburton; Rouse Collier*².   fantasy,] *F; fantasie; Theobald.*

---

as the air. 'Toys' sometimes had the sense of 'objects lacking substance', sometimes that of 'idle fancies' (cf. I. iv. 40). Theseus' 'I never may believe / These antique fables nor these fairy toys' (*MND.*, v. i. 2–3) suggests that 'fairy' and 'toy' were associated in Shakespeare's mind.

44. *Cricket*] Apparently one of the traditional personal names for a fairy.

45. *unrak'd*] not properly 'raked' to keep smouldering over-night and be still alight in the morning.

46. *pinch the maids . . .*] A traditional occupation, or function, of fairies. (Caliban dreads the pinches of Prospero's spirits in *Temp.*; and Nashe in *The Terrors of the Night*, quoted by Hart, has 'The Robin-good-fellowes, elfes, Fairies, Hobgoblins of our latter age . . . pincht maids in their sleep that swept not their houses cleane . . .'. Cf. also *Err.*, II. ii. 191–4.)

bilberry] The bilberry (or 'whortle-berry') is a particularly deep blue.

47. *Queen*] Probably the word refers both to the Fairy Queen and to the Queen in Windsor Castle—Elizabeth herself.

sluts] Used in the weaker sense, implying only untidiness or slovenliness (*O.E.D.* 1).

48–9.] If Falstaff, unexpectedly, also speaks in rhyme, that is probably not because Shakespeare forgot to adapt earlier material but because the play is intended to become less realistic as it takes on more of the character of a masque.

49. *wink and couch*] close my eyes and hide by lying down.

50. Evans] The speech of Evans, like that of Quickly and Pistol, loses its former character so far as the appearance of the words on the page is concerned—but the actor is apparently relied on to continue with the accent, for Falstaff (ll. 82–3) identifies Evans as a 'Welsh fairy'.

Bead] Q has Evans call one fairy 'Pead', another 'Peane', showing that the reporter understood the name that F spells 'Bede' to mean 'Bead'—which is, of course, appropriate for a small fairy.

52.] i.e. give her imagination free rein, let her have pleasing dreams—perhaps with a quibble.

53. *Sleep she*] though she is sleeping. The alternative is to replace F's comma after l. 52 by a semi-colon and interpret as 'may she sleep'.

careless] carefree.

54. *as*] who.

Pinch them, arms, legs, backs, shoulders, sides, and
   shins.   55

Quick. About, about;
   Search Windsor Castle, elves, within and out;
   Strew good luck, ouphs, on every sacred room
   That it may stand till the perpetual doom
   In state as wholesome as in state 'tis fit,   60
   Worthy the owner, and the owner it;
   The several chairs of order look you scour
   With juice of balm and every precious flower;
   Each fair instalment, coat, and sev'ral crest,
   With loyal blazon, evermore be blest;   65
   And nightly, meadow-fairies, look you sing,
   Like to the Garter's compass, in a ring:
   Th' expressure that it bears, green let it be,

56, 85. *Quick.*] *As F (Qu.)*; *Queen* / *Collier*; *Anne* / *Halliwell*.   60. state as] *F;* site
as *Hanmer.*   62. several] *F* (seuerall).   63. balm . . . flower;] *As Rowe;*
Balme; . . . flowre, *F.*   64. sev'ral] *F* (seu'rall).   66. nightly, meadow-fairies]
As Capell; Nightly-meadow-Fairies *F.*

59. *the perpetual doom*] the final
judgment; Day of Judgment. Hart
suggested that in these lines there may
be an allusion to Elizabeth's motto
semper eadem ('always the same').

60.] i.e. as 'healthy' in state (condition) as it is fitting in state (dignity).

61. *and the owner it*] and the owner
worthy of—indeed the only appropriate owner of—it.

62. *several chairs of order*] various
stalls (in the choir of St George's
Chapel, Windsor) assigned (one each)
to the knights who are members of the
Order of the Garter. Each knight's
crest, helmet, and mantlings are above
his stall; and his banner is on a stave
projecting from the wall above these.

63. *balm*] Originally the aromatic
gum of specific trees, 'balm' was used
of aromatic herbs and indeed of
practically any fragrant plant or oil.
It was customary to perfume rooms
for special occasions; and the allusion
here is almost certainly to the coming
ceremony of installing the new
Knights of the Garter. See Introduction, pp. xliv ff.

64. *instalment*] place where one is
installed; here the individual stall of
the particular knight.

coat] coat of arms, referring either to
that on the banner or to the stall-plate
nailed to the back of the stall.

crest] 'A figure or device (originally
borne by a knight on his helmet)
placed on a wreath, coronet, or
chapeau, and borne above the shield
and helmet in a coat of arms' (*O.E.D.
sb.* 3); also used of the helmet itself.
The crests of the Garter Knights are
set on the helmets.

65. *blazon*] Used both of the heraldic
shield and of the banner bearing the
coat of arms. The verbal construction
in ll. 64–5 is not 'be blest with' but 'be
blest, as well as the loyal blazon'.

67. *compass*] circle, circumference
(*O.E.D. sb.* IV).

in a ring] An easy order for the
fairies, who normally danced in a
'fairy ring'.

68. *expressure*] expression (cf. *Troil.*,
III. iii. 203–4, 'an operation more
divine / Than breath or pen can give
expressure to') and so, conceivably,

More fertile-fresh than all the field to see;
And *Honi soit qui mal y pense* write   70
In em'rald tufts, flowers purple, blue, and white,
Like sapphire, pearl, and rich embroidery
Buckled below fair knighthood's bending knee:
Fairies use flowers for their charactery.
Away, disperse; but till 'tis one o'clock,   75
Our dance of custom round about the oak
Of Herne the hunter, let us not forget.

Evans. Pray you, lock hand in hand; yourselves in order set;
And twenty glow-worms shall our lanterns be
To guide our measure round about the tree.   80
But, stay, I smell a man of middle earth!

Fal. Heavens defend me from that Welsh fairy, lest he
transform me to a piece of cheese!

Pist. Vile worm, thou wast o'erlook'd even in thy birth.

Quick. With trial-fire touch me his finger-end: 85
If he be chaste, the flame will back descend,
And turn him to no pain; but if he start,
It is the flesh of a corrupted heart.

---

69. More] *F2;* Mote *F1.*   71. em'rald tufts] *F* (Emrold-tuffes).   82–3.] *Prose as Pope;* Heauens . . . Fairy, / Least . . . Cheese. *F.*

impression or imprint. The fairy ring manifests itself in grass greener and fresher looking than is the other grass. The Garter ribbon itself is blue, as Shakespeare possibly recognizes in ll. 71–3, and the motto is normally, but not invariably, in gold lettering.

70. *Honi soit . . . pense*] Evil be to him who evil thinks—the motto of the Order of the Garter, woven into the garter itself.

74. *charactery*] script. It is not clear whether in this line 'flowers' is to be pronounced as a monosyllable (F does spell 'Flowres' both here and in l. 71) and 'charactery' as four syllables, with the main stress on the second, or whether 'flowers' has two syllables and 'charactery' three, with the main stress on the first.

76. *dance of custom*] customary dance.

81. *middle earth*] Described by *O.E.D.* as 'an etymologizing perversion' of

ME *middelerd*, the term was originally used because the earth was theoretically midway between heaven and hell; it came to be applied to the 'real' or human world as distinct e.g. from the world of fairy.

82–3.] See notes on I. ii. 12 and v. v. 50; and cf. ll. 138–40.

84. *o'erlook'd*] looked at by one with the evil eye, and so bewitched, destined for evil (*O.E.D.* 'overlook' *v.* 7—discussed also by Hilda Hulme, pp. 19–20).

85. *trial-fire*] Hart quotes from Fletcher's *Faithful Shepherdess* a parallel passage (a flame 'which will burn him if he lust'). Fletcher may only have been imitating Shakespeare, but there may well have been such a popular superstition, ingeniously adapted for the purpose of Falstaff's 'trial'.

me] Another example of the ethic dative.

Pist. A trial, come.

Evans.   Come, will this wood take fire?
                           [*They burn him with their tapers.*]

Fal. Oh, oh, oh!   90

Quick. Corrupt, corrupt, and tainted in desire!
       About him, fairies, sing a scornful rhyme;
       And, as you trip, still pinch him to your time.

Song.

          Fie on sinful fantasy,
          Fie on lust and luxury!   95
          Lust is but a bloody fire,
          Kindled with unchaste desire,
          Fed in heart, whose flames aspire,
          As thoughts do blow them, higher and higher.
          Pinch him, fairies, mutually;   100
          Pinch him for his villainy;
       Pinch him, and burn him, and turn him about,
       Till candles and starlight and moonshine be out.

*During this song they pinch Falstaff. Doctor Caius comes one way, and
steals away a fairy in green; Slender another way, and takes off
a fairy in white; and Fenton comes, and steals away Anne Page.
A noise of hunting is heard within. The Fairies run away.
Falstaff pulls off his buck's head, and rises.*

89. S.D.] *As Q; not in F; They burn him with their Tapers, and pinch him. Rowe (before
'Come').*   103. *During . . . rises.*] *As Steevens, after Theobald; not in F; Here they
pinch him, and sing about him, & the Doctor comes one way & steales away a boy in red.
And Slender another way he takes a boy in greene: And Fenton steales misteris Anne, being in
white. And a noyse of hunting is made within: and all the Fairies runne away. Falstaffe
pulles of his bucks head, and rises vp. Q; He offers to run out. Rowe.*

89. *wood*] The reference can hardly
be, as some editors suggest, to Falstaff's
horns, made of oak (if they were); the
word must be used ironically, of his
finger.

94. *fantasy*] imaginings, and so
aspiration.

95. *luxury*] All but synonymous with
'lust'; lechery.

96. *bloody fire*] fire in the blood.

98. *aspire*] rise up, like smoke
(*O.E.D.* III. 5).

100. *mutually*] together, in unison
(*O.E.D.* 2).

103. S.D. *During . . . rises*] This is
based on Q but differs from it, largely
because Q again gets the colours
mixed. Earlier editors point out that
the scene may have been influenced by
IV. iii of Lyly's *Endimion* in which,
while dancing and singing such words
as 'pinch him, pinch him, black and
blue', the fairies pinch Corsites.
(Although *Endimion* was published in

Enter PAGE, FORD, MISTRESS PAGE, *and* MISTRESS FORD.

Page. Nay, do not fly; I think we have watch'd you now.
 Will none but Herne the hunter serve your turn?   105
Mrs. Page. I pray you, come, hold up the jest no higher.
 Now, good Sir John, how like you Windsor wives?
 [*Pointing to the horns*] See you these, husband? Do
  not these fair yokes
 Become the forest better than the town?
Ford. Now, sir, who's a cuckold now? Master Brook,   110
 Falstaff's a knave, a cuckoldly knave; here are his
 horns, Master Brook; and, Master Brook, he hath
 enjoyed nothing of Ford's but his buck-basket, his
 cudgel, and twenty pounds of money, which must
 be paid to Master Brook; his horses are arrested for   115
 it, Master Brook.

103. *Enter Page . . . Mistress Ford.*] *As Capell; not in F; And enters* M. *Page,* M. *Ford, and their wiues,* M. *Shallow, Sir Hugh.* Q; *Enter* Page, Ford, *&c. They lay hold on him.* Rowe; *Enter Page, Ford, Mistress Page, Mistress Ford, and Sir Hugh Evans.* Alexander. 104–5.] *Verse as Rowe; prose F.* 108. S.D.] *Hanmer; not in F.* yokes] *F1* (yoakes); Okes *F2.* 110–12.] *Prose as Pope;* Now . . . now? | Mr *Broome . . .* Cuckoldly knaue, | Heere . . . hornes Master *Broome:* | And . . . *F.*

1591, the words of the song first appear in the play in Blount's edition of 1632, and their authorship and date are open to question.)
 S.D. Enter . . . Ford] Q also brings on Shallow and Evans (who has not left the stage, unless he ran away with the 'fairies', as Pistol and Mistress Quickly presumably did), and gives Shallow the words 'God saue you sir *Iohn Falstaffe*' in reply to Falstaff's first speech. F has neither entrance nor dialogue for Shallow, but his presence would be natural enough in the finale. Perhaps also the Q S.D. implies that Evans left the stage to drop his disguise; it may conceivably be relevant, as Hart suggested, that he resumes his Welsh accent hereafter (but see note on l. 43). Neither Pistol nor Quickly speaks again in Q or F, and they could hardly be included in Mistress Page's final invitation (ll. 238–40). In Q the dialogue begins after the S.D. with a speech by Falstaff that includes

another attempt to link the action with the *H4* plays: 'What hunting at this time of night? / Ile lay my life the mad Prince of *Wales* / Is stealing his fathers Deare'.
 104. *watch'd*] caught by spying upon or lying in wait for; cf. *2H6,* I. iv. 45 and 58.
 106. *hold up*] keep up, maintain.
 108. *yokes*] Falstaff's horns, so called apparently because they resemble the oxen's yoke in shape. See l. 121 and note. Hart's suggestions that the 'horns' were made of 'oak' and that there is a pun on 'oak' are unconvincing. (It would presumably be easier for Quickly—see v. i—to obtain for him the mounted head of a buck or the horns from one.)
 109. *Become*] suit.
 110–16.] Ford's mockery of Falstaff includes a parody of his style, with, particularly, the over-frequent use of 'Master Brook'.
 115. *arrested*] seized by law, to be

Mrs. Ford. Sir John, we have had ill luck: we could
  never meet. I will never take you for my love again,
  but I will always count you my deer.
Fal. I do begin to perceive that I am made an ass.   120
Ford. Ay, and an ox too: both the proofs are extant.
Fal. And these are not fairies? I was three or four times
  in the thought they were not fairies; and yet the
  guiltiness of my mind, the sudden surprise of my
  powers, drove the grossness of the foppery into a   125
  received belief, in despite of the teeth of all rhyme
  and reason, that they were fairies. See now how
  wit may be made a Jack-a-Lent, when 'tis upon ill
  employment!

118. meet] *F;* mate *New Camb.*   122. And . . . fairies? I] *Prose as Pope;* And . . .
Fairies: / I . . . *F.*

held until the debt is paid. This is what
Mistress Ford said would be Falstaff's
punishment, at II. i. 93–4. There is no
direct connection between this part of
the plot and the stealing of the Host's
horses; and indeed the plan that some
editors see—to replace the Host's own
horses by letting him have Falstaff's—
would contradict, not enhance, the
plans for vengeance on the Host made
by Evans and Caius. At most, Falstaff's
loss of his horses is an ironic parallel to
the Host's. In Q Mistress Ford does
later ask her husband to let Falstaff
off his debt; F leaves the question
open.
  118. *meet*] *New Cambridge*'s emendation 'mate' is defended by the argument that 'they had "met" three
times, but never "mated" '. 'But', as
C. J. Sisson says, *N.R.*, p. 73, 'surely
there are meetings and meetings'. The
two words may have been closer in
pronunciation than they are today and
conceivably a quibble is involved.
  121. *an ox too*] *New Cambridge* says
that 'to make an ox of one' means 'to
make one a fool' and compares *Troil.*,
v. i. 66, which does not necessarily
support this. May the reference not be
to a proverb that Tilley does list, O107:
'an ox is taken by the horns and a man

by the tongue'? Certainly 'both the
proofs' in the second half of the line
refers to the horns; and the 'ox' image
refers back to 'yokes' in l. 108.
  extant] Another quibble, on the
surviving meaning 'still in existence'
and the literal meaning 'standing up',
'protuberant' (*O.E.D. adj.* 1).
  124. *guiltiness . . .*] Hart complains
that 'this is most un-Falstaffian
language' and *New Cambridge* adds that
'the passage must be a relic of the old
play'. Alternatively one may see
Shakespeare skilfully modulating into
the key of the final passages—perhaps
at the cost of consistency in characterization but not necessarily so: this is not
the first time in the Falstaff plays that
Falstaff has admitted to being the
dupe ('Ah, no more of that, Hal, an
thou lovest me!') and the balancing
of the phrases sounds 'authentic'.
  125. *powers*] mind and senses.
  foppery] cheating (cf. *O.E.D.* 'fop'
v. 2—the same as 'fob' in 'fob off').
  126–7. *in despite . . . reason*] 'In spite
of the teeth' (originally, perhaps, the
teeth of an animal) was a proverbial
phrase (Tilley S764), as, of course,
was 'neither rhyme nor reason'.
  128. *Jack-a-Lent*] See note on III. iii.
23.

Evans. Sir John Falstaff, serve Got, and leave your 130
    desires, and fairies will not pinse you.

Ford. Well said, fairy Hugh.

Evans. And leave you your jealousies too, I pray you.

Ford. I will never mistrust my wife again, till thou art
    able to woo her in good English. 135

Fal. Have I laid my brain in the sun and dried it, that it
    wants matter to prevent so gross o'er-reaching as
    this? Am I ridden with a Welsh goat too? Shall I
    have a cockscomb of frieze? 'Tis time I were
    choked with a piece of toasted cheese. 140

Evans. Seese is not good to give putter; your belly is all
    putter.

Fal. 'Seese' and 'putter'? Have I lived to stand at the
    taunt of one that makes fritters of English? This is
    enough to be the decay of lust and late-walking 145
    through the realm.

Mrs. Page. Why, Sir John, do you think, though we
    would have thrust virtue out of our hearts by the
    head and shoulders, and have given ourselves
    without scruple to hell, that ever the devil could 150
    have made you our delight?

Ford. What, a hodge-pudding? A bag of flax?

Mrs. Page. A puffed man?

Page. Old, cold, withered, and of intolerable entrails?

---

152. hodge-pudding] *F;* hog's pudding *Pope;* hog-pudding *Collier.*   flax] *F;*
flux *conj. New Camb.*

---

137. *wants*] lacks.

138. *ridden with a Welsh goat*] There
were said to be many goats in Wales,
and the devil was said to transform
himself often into a goat. There need
be no direct allusion to Evans's
costume.

139. *cockscomb of frieze*] a jester's cap,
made of frieze, a coarse woollen cloth
variously thought to be typical of
Wales and of Ireland (both being
considered poverty-stricken). Cf. *The
Two Noble Kinsmen,* III. v. 8, 'You most
coarse frieze capacities'.

140. *cheese*] See note on I. ii. 12 (the
Welsh fondness for cheese).

144. *fritters*] Literally, pieces of fried
batter. (The other meaning, 'shreds'
or 'fragments', would seem to have
been later.)

148–9. *thrust . . . shoulders*] 'To thrust
out (or in) by the head and shoulders'
was a stock phrase (Tilley H274).

152. *hodge-pudding*] a pudding or
sausage made of 'hodge' or pig's
entrails (cf. II. i. 31, and l. 154 below).

bag of flax] sack full of flax, or flax-
pods (from which linseed is extracted).
Emendation is unnecessary: Hal calls
Falstaff 'wool-sack' in *1H4,* II. iv. 148.

154. *intolerable*] No doubt again with
a quibble: excessive (*O.E.D.* 1.c) and

Ford. And one that is as slanderous as Satan?   155
Page. And as poor as Job?
Ford. And as wicked as his wife?
Evans. And given to fornications, and to taverns, and
sack, and wine, and metheglins, and to drinkings,
and swearings, and starings, pribbles and prab-   160
bles?
Fal. Well, I am your theme: you have the start of me.
I am dejected; I am not able to answer the Welsh
flannel; ignorance itself is a plummet o'er me; use
me as you will.   165
Ford. Marry, sir, we'll bring you to Windsor to one
Master Brook that you have cozened of money, to
whom you should have been a pandar. Over and
above that you have suffered, I think to repay that
money will be a biting affliction.   170

---

164. is a plummet o'er me] *F;* has a plume o' me *conj. Johnson;* is a planet o'er me
conj. Farmer.   170.] *Theobald inserts, from Q,* 'Mrs *Ford.* Nay, husband, let That
go to make amends: / Forgive that Summ, and so we'll all be Friends.'

---

impossible to bear or carry (literally).

155–7.] The allusions are to Satan as the slanderer of Job (Job, 1:9–11 and 2:4–5) and probably, as Noble points out (p. 272), to a marginal gloss on 2: 9 in the Bishop's Bible (1568 and 1572): 'A cruel temptation of an euyl and vngodly wife'.

159. *metheglins*] The plural is perhaps Evans's own (unless it is the variant 'metheglings') but 'metheglin' is the well-known name of a potent spiced mead, first concocted in Wales. Cf. Wasp's insults in Jonson's *Bartholomew Fair*, IV. vi. 47–51, 'You are a welsh Cuckold . . . You stinke of leeks, *Metheglyn*, and cheese'.

160. *swearings, and starings*] Hart shows, by relevant quotations from Nashe, that 'swearing and staring' was 'evidently an established phrase': 'staring' meant 'glaring' or 'raving' as if mad (*O.E.D.* 'stare' *v.* 3.a).

160–1. *pribbles and prabbles*] Evans falls back on another ready-made phrase: cf. I. i. 51–2 and note.

162. *your theme*] the subject of your jests.

you have the start of me] A standard phrase (Tilley S828); the modern idiom might be 'have the advantage over me' or 'have the whip hand'.

163. *dejected*] Probably yet another quibble on secondary and primary meanings: downcast and cast down (in status if not physically).

163–4. *Welsh flannel*] Cf. l. 139 and note. (A conjecture that the English word 'flannel' is a corruption of Welsh *gwlanen* is called 'plausible' by *O.E.D.*, which sees some difficulties in the theory.)

164. *plummet*] *New Cambridge* saw another quibble, 'plummet' being (1) the nautical apparatus for testing depth (and apparently Falstaff means that he has now sunk even deeper than the plummet: ignorant people—like Evans—can find him out to be more ignorant) and (2) plumbet, defined by *O.E.D.* as 'a woollen fabric' (and thus a 'flannel').

Page. Yet be cheerful, knight: thou shalt eat a posset
to-night at my house, where I will desire thee to
laugh at my wife that now laughs at thee. Tell her
Master Slender hath married her daughter.

Mrs. Page. [*Aside*] Doctors doubt that; if Anne Page   175
be my daughter, she is, by this, Doctor Caius' wife.

Enter SLENDER.

Slen. Whoa, ho, ho, father Page!

Page. Son, how now? How now, son? Have you
dispatched?

Slen. Dispatched? I'll make the best in Gloucestershire   180
know on 't; would I were hanged, la, else!

Page. Of what, son?

Slen. I came yonder at Eton to marry Mistress Anne
Page, and she's a great lubberly boy. If it had not
been i' th' church, I would have swinged him, or   185
he should have swinged me. If I did not think it had
been Anne Page, would I might never stir—and
'tis a postmaster's boy!

Page. Upon my life, then, you took the wrong.

Slen. What need you tell me that? I think so, when I   190
took a boy for a girl. If I had been married to him,
for all he was in woman's apparel, I would not have
had him.

Page. Why, this is your own folly. Did not I tell you how
you should know my daughter by her garments?   195

175. *Aside*] *Theobald; not in F.*   176. S.D.] *Q; not in F.*

171. *eat a posset*] See note on I. iv. 7.
'Eat' is used in a general sense: the
modern idiom would be 'take'.

175. *Doctors doubt that*] Apparently
proverbial; cf. 'You need not doubt,
you are no doctor'. Tilley D425, and
'That is but one doctor's opinion',
D426. The pun on 'daughter' and
'doctor' suspected by Hart may not
be there.

176. Enter Slender] Q reverses the
order of the entries of Slender and
Caius.

179. *dispatched*] settled the business
(*O.E.D.* 'dispatch' *v.* II. 10).

185. *swinged*] thrashed. *New Cambridge* sees a (somewhat improbable)
quibble on the sense 'have sexual
intercourse', citing *O.E.D.* 'swinge'
v.[1] I. e.

187. *would . . . stir*] Not Slender's
invention but a stock phrase ('I would
I might never stir else', Tilley S861).

188. *postmaster's*] The postmaster
was the official in charge of the post-
messengers or post-horses.

Slen. I went to her in white, and cried 'mum', and she
cried 'budget', as Anne and I had appointed; and
yet it was not Anne, but a postmaster's boy.

Mrs. Page. Good George, be not angry: I knew of your
purpose, turned my daughter into green, and   200
indeed she is now with the Doctor at the deanery,
and there married.

Enter CAIUS.

Caius. Vere is Mistress Page? By gar, I am cozened: I
ha' married *un garçon*, a boy; *un paysan*, by gar; a
boy; it is not Anne Page; by gar, I am cozened.   205

Mrs. Page. Why, did you take her in green?

Caius. Ay, by gar, and 'tis a boy; by gar, I'll raise all
Windsor.   [*Exit.*]

Ford. This is strange. Who hath got the right Anne?

Page. My heart misgives me: here comes Master   210
Fenton.

Enter FENTON *and* ANNE PAGE.

How now, Master Fenton?

Anne. Pardon, good father; good my mother, pardon.

Page. Now, mistress, how chance you went not with
Master Slender?   215

Mrs. Page. Why went you not with Master Doctor, maid?

Fent. You do amaze her. Hear the truth of it.
You would have married her most shamefully,
Where there was no proportion held in love.

196. white] *Rowe³;* greene *F;* red *Q.*   200. green] *Rowe³;* white *F.*   202.
Enter Caius] Q; not in F.   204. *un garçon] Capell;* oon Garsoon *F1;* one Garsoon
F2.   *un paysan] As Capell;* oon pesant *F.*   206. take] *F;* not take *Pope.*
green] *Pope;* white *F.*   207. by gar, and] *Hanmer;* bee gar, and *F.*   by gar,
I'll] *Hanmer;* be gar, Ile *F.*   208. *Exit] Capell; not in F.*   211. S.D.] *Q; not in F.*

196. *white*] Why F should have
mixed up the colours here and in l. 200
is not clear. A desperate hypothesis
would be that the scribe, thinking that
Slender was bound to get his instructions wrong, made the alteration in
l. 196 and then changed 200 to be
consistent (but of course Mistress Page

could not rely on Slender's being
wrong). Q adds to the confusion by
saying 'red' (it has no line corresponding to 200).

204. paysan] peasant or rustic.

217. *amaze*] bewilder (here by asking
two questions simultaneously). Cf.
l. 228.

    The truth is, she and I, long since contracted,   220
    Are now so sure that nothing can dissolve us.
    Th' offence is holy that she hath committed,
    And this deceit loses the name of craft,
    Of disobedience, or unduteous title,
    Since therein she doth evitate and shun   225
    A thousand irreligious cursed hours
    Which forced marriage would have brought upon her.
Ford. Stand not amaz'd; here is no remedy.
    In love the heavens themselves do guide the state;
    Money buys lands, and wives are sold by fate.   230
Fal. I am glad, though you have ta'en a special stand to
    strike at me, that your arrow hath glanced.
Page. Well, what remedy? Fenton, heaven give thee joy!
    What cannot be eschew'd must be embrac'd.
Fal. When night-dogs run, all sorts of deer are chas'd.   235
Mrs. Page. Well, I will muse no further. Master Fenton,
    Heaven give you many, many merry days!
    Good husband, let us every one go home,
    And laugh this sport o'er by a country fire,
    Sir John and all.
Ford.   Let it be so.—Sir John,   240
    To Master Brook you yet shall hold your word,
    For he to-night shall lie with Mistress Ford.   *Exeunt.*

224. title] *F; guile Collier².*   233–4.] *Verse as Rowe³; prose F.*   240. so.—Sir
John,] *As Theobald; so (Sir Iohn:) F; so, Sir John: Rowe.*

221. *sure*] firmly bound together.
   225. *evitate*] avoid. Fenton, speaking in a high moral tone, is again using formal language.
   229–30.] The rhyming couplet indicates the finality of the epigrammatic statement; the second line is a variant of the proverb 'Marriage and hanging go by destiny' (cf. Tilley M682).
   231. *stand*] hunter's hiding place from which to shoot. Cf. e.g. *3H6,* III. i. 3.
   234.] A variation on proverbs such as 'What cannot be cured must be endured' (Tilley C922): 'eschew'd' means

'avoided'; 'embrac'd', 'accepted'.
   235.] This sounds like a proverb but Tilley does not list any closely parallel to it. The meaning and relevance at least are clear: when dogs run loose at night, out of control, the hunting will not be according to the rules; and so those who set out to deceive each other over Anne's marriage cannot complain that matters were taken out of their hands, that they wanted to hunt true 'deer' but acquired unexpected trophies.
   236. *muse*] Either 'wonder' or 'complain' (*O.E.D. v.* 3, 6).